RETURN FROM DENIAL

... MEMOIR OF LEON GAROYAN'S FAMILY IN AMERICA

LEON GAROYAN, PH.D.
NOVEMBER 2016

Published by Leon Garoyan, April 2015
Revised November 2016
Davis, California

Dedicated to the memories of my parents,
Leon and Beatrice Garoyan,
and my siblings, Arpie, Isabel, Marian, and Charles
who made this possible,
and my brother-in-law George Kaloostian,
who I really considered a brother.

This is also dedicated to Leon III and his son Ben,
and my daughter Elizabeth Ann (Lisa).

And of course, to my spouse Nina, who first
suggested I undertake this story.

CONTENTS

ACKNOWLEDGMENTS

This memoir would not have been written without the suggestion of my wife Nina, who tired of my family stories and my professional activities that carried me around the world. I suspect that had she not been my travel agent for some of the time, she might have thought I exaggerated. But she knew better—after all, she earned a part of her commissions by writing my air tickets. But some things I did were confidential and secret, even to a spouse, to my children, and certainly to my parents. About six years ago, Nina suggested I write a memoir and the thought simmered for a year before I began the task of bringing it to life. Nina, thanks for your idea and your support.

Next, two individuals have guided me through several publications not related to my professional interests, and I have learned to rely on them for such guidance and assistance. One of these is Nancy Ottum, a long-time friend from her professional days at UC Davis. Nancy has previously served as the editor and production director, typesetting some of my non-collegiate publications. I wouldn't know how to begin without her friendly, supportive help.

It was Nancy who introduced me to the third person whose assistance I wish to mention. David Davies, also of Davis, has many skills, of which I have called on only two: A patient photographer who insists there is nothing relating to photographs he cannot perform and he has made me a believer. He doesn't brag. Some of the family pictures in this memoir were taken about 100 years ago with a Kodak box camera; he brought them to life and made them a wonderful addition to this book. I am grateful to David, who remains a close friend.

Thanks Nina, Nancy, and David. I am indebted to you.

INTRODUCTION

This memoir is about a small family, its development and achievements in the United States — a story with widespread implications to others, including those wishing to legally immigrate. I focus on the development of the Garoyan family, of which I have had the privilege of observing through experience. I am the surviving member of that nuclear family.

It is a story worth reading because it tells and reflects the pioneering nature of my parents that influenced each of their five children. As the last of those children, I have had the opportunity to view much of this family, and to endorse what I have experienced.

I considered several alternative titles for my life story before I chose the title on the cover. One I considered briefly was "The Organized Life of an Unorganized Person: The Life of Lee Garoyan and Family." I felt that the survivors of the nuclear family and probably those who know this story, or who think they do, might be offended by such a title.

During my lifetime of 91 years I have been known by various names, depending upon when we were acquainted, these include "farm boy", "man of the earth", "farm advisor", "horticulturalist", "professor", "personal advisor to friends", "confidant", "car collector", "economic advisor", "arbitrator", "organizer of cooperatives", and "friend to many people in many lands". Add a few, or select one or more. They would all be correct during some segment of my life.

WHO ARE THE GAROYANS?

Who is this memoir about? It begins with a family that was victimized in its historic lands in ancient Armenia. The male members were taken by the Turkish military to unknown destinations and the female members (including infants and young girls) and some male adults were also moved under direction of the military and police. The destination of the females was known, while the men just disappeared. Many of the women and children traveled without food and water except for what they could bribe from the troops herding them southwesterly.

My mother saw many die, with their bodies thrown into the river, or left for the vultures to feed on. At age 6, my mother and her sister Lucy, 3 and their mother survived the march across the Syrian desert to the Syrian coast and from there the French navy rescued them and took them to Marseilles. My mother's father (a goldsmith and jeweler) possessed a supply of gold coins and jewels which her mother had sewn in the hem of her coat and in the children's clothes so they had valuables for bribing the soldiers. Apparently the valuables served them well, and ultimately provided transport money for travel to the U.S.

The other part of this story involves my father and his brother Avak, who took a different direction. Both brothers had been students at Euphrates College, an educational institution operated by American and British Protestant organizations. The college had sent Avak to Johns Hopkins University to study medicine. My father had been sent to Liverpool, England for advanced studies in journalism. Thus, they both survived the Turks' first wave of genocide during 1895–1905, during which 14 households of Garoyans were killed.

I despise the continuing 100 years of Turkish denials of these genocides that are well documented in international government records. Thus, I do make references in my memoir to this episode of Armenian history. **Simply put, it is also my personal history.** But I include descriptions of the ordeals as told to me by my parents. Our family history would be different had it not occurred.

How did it happen that there were Armenian survivors to the Turkish Genocides? The Turks were poorly organized and their government was fiscally underfinanced. Besides the destruction of Armenian presence in their historic land, the Turks' motive was to curry peace with the Kurds as mercenaries, with whom they feared there would eventually be conflicts. Turkey's leaders offered Armenian properties and possessions to the Kurds if they joined with the Turkish military to drive the Armenians out.

During a period of the genocide, Turkey was also involved with four, and sometimes five, widely dispersed international military conflicts involving Britain, France, United States, Canada, and Russia. As word of the Turks' motives and killings became apparent, Armenians throughout Turkey, outside of where the killing was occurring, began to emigrate. They moved to neighboring countries, the U.S., Canada, France and scattered worldwide wherever fellow Armenians had previously moved. Despite this massive flight, the U.S. Embassy claims Turkey killed 1.5 million Armenians whose families had lived in the area for hundreds of years. The number who escaped is considered to be about half of the world's Armenian population. The Genocides occurred in three periods: 1895-1905; 1910-14; and 1915-21.

THIS BOOK IS A MEMOIR AND NOT AN INDICTMENT OF TURKEY

The foregoing very brief history of the Turkish Genocide of Armenians is a necessary part of the history of nearly all Armenians who emigrated out of the region. It is necessary to understand this history to understand the story of any American of Armenian descent. It made necessary the immigration of my parents, and caused the deaths of at least 150 of my grandparents, aunts, uncles and cousins whom I never knew.

Despite this, there were happy events and years in our family's story, and this memoir focuses on those events and accomplishments, some tragic, and many of proud achievements. That's what I hope a person will take away from reading this memoir. But the Turkish genocide is a critical piece of history and cannot be overlooked for most Armenians. If the leading countries in Europe had taken a hard look at the Armenians' genocide, the genocide of 6 million Jews may not have occurred in the 1930s. Hitler is frequently quoted, "Who remembers the killing of the Armenians?"

WHY IS THIS STORY OF INTEREST?

This is a story that begins humbly, though painfully, about my father and mother, who escaped a life made intolerable by terrorists, a situation not uncommon in many regions of the world even as this is being written. Over time, the family that developed here in America grew out of poverty to become middle-income citizens while contributing to American society and culture. It is a story of a couple who individually immigrated to the United States during hard economic times and their five children who were all born there. Theirs is a story to be understood, and held up as an example of the greatness of a nation that enables individuals and families to prosper. Ours is a story of encountered prejudice, met head on and overcome. I believe the story of the Garoyan family is worth remembering, and I am proud to be able to describe this epoch.

WHO SHOULD READ THIS MEMOIR?

The U.S. is like a magnet, attracting people to its shores who desire an opportunity to survive, to develop a better life than they can achieve in their native country. The story of my family indicates that we have become good members of American society, who not only raised ourselves up by our bootstraps, but also did so without diluting opportunities of existing members of society.

My family's experiences indicate such results can occur within a single generation when opportunities are not artificially restricted. Such achievements start with family aspirations and opportunities sometimes fettered with prejudice.

I hate what the Ottoman Turks did to my greater family, just as I can understand why Jews likely despise the killing of their families by the Nazis. But, I am unable to document the aggregate national acts of Turkish atrocities, and I wasn't there at the time to write my observations. Fortunately there are others who can and have done so more effectively than me.

I focus on the development of the Garoyan family in America as I have observed and experienced it. It is a strong story worth writing about even as a memoir, because it reflects the pioneering nature of my parents that influenced their five children. **This I know**.

AUTHOR'S NOTE

The causes for the genocide of Armenians is complex, and cannot be properly (nor adequately) explained in a memoir. It was partly of religious origin; the Armenians are Christians and the Turks are Muslim. It was partly economic—the Armenians were financially more successful. It was intellectual—the Armenians were better educated. It was partly because the Armenians were successful business people—and it was partly greed, because the Armenians were native to the region before the Turkish invasion of centuries ago.

PART A

THE EARLY YEARS

CHAPTER ONE

WHERE IT ALL STARTED

This is the story of my life as I remember it. But that story is only a small, residual to the story of the family, of which I was the youngest of five siblings. While I intend to focus on my life story, that would be incomplete without placing it in its proper context. The Garoyan family is the real story, and I shall try to talk about my memories within the context of the family.

WHAT'S IN A NAME?

Variously known over time as Garabedian, Garoian, and Garoyan, one may wonder what's up about this family that can't decide on what it should be known as? It's pretty simple, really. In the Armenian vernacular, the "ian" and "yan" are interchangeable, and mean "of". So, the prefix in my grandfather's time could have been Garabed", which is the formal version of his name "Charles". Let's assume that is the case, so offspring of my grandfather on Dad's side would be "of Charles". But here's a fly in the ointment; the nick-name of Garabed is Garo, meaning "Chuck", somewhat less formal a name for Charles, as it is also in the English language. Theoretically, a generation's name within the family would change, depending on the father's first name. In my case, my father was Leon, which is Levon in Armenian, so my siblings and I could have been known as "Levonian" instead of Garoian or even Garabedian. This is a common practice in a number of cultures. I don't know when this practice changed with Armenian family names, but I suspect it was many generations ago even in Armenia. It would be difficult for succeeding generations to trace relatives because of this system of naming.

This transition of surnames evolved over time, and when Dad came to the U.S. in about 1902, his family name could have been Garabedian, but it was Garoian. It remained with that spelling until sometime during the early 1940s, when Dad changed it to Garoyan, substituting a "y" for the "i". The only other family members besides my parents who carried on the family name were my brother Charles and me. Chuck went along with the new spelling, but I retained the old spelling, since all of my records were with that spelling. When I returned to California in 1969, my brother asked if I was going to "join the family" by also adopting the "y". So, I did, and that's how it happened. However, my children have retained the traditional spelling, with an "i". I understand that my grandson Ben, the son of my son Leon, sometimes uses the Garoyan spelling of our name, because phonetically, he finds it easier.

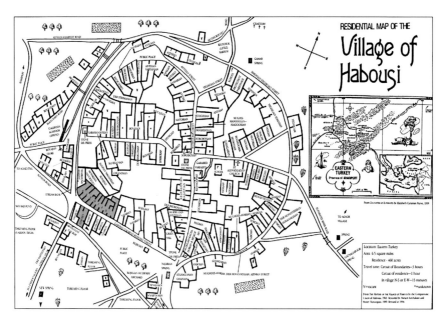

A residential map of the Village of Habousi, in historic Armenia where the Garoian family originated many centuries ago. There are 14 Garoian properties in the southwest section of the map that are shaded. The map is from *The History of the Village of Habousi* (1963) reprinted with permission from the authors, Mayreni Publishing, 1997. Map is restored by Miriam Kochakian and Henry Manoogian, 1969, published by the Compatriotic Union of Habousi. The mothers of both of the authors are from the Garoian family, and are cousins to the Leon Garoian family.

In my Dad's home town (Habousi) in ancient Armenia there was a Garoian street, with 14 households, descendants of Garoian. Apparently this system of surnames was in effect in the late 19th century, which is when the Turkish massacres wiped out most of my Garoian relatives between 1895-1899.

THE FAMILY TREE

Because of the Turkish genocides, it is difficult to track an Armenian family whose generations extended for over 500-600 years in Ancient Armenia (now Ottoman Turkey).

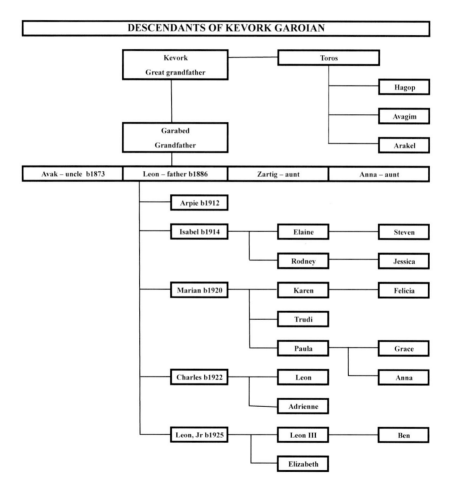

DESCENDANTS OF KEVORK GAROIAN

Source: Miriam Kochakian. Miriam Kochakian, whose mother was a surviving member of the Garoian family from Haubousen, the town along the Euphrates River where the Garoian clans lived for centuries, has provided me with a family history that extends into several generations.

Now I live in Davis, California and my neighbors are two families of Chinese descent. One can trace his ancestry for over a 3,700-year period. The second has his family ancestry going back over 1500 years. I can't come close, can I? Yet, I am told the Armenians were descendants of Noah, whose Ark landed on Mount Ararat, in Armenia.

CHILDREN OF LEON AND BEATRICE {KALAJIAN} GAROIAN

Arpie, born in 1912 in Providence, R. I., died in 1943 from complications of the flu that turned into a bacterial infection of the heart. She was 31 years of age when she succumbed to this illness, which penicillin, developed in England would have cured. Unfortunately it was available only for military use, and was not released to civilian use until several months after Arpie's death. At the time of her death, Arpie was a faculty member at the University of California, Berkeley, from which she received her Ph.D. Arpie was unmarried.

Isabel, born in 1914, also in Providence, married George Kaloostian, a neighbor in Fowler, in 1935. Isabel received a B.S. degree from Fresno State College, and a Master's Degree in Human Nutrition from Utah State University. After raising 2 children (Elaine and Rodney), she became a fourth grade teacher in Riverside, California. She died in 2011 at the age of 96. Her husband, George died in 2008 also at the age of 96.

Marian, born in 1920 in California, received a B.S. degree in Nursing and a Master's in Public Health from the University of California. She married Karl Schmidt, who received his M.D. degree from UC Berkeley. Marian had three children: Karen, Trudi, and Paula. Marian died of pancreatic cancer at age 55. Amazingly, Karl died of the same cancer 10 years later.

Charles, born in 1922, received a Master's Degree in International Trade from the American Institute for Foreign Trade after having spent 7 years with the U.S. Air Force, much of it in the India-Burma Theater. Starting out as a tail gunner on a B-24 bomber, he quickly became fluent in the Hindi language, and became the personal translator for the base commander. As a result, he was among the last to return from India after the Japanese surrender. In California he married Mary, a woman from Jerusalem, whom he later divorced, and with whom he had two children, Leon, and Adrienne. Chuck died in 1988 from pancreatic cancer at the age of 66.

Leon (me), was born in 1925, and lived on the family ranch in Fowler, California until I went to college at age 18. All of the Garoian children attended Fowler schools. My sisters were outstanding students, and were a tough act for Chuck and me to follow. After Fowler, I attended Fresno State College from

1944-45, and transferred to California Polytechnic State University, San Luis Obispo from 1945-47 where I earned a B.S. in Plant Sciences.

Then There Was George

For as long as I can remember, George Kaloostian was a member of our family. When I was 2, our family would go to the Kazarian house, located one-half mile distant, and visit with the Kazarians. Our family was not socially close to the Kazarian family, but George Kaloostian and his father Hagop lived with the Kazarian's. Isabel was 14, and George was 16, and their budding romance was probably the reason for our visits to that family. (George and Isabel never dated anyone else and were married for 72 years until George's death.)

When visiting, I would sit on George's lap, and I recall to this day what a great guy he was, and how much I loved him. Of course, I had no awareness of Isabel being 14 and George being 16. I was told by George, when visiting a few years before his death, how much of a pest I was as a two-year-old, snuggling up to him, and sitting on his lap. He'd have preferred to be alone with Isabel rather than having her youngest brother next to him.

George had many relationships within our family. He was like a son to my parents, became a husband to Isabel, was a classmate to Arpie, and was viewed as a brother to Marion, Chuck, and me before he became our brother-in-law. We all loved him greatly.

True, we were poor, but the stability I felt living on the farm was significant, and I never knew we were poor. I was secure with my siblings, and we always had company several times a week. I was often with the adults as they visited and talked with my parents. In recent years, I have thought about how fortunate I had been that my parents had not considered aborting me; after all, they had a full family of four children when I was born. But I am sure because of the piety of my parents they did not even think of such a thing.

The Family Takes Roots — My Return From Denial

My life story begins with the family farm in Fowler, CA though at the time of my birth, we lived in the small rural town of Parlier, where Dad was a farm laborer. The family returned to the "ranch" at Fowler, which my uncle Avak had bought in 1922, and lost in 1924. However, first I will go back into history with my parents and their ancestors in the old country.

It is presumptive to write a life story, because it assumes there are people who will read what is written. Often the people about whom this story is written have been partial witnesses to that life, and thus have their own concepts, viewpoints, and memories, that could be different from that which I write. They likely would consider this an effort in futility. And well it may be for them. None of my nuclear family, all deceased, left a personal or family history. In my case, there are warts and pimples that I would like to overlook, but should not. I presume the reasons why one writes a life story is to provide understanding through information to others, including family survivors, to feel there is something to be remembered long after the writer is dead.

The main recipients of this history are my son, Lee; his son Ben; my daughter Lisa, and my spouse Nina. I hope my nieces and nephews will have an interest in their family's history, to understand where we came from and what we have gone through. I would also hope it would be of interest to my step-children Peggy, Tami, Julie, Sandy, and Tom. It is Nina who has asked me to write my story, as I have unfolded it to her since we married. In a way, she must think I was unable to do all of the things that I talk to her about, because my life, in my opinion, has been blessed with a large number of events and a great variety of activities. Life has not been boring; it has been extremely enjoyable and rewarding. I hope I shall be able to get this excitement and enthusiasm across in this profile.

The title to this section needs to be explained. It came to me while sitting around the breakfast table on the top of a grassy, mountain knoll in Mendocino County, about 5 miles off a paved state highway and up a dirt road. It was in the mid 1990s when I was visiting my dear friends Roland and Barbara Wentzel. They had just bought a large house built in the style of a Santa Fe adobe, using solar electricity and with a spring that supplied clean, refreshing water. Roland was a former graduate student of mine at Oregon State. His father and I were classmates at Cal Poly.

On that sunny morning, Roland, Barbara, Vincent (a Belgian friend of the Wentzel's) and I were enjoying a pleasant breakfast and somehow, the conversation turned to prejudices. Soon I was relating my experiences of growing up Armenian in the Central Valley of California, where an atmosphere of prejudice against Armenians and their descendants prevailed.

In many ways there was denial of opportunity to many of Armenian descent, which is described in later chapters. For the most part, the prejudices against Armenians also applied to Greeks, Italians, Germans, Jews, Orientals, and Mexicans. I personally don't recall prejudices during my elementary and high school years, but I was aware of them affecting other students of Armenian descent. It took a long time and considerable mental effort to overcome the feelings of this prejudice—even years after I had left the Central Valley, and after the degree and type of discrimination was watered down. Is it still there?

Perhaps some, but there have been many other ethnic groups that have moved into California and much of the prejudices are now directed to them.

It is interesting that my professional reputation was earned outside of California, and only once established, did I actually return to California to work and live. Prejudice against Armenians was not pervasive throughout California; it occurred mostly in regions with dense populations in the Central Valley and in parts of southern California.

In my mind, I was denied privileges available to my friends, but seldom available to me. This became explicit when I enrolled at Fresno State College (now California State University, Fresno) when some social activities like dating, and fraternity living were off limits to me. During my first semester at Fresno State, I met a very attractive girl from Marysville, north of Sacramento, with whom I studied in the library. As time went on, and our studying became helpful to our learning, we also became good friends. It took a long time for me to act on my feelings, and when a holiday dance event was held on campus, I got enough nerve to ask her to be my date—our first date actually. She came from a middle-income family, and this was our first social event of the fall.

I went to pick her up at the room she rented from a Fresno State College Professor. My date was splendid in a light blue gown, and I had splurged for a color-coordinated, lovely corsage that matched. The night went well. We liked the evening, and each other. A week later, I asked her out for another campus event and she said the family had told her after the prom, that she should not socialize with me, since I was of Armenian descent. We never studied together, nor dated again. This was my first direct experience with discrimination because of my ancestry. I was angry because of their prejudice.

At the end of the semester I left Fresno State to attend Cal Poly in San Luis Obispo, where I did not meet with prejudice. The first year at Cal Poly, as a junior, I became editor of the student newspaper and the following year I was elected student body president. I also became an Honorary Rotarian in San Luis Obispo. In subsequent years, I overcame feelings of earlier discrimination; the denial of jobs, activities, groups and clubs in which I could join or participate. I deliberately looked for professional work outside California, and found a great reception at Oregon State University and in Oregon generally. Because I had not experienced prejudice outside of California, and I had achieved a successful professional reputation, I felt safe in returning to California in 1969. Even George Alcorn, administrator of Cooperative Extension at the University of California said after I was hired, "We don't have any prejudices in our unit, we have Garoyan". Thus, the title, "Return From Denial".

Our Epic Story

My family's and my story is one of the epics that makes the United States a great nation equaled by none other during the past several hundred years. My family's religious and racial existence was challenged by Turkey in the first of the murders of Armenians that began in 1896-1905. Only two of my paternal family members survived. They escaped because American protestant missionaries had selected them for a higher education than they could have achieved had they remained in a "peaceful" Turkey. That didn't seem to be a reality.

My grandmother on my mother's side, a mother with two children, one 6 or 7, and one about 3, were driven into the desert like cattle, required to fend for themselves. They were provided no water or food except that which they carried with them or could scrounge from the desert. How they survived this dastardly crime against humanity remains a question, not just for my maternal survivors, but for the untold story of others who survived. Official American government records compiled by U.S. Ambassador Morgenthau during the period indicate at least 1.5 million Armenians were killed by Turkish and Kurdish brutality. This represented about 50% of the world's Armenian population at the time.

I hate prejudices as I have experienced because they can prevent people from achieving their potential, but I have prevailed. (In a later chapter, I describe my professional achievements.) During my career I have served appointments from three U.S. presidents. I have served as trustee for two national organizations for education on cooperatives. I have been a professor on the faculty of three world-class universities, and consulted on international problems with the World Bank and International Finance Corporation. I have consulted on professional matters with numerous American and foreign universities, governments, and businesses on economic development projects.

MEMORIES OF LIFE ON OUR FARM, AS A VERY YOUNG BOY

We called our 20-acre grape vineyard the "ranch", a term still used by people in the San Joaquin Valley. It took a long time—over 75 years—for me to realize a small vineyard is not correctly called a ranch.

Today, I don't have much recollection of the first several years of my life.

Before my time, Dad's brother Avak, about 13 years older than Dad, had purchased a 20-acre farm that had less than 10 acres planted to Thompson grapes for drying into raisins. In Armenian culture, the eldest son was the master of the house, and that relationship prevailed between Avak and Dad. When the family moved in with Avak, he was a pretty dominant person, and felt in charge of Dad's family.

At this time, the family consisted of Dad (Leon) born in 1885, and Mom (Beatrice) born in 1896, and children Arpie, born in 1912, Isabel, born in 1914, Marian, who was born in March, 1920, and Charles, born in 1922. Even before the family moved in with Avak, he enforced his rights as head of the Garoian family. He had wanted to name Isabel "Hyastan", which was the name for Armenia. Mom's will prevailed, and she was named Isabel Margarite. I don't recall what he intended Marian to be named.

Having a dominant older brother of Dad's living with us could have led to a lot of friction within the family. Avak had owned the farm for only a few years when the farm was foreclosed and he lost ownership. That was during the depression of 1922-23. But, because no one came forth to buy the farm, he was able to buy it again in 1925, the year I was born. He struggled to keep ownership for the next 7 years, when, in 1931 or 1932 he died from a combination of alcoholism and pneumonia. In his will, the farm was left to Dad and Mom. It was a tough period because it was the beginning of the Great Depression, and we had little income from the farm. Some of the neighbors were better off, but that was not because they were better farmers, but because they had more acres in grapes producing a crop.

Most farms in our neighborhood consisted of 20 acres. Our farm consisted of about 18 acres, when you subtracted the acreage of the house, outbuildings, barn, streets and "avenues" or vacant areas for turning between the rows. We had only about 10 acres producing a cash crop, and the remainder of our land was planted in alfalfa to produce feed for our two horses and a cow and miscellaneous crops that didn't produce income.

There was a fence between our farm and the adjoining Kevorkian farm that was planted to grapes, and they claimed those grape vines as theirs. For about 20 or more years they harvested the grapes from that fence. Dad always believed that fencerow was on our farm, but lacking money to have the property surveyed and then to hire an attorney, he let it go until our farm was paid for, and he had enough money to get it settled. The survey confirmed our ownership, and one night the Kevorkians cut all the vines down to the ground, to keep us from harvesting the grapes. Needless to say, relations between neighbors, even Armenian, were not always cordial when property or income was involved.

It was tough to support a family of 5 kids and two adults off 10 acres of grapes, but planting additional grapes was expensive, and it took 4 years for the new plantings to bear a crop. So, for a long time, because we were short of money, Dad planted annual crops, but that was not a profitable idea either. For example, we planted about one acre of cotton for several years. According to USDA regulations, any farmer could plant one acre of cotton without a quota. So we planted one acre, and did all the work ourselves, including hand picking the 4-ft. tall plants, a terrible bit of work. A neighbor loaned us 6-ft. long cotton picking bags that we placed over our head and shoulders and dragged behind us as we moved down the narrow rows. We walked down a row, dragging the bag along and "snatched" the cotton fiber from the opened boll by hand, and placed it in the bag. The bolls were dry, and the tips were pointed and sharp, and were very painful on the hands. All of us picked cotton, with Chuck and I "chopping" cotton after planting and germination of the seed, when the plants were about 2 inches high. To chop cotton, you walked down each row and chopped out the extra plants using a long-handled hoe with a 9-in. blade. This left young plants spaced about 9 inches apart. Chuck and I had additional work to chop out weeds as they germinated following irrigation. We also were responsible for irrigating the crop. On a per acre basis, we made more money from the cotton, because of subsidized prices to avenge the southern political powers, than we made from raisins. But, we could not plant more than 1 acre of cotton because we did not have a history of farming cotton, as designated by Congress and the U.S. Department of Agriculture.

Other crops Dad planted included an acre of watermelons, and he was a good watermelon farmer for several years. He grew very nice, large, tasty watermelons, but he was unable to attract buyers for such a small acreage compared to the west side melon farmers who would deliver truckloads to their wholesale buyers in the produce market. These large farmers had been delivering melons for years and years. Unable to compete with the large growers from the west side farms, our melons went to waste. One year, Dad insisted on making watermelon jelly. We picked the watermelons, hauled them to our house, cut out the hearts which were seedless, and Dad tossed in a bunch of sugar, and placed the cut melons and the sugar over the kitchen stove under high wood heat, to make his jelly. Mom had somehow found a way to leave the house, so Dad was on his own. Well, he did make a jelly, but it got scorched from the high heat, and it was not edible. That was a waste of sugar that we could not afford, and it didn't use up many of the melons.

As an 8-10 year old kid, I would pile about 5 or 6 large watermelons in my little red wagon and pull them one-half mile to Highway 99, and wait for someone to stop to ask about the melons. I sold them for 25 cents which was a pretty good price, though it amounted to only one penny a pound. Then, during grape harvest season, a neighboring farm allowed a Mexican family to pitch a tent on their property. I would sell them a watermelon each night, and several times a week, a pound of Mom's Armenian cheese for 50 cents. They would give me a flour tortilla hot off the stove, topped with a bit of our cheese and I was in heaven. They were a nice family, and would return each year to the Sorenson's ranch to pitch a tent.

Dad finally decided he needed to plant more grapes if he was to increase farm income. In the winter, he would make cuttings from our vines, and root them in a small underground cellar made each year for that purpose. We had an acre that had been in alfalfa in the middle of the farm, but it was full of Bermuda grass, a weed grass that spread by its rhizome roots. The common belief was that the roots would germinate again even if hung on a fence all summer in the 100-degree weather.

One summer Dad decided Chuck and I would rid that piece of land of Bermuda grass. Dad would plow a furrow around the land, and with hooked "potato" forks, Chuck and I would comb the roots out and place them in a row behind us for the sun to dry them out. What we missed the first time, we would have to go back later as the roots re-sprouted. It took us all summer, but we cleaned the field of Bermuda and next spring the new vineyard was planted. It was hot, dirty, sandy, and even dusty work, and pretty tough on us as kids about 10 and 12 years old. I do not remember if Chuck or I had straw hats to shield us from the sun. But if it got too hot, we could go lay down under the shade of an adjoining grape planting to cool off.

Growing grapes was hard work in those days, and there was always something to do in the vineyard 10 months out of the year. Much of the time, we worked behind a team of horses, breathing the dust, and spitting up black mucous at the end of the day. It's a miracle none of us developed lung diseases.

The farm was a terrible place for our family, and all of us hated farm work. It was hot, dirty, tiring work during the 1930s, and the rewards from such small acres of grapes was not enough to maintain a family. To earn money for school, Arpie and Isabel worked in the cannery in Selma cutting apricots and cling peaches for canning. It was hard work, cutting the fruit with a knife, and then using a small hand pitter to remove the seed in a very precise manner. Arpie and Isabel were slight and slender, and it was very tiring work, the peach fuzz was irritating and caused rashes, and their wrists would get sore. I recall how they would tape their wrists each day just to be able to continue working.

I don't recall if Marian worked in the cannery, and I do not know how she could have avoided that experience. Chuck worked for the Forest Service cutting out gooseberry and currant plants. When I was 14, I tried to get on the cannery crew as a "pie" boy, someone who would carry away the seeds and remains from the cutting work by ladies, but I was not able to get that kind of job. That was the lowest scale job in the cannery, with no skills required.

So, after an unsuccessful week of trying to find a job in the cannery, I decided to change my approach and wear my school shop coveralls. I placed a crescent wrench, screw driver, pliers, and a clean rag in my back pockets and asked for a job as a grease monkey. They hired me that day, and I was placed in charge of the can delivery system, making sure the automatic feeder of cans to the filler lines did not get clogged. I made about 50 % more than a pie boy and it was good, clean work that I kept for several years during the canning season. It was while doing this work that I first realized I had low blood pressure: I found that out when I would become dizzy and had fallen a few times even as a kid doing farm work, but I didn't realize the cause. Chuck thought I was just lazy and he was not very sympathetic and I suppose Dad may have thought the same thing.

It is little wonder that I hated working on the farm. We could have rented some farms when I was just out of high school, but Mom was not in favor of that, and now I understand why. She grew up in a large Armenian city in southern Turkey, near the Iran border, where her father was a goldsmith and jeweler. Mom was never happy on the farm at Fowler. Dad was educated as a writer-journalist, and I am sure he was not happy on the farm either, but I never heard him say much about it. Dad kept busy with our church, where he was elected as a member of the Council, and served as the deacon. He was also very active in Armenian politics, and would write and deliver rip-roaring speeches, and get lots of applause from audiences of several hundred people.

WORKING FOR GEORGE'S FATHER HAGOP (JAKE)

Hagop did not have a farm, but made his living by being frugal, and by buying apricots and peaches on the trees from small parcels, with 15-20 trees and harvesting, cutting, and drying the fruit for sale. I suppose he didn't pay much for the fruit; Chuck and I constituted his harvest crew. Hagop would shake the ripe fruit, and Chuck and I would pick them from the ground and place them in boxes. In the afternoon, Hagop would have the fruit cut, and then sulfured in a special tight building made with roofing paper in which he would place the cut fruit in single layers on the wood trays. Then, he would burn sulfur in the shack, and close the door tightly to avoid the sulfur fumes from escaping. The next morning he would open the small building and the trays would be carried out and placed on the ground in the sun for the fruit to dry. Chuck and I were involved with much of this effort. In our younger ages, like around 9 or 10, we would make 50 cent a day but as we grew older, we could each earn about a dollar a day.

Chuck and I would go to the National Dollar Store, run by a Chinese group, or Gottschalks, a large department store, with our summer's earnings. We each used our own money to buy our upcoming school year's clothing and shoes and our parents would allow us to make most of the purchase choices.

The awareness of being poor became evident to me in 1932 by age 7, when I was in the second grade at Fowler Grammar School. That was a very low point of our family's financial status, and I would hear talk around the table of having to sell our team of horses to pay the mortgage and interest, and about Fresno Agricultural Works repossessing the plow and cultivator that Dad used on the farm that had been purchased on credit. Each afternoon at school, I would cry with the fear that Mom would not be home when I arrived home from school, fearing she had been taken to jail because we could not pay our bills. Mrs. Gower, my teacher that year, must have wondered about me, not knowing the sad financial shape we were in as a family and how it affected me. She would come to my desk, put her arm around me, and ask if I was not feeling well—little did she know.

Once I understood what it meant to be poor, I became ashamed of being among those considered to be poor. I suspect that feeling still carries on today and is the cause of my being a spendthrift. Finances were really bad during the Great Depression when I was about 9 to 10 years old and in grades five and six. During 1934 and 1935, which were our worst years for low income, our lunch consisted of sandwiches of home-made jams spread on Armenian flat bread. These flat sandwiches, wrapped in Armenian newspaper were very embarrassing to me. I would try to go off by myself to eat those sandwiches because they were different from the other ones made with regular, store-bought bread. On days when I could not go off by myself, I would throw my lunch away instead of eating something in public that was so different.

CHAPTER TWO

ABOUT THE FAMILY

As I embark on this rare opportunity to remember my family's and my memories, I wish to remind readers of one fact they probably have not thought of: *I was born 60 years, three generations, **after** the end of the American Civil War.* I hope you will keep that lengthy time-frame in mind if you get crotchety about dates and events I write about.

Most of the chapters in this memoir have a clear focus, or at least that has been my objective. Now, I have finally reached a topic whose purpose will be less defined. What is it that I want to communicate that would help non-family readers understand us? I'm restricted by my knowledge of the family about which I have memories. But circumstances that will unfold allow me to talk about only my immediate family and Avak, my father's brother. Some would refer to him as "my uncle".

Avak was the first of the Garoian family to be offered an opportunity for a foreign education by American (Christian) missionaries, at Euphrates University in central Turkey. Through their efforts he enrolled at Johns Hopkins University for medical training. Previously he had married an Armenian girl who remained with the Garoian household in Habousi while Avak was in the United States.

Avak kept encouraging Dad to immigrate to America to join him. At the time, Dad had been sent by the same Euphrates University missionaries to take

Leon (Levon) on the left and his brother Avak, believed to be taken in about 1905, likely in Boston. Avak was about 13 years older than his brother and about 6 inches taller. The Garoian families were considered to be prosperous farmers in their home village of Habousi, Turkey.

advanced courses in journalism in the coastal city of Liverpool, England. He attempted to travel to America but failed to meet the health requirements for immigration due to a medical problem with his eyes, an infection of sorts. Convinced by Avak of the potentials in America, Dad stowed away on a ship, which actually took him to Newport News, Virginia. There he jumped ship, somehow got to shore (I think the story is he swam to shore) and walked to Boston. He lost touch with his brother (that is another story I have written about in another section). He found friends in Boston or Providence, and found work sweeping floors at the Brown Shop, a machine shop. About 6 months later, the Immigration people came looking for him and sent him back to Liverpool. (He must have been a model for the Mexicans of present times, who are sent back to Mexico, only to return to the U.S.) Anyway, he stowed on board another ship and found his way back to Boston. Again the authorities found him and he was shipped back to Liverpool a second time. Consequently, he had his eye problem taken care of in Liverpool and passed the medical tests for immigration, and legally entered the U.S.

Dad found work as an ironer of men's shirts where he met Beatrice, who a few years later became his wife. Within several years they had two children, Arpie and Isabel. During WWI he tried to enlist in the American army as a soldier but was not accepted because he had two children. Later he was accepted into the National Guard.

Meanwhile Avak had received word that his wife still living in Habousi had been kidnapped. He dropped out of college so he could return to Turkey and take his revenge on the Kurdish Bey who had claimed his wife (as described in another chapter). Upon his return to the U.S., Avak left medical school without finishing and moved to southern California. Avak encouraged my parents to come to California too. I don't know much about his activities there, but I recall from my parents that he hung around with other immigrants, including Greeks. One of these was dabbling with silent movies, and he encouraged Avak to join him in a new venture. Who was this Greek? Could he have been the young Zanuk? Or, who?

Avak saw no future in making movies, so he moved to Yettem, a rural town in the San Joaquin Valley, where he worked on the large Arakelian grape ranch. While there, he arranged for my parents to move from Providence, R.I. to California where Dad also worked for Arakelian. By 1920, Avak had saved enough money to buy a vineyard at Oleander, south of Fresno. Within several years during the post-WWI financial depression he lost that farm. In 1922 he put together enough money to make a minimum down payment on a 20-acre grape ranch at Fowler, to which the entire family moved. He lost that farm too, but

Mom and Dad shown in an early scene believed to be on the Fowler farm about 1928.

since there were many in the same financial condition, he was able to buy the farm again in 1925. When Avak died, Dad and Mom inherited the vineyard. During the Great Depression of the 1930s, my parents nearly lost that farm.

It was through the efforts of a Fresno Attorney, Mr. Snow, that Dad was able to get one of the first farm loans from the Federal Land Bank in 1933, a depression-era agency set up by President Franklin Roosevelt. That loan saved the farm for us, and my parents were able to pay off the mortgage following the 1939 harvest. It is no wonder that I have so much admiration for the programs of President Roosevelt, and that our family has been registered as Democrats all these years.

In a sense, the Garoian family survived and modestly prospered because of the opportunities created during the Roosevelt era. I hate to conjecture what our lives would have been without Roosevelt's programs: 5 children received university educations, two with Ph.D.s and the other 3 with Master's degrees, all done with mutual help, hard work even when going to school, and the struggles of remaining on the 20-acre farm at Fowler despite low income.

Arpie and Isabel attended Armenian school on Saturdays, but I do not recall Marion doing that. Chuck and I attended for several years, but we were both pretty bad students at these Saturday schools. That is surprising for Chuck, who was gifted in languages.

Arpie with a large bow and Isabel on the left. Arpie was 6 and Isabel about 5 years old. Photo taken in Providence, RI about 1917.

MY FAVORITE SISTER, ARPIE

Arpie was (and remains) my favorite sibling. She left home in 1933 to attend Fresno State and she lived with the Markar family supporting herself by working as a maid while attending classes. Because of that relationship, our two families became close friends and remained so until we left home for school or deaths separated us. Peggy Markar had served as a nurse in the battlefields of Europe during WWI. After Arpie left Fresno to attend UC Berkeley, we'd see her mainly during Christmas holidays. I don't remember much about

Thanksgiving being a big event with our family that would bring Arpie home, but my memory may be a bit shy. After receiving her doctorate, Arpie became an instructor at the university beginning about 1939. She worked for the WWII war effort as well as keeping up her academic work. While continuing this brisk schedule, she came down with a case of the flu. Instead of improving, her illness turned more serious and she developed a bacterial infection in the heart (bacterial endocarditis). She remained hospitalized for nearly a year, with no medication helpful to cure the bacterial infection. It was in April 1943 that Arpie died in the UC hospital. The English had developed penicillin during WWII, but kept it for military use. Several months after

Arpie enjoyed the S.F. Bay Area, taking opportunities to spend time at the sea shore whenever she could. Photo about 1933.

Arpie's death, it became available for civilian use: It would likely have saved her life if it had been available when she needed it.

Our family desperately tried to keep in contact with Arpie all through her hospitalization. Marion was in nursing school at UC San Francisco, so she would frequently see Arpie. Arpie would regularly write letters to the family during the beginning of her illness, and our family in Fowler would respond. Dad and Mom were not able to go to San Francisco as often as they desired. Chuck was in the military stationed in India so he could not come home. I was still in high school, working at Aivasian's truck service station in Fowler. I was able to get rides with truck drivers to the Bay Area, so I'd do this about once a month until Arpie's death. I last saw Arpie about a week or 10 days before her death.

I was very attached to Arpie, and remain so to this day. She was a great scholar like Dad, very nice and so caring like Mom, she worked hard to get an education in the UC system where she also taught, and she had great compassion for others.

When Arpie moved to Berkeley she found a room near the campus on Channing Way, and after paying for her fees and year's rent, she had about ten dollars left. She bought a bag of potatoes and lived on potatoes and milk until she received her salary the next month. She took great interest in my development, and when I told her I wanted to become a lawyer, she bought me a book I still have, titled *Country Lawyer*. Arpie took interest in Chuck too, and she found him a job washing pots and pans in a large restaurant in Berkeley one summer, while he lived with her in her small apartment.

I didn't know Arpie for as many years as my older siblings did, and I know they all loved her as I did and still do. Her death did affect me profoundly, but I cannot imagine how hard Arpie's death was on Mom and Dad. Just that thought makes me very sad even to this day.

I have kept her last zippered leather note book with a few notes left from Arpie's personal papers, and probably these few sheets from Berkeley are all that remain. One sheet contains a brief verse:

"Arpie's the lass,
Who's first in our class.
She's A number one
With us all."

Arpie, with a friend, relaxing by the sea in San Francisco. We believe this photo was taken about 1937 after both had completed graduate studies.

CHAPTER THREE

MEMORIES OF MY FATHER

I am writing this on Father's Day June 17, 2009, an appropriate day to write memories of my Dad. He would like to have been thought of as a simple soul, but in reality he was a complex person whose life was spectacular when you consider the following:

- his origins,

- his escape from a genocide that took all of his family and 14 households of Garoian relatives except his brother Avak and him,

- his immigration as a stow-away twice and being deported twice until he was able to clear U.S. health regulations,

- his struggles that strained his body and maintained a strong mind to raise and educate five children to adulthood, and

- remaining a pious individual and raising his family to serve their church.

Surely you would agree that he was a remarkable man whose life was complex.

As his son, my memories are of a father with high standards of integrity, with a spirit who enjoyed telling stories that indicated a sense of humor, a practical joker wrapped in the body of a gentle man. I'm sure each of my siblings would have different memories of Dad, and all of them would be correct, except for any factual matters that were in error.

When Dad and Mom worked together in the laundry, Mom called him a dapper, dynamic, and handsome young man. Dad was about 24 years old in this picture.

My birth certificate says Dad was 39 years old when I was born in 1925. That would have him born in 1886 in a little village in ancient Armenia, as we refer to the eastern region of present day Turkey.

The Garoian family tree (see Chapter 1) indicates he had two younger sisters, too, who did not survive the first Genocide (1895-1905). I do not recall Dad ever talking about his family, all of whom were killed in that Genocide, except for Dad and Avak.

It was typical for Armenian families to live in villages and to tend their farms on adjacent lands. This was a fertile region of river bottom soil that produced multiple agricultural crops, including fruits, grapes, grains, animal culture, etc. Dad grew up in the town of Habousi that no longer exists. It was inundated by water when the Keban Dam was built for irrigation and hydroelectric generation. During years of drought and low water levels, the foundations of former houses can be seen. Dad always talked about the flavors of fruits of his home region and it was hard for me to understand how they could be better than those we grew on our farm at Fowler. I thought he was just being nostalgic, until many years later I had the experience of eating fruits and vegetables from Armenia during my frequent trips there as a member of an agricultural development team of professionals. Dad's memories were not mere nostalgia, and he had good memories that I am able to vouch for.

A bit more about Dad and his older brother Avak will help to give an understanding of my Dad and his persona. American missionaries were very active in the rural areas of Christian Turkey where Dad's family lived. This region was laced with many Armenian villages, since it was Ancient Armenia before the Turks and Tartars invaded Armenia in about the 1700s. This Christian population was fertile ground for Protestant missionaries from America and Europe. In fact, the Garoians were Protestant Christians, as distinguished from families that were members of the orthodox Armenian Church. Dad remained a Protestant until he immigrated to New England and there he became a member of the orthodox Armenian Church. The Armenian Church was an important part of his life and that of all of our family, about which I will describe more. Religion has been important to my family's life, both as Protestants and the traditional Armenian Church. Avak was selected by the missionaries to be sent to America to attend Johns Hopkins University Medical School, but I do not know the year. Obviously, it was before 1905 when the family had been exterminated. The same missionaries selected Dad to attend college in England to study journalism, and that was also before the massacres. Avak, like Dad, had been a student at Yehprat (Euphrates University). Dad was very proud to have been enrolled there when the missionaries selected him for advanced education.

Except for Avak and Dad, no one else from their direct family survived the genocide. You now can understand why the Garoian family survivors and their offspring grew up with strong religious ties.

Throughout his life, Dad was a terrific writer and served as the Central California correspondent to *Baikar*, a prominent Armenian language newspaper distributed throughout America. He later became correspondent for other Armenian language newspapers, all without pay or income, but *Baikar* did provide him with an Armenian language typewriter. And, he got his bylines, which meant a lot to him and his friends in New England. Our family could have used money instead of recognition for Dad's efforts, but he was happy as the designated correspondent to the equivalent to the New York Times of the Armenian press.

My memories of Dad include his spending long evenings at the kitchen table (the only table we had in our house), writing articles by long-hand for publishing in Baikar. Long into the night he would write, often with a dictionary at his side. Besides being a good writer, his penmanship was lovely.

He became a political writer for the *Baikar* and other publications, because from the 1920s and all through the 1930s, serious political issues divided the Republic of Armenia. During WWI, U.S. President Woodrow Wilson recommended that Armenia be designated as a protectorate of the United States, but the isolationist mood of Congress did not agree. This became a major political issue as to which country Armenia should align itself with: America that did not want them, or Russia, that did. And so this political issue dominated the Armenian diaspora throughout the world, and not just within the tiny country of Armenia. The Armenian Church became split into the Eastern and Western branches along political lines, and that prevailed for anything doing with Armenia except its language. Dad sided with those who wanted America to protect Armenia from Turkey, but when that proved to be impossible because of America's isolationism, the main thought of these people was for Armenia to remain independent of any alliances. Dad then joined the pro-Russian group because he was convinced Armenians were potentially incapable of surviving or protecting themselves from another, even larger, attack from Turkey. He remained supportive of the protection needed from Russia on that political issue. He not only wrote columns, and not just articles on the issue, but also was invited by his party leaders to give long orations at meetings on Sunday afternoons in Fowler High School's auditorium to crowds of 300 people and more. As a kid, I thought he talked too long, often over an hour to 1½ hours, to conclude with standing ovations. He was certainly in his glory. I was impressed and proud of Dad.

The Fowler Armenian Church favored the idea of Armenia becoming a republic of Russia, and so Dad had another cause to serve. Sometime while he lived in New England or before moving to California with Mom and their two children, Arpie and Isabel, Dad had converted to the Orthodox Armenian Church. I don't know when it happened but he became a deacon in the church. As my siblings and I reached a certain age, we were recruited into the choir and at one time the choir of 10 people had four Garoians in it: Arpie, Isabel, Marian, and Chuck. As the youngest, I served as altar boy. Dad also served as a trustee at St. Gregory church in Fowler for years and years, probably until his death.

It was politics and the church that were Dad's main interests, and he spent many hours at both. As I look back, I think Dad lacked balance between church and political interests and farming. He received public recognition through politics and the church, and not for his financial achievements, or lack thereof from farming.

Dad was a perfectionist in everything he did, even his farming. It was not until 1939 that Dad could afford a tractor and he bought a Ford that was delivered to our ranch. In 1939, Chuck was in the California National Guard and therefore didn't use the tractor. Even though I was underage for an automobile driver's license, I drove the tractor along the highway apron on weekends, the two miles from the ranch to the 99 Service station in Fowler, where my friends tended to gather.

Until the purchase of the tractor, all work was done with a team of horses. Each spring Dad plowed the cover crop into the soil in very straight furrows with a single plow over every acre of our vineyard. Everything he did on the farm was very straight. In 1938 we installed an underground concrete pipeline to save water. Because we could not afford to hire the trenching done by machine, Dad marked the lines and Chuck and I hand-dug the trenches with shovels to be exactly 36 in. deep, and 24 in. wide. We would wait for Dad's final approval. The walls were so neat and perfect that I recall the pipe installers complimenting us about the work. I was 13 and Chuck was 15. Chuck was a bit of a perfectionist too, but not to Dad's extent; I seem to have missed out in that respect.

Of course, our family did all the grape harvesting and dried them in the sun until they became raisins. Each of us would be assigned his/her own row of grapes to pick and to spread them on trays to dry. Dad's trays were works of art; he was slow and pokey, but each tray was picture-perfect.

I'm a bit baffled by the ability of a writer to also be a perfectionist in something that was not necessary to his profession as Dad was in everything he did.

Today some writers often do not deal with truth, and so they may not be professional perfectionists. Maybe I have missed something in my observations.

Dad was very generous too, even when we couldn't afford to be. In the 6th grade through 8th grade, I was pretty popular with the "rich" kids in my class and I would be invited to their parties- usually about 5 to 6 of us. The parties would be at their nice homes, on big farms, and kids would be delivered by parent's driving new cars. I would arrive in our 1928 Chevy 2-door, and that embarrassed me. I'm sure the kids didn't give it any thought, since these parties lasted over a 3-year period with me invited to them all. In retrospect, I believe my values system was out of whack; I had a loving family, willing to help each other, wonderful parents who supported college education for each child. I probably was the most spoiled of my siblings, because I was the youngest, and as each matured, there was less competition for the limited income we had.

Dad was proud. When many people better off than our family received federal foods and other welfare, he would not even consider such handouts. He was very happy to be in America and have the opportunity to vote as a naturalized citizen. When it was election time, he and Mom would arrive at the nearby Elm Farm voting precinct to be at the front of the line and be the first to vote.

To cope with income needs, Dad took a seasonal job at Sun-Maid Raisin Growers Cooperative working at lifting heavy boxes of raisins and dumping them onto belts to be graded and sorted for packing. Dad was about 5 feet 5 inches tall, and of slight build, so lifting the boxes of raisins of over 200 pounds with another worker was a very grueling job. He did this every day, 8 hours daily. When he'd come home, he still did the farm work too. Even in winter months there was work to be done on the farm. Of course, he'd spend many evenings writing news articles, or political columns, and I now realize he didn't get enough rest.

Dad was extremely honest and never forgot an obligation. In order to move his family from New England to California, he borrowed money from friends and what few relatives he had, but he could not immediately repay them. The family moved to California in either 1917 or 1918 and it was not until 20 years later that Dad and Mom had enough money to repay their lenders. We went to the bank where he explained the problem to the bank manager and asked him to calculate the amount he owed plus 20 years of interest. He then sent the money back to those who had probably forgotten or given up hopes of ever getting repaid.

Dad and Mom always shared the blessings of our ranch with friends and relatives in New England. Each fall they would prepare lug boxes of dried fruit, raisins, and walnuts from our farm, along with Armenian candy they prepared from our grapes. My parents sent them each a box (about 25 pounds) by Railway Express, the only way to get such packages shipped the 3,000 miles away. This was an annual fall project after the raisins had been put away and probably sold. In recent years Nina and I have started this tradition, but not from our own effort, but what we buy from farmers in our region. Some of these packages go to members of families that received these good foods from "Uncle Levon and Aunt Beatrice", as my parents were called.

MEMORIES OF DAD IN A NUTSHELL

This chapter started out with the intention of remembering Dad on Father's Day, and I got into a bit of history, too. So, what are my memories in a nutshell? I recall a very hard-working father, who by destiny worked as a laborer in agriculture instead of his professional training. I never heard Dad complain about that fate. He was a father who was extremely proud of his five children and their accomplishments. I sometimes think he took solace of his inability to work at his professional training through the accomplishments of his children. His integrity and commitment to obligations is something I am reminded of almost daily. Sure, we grew up as a poor family, but we grew up together, helping each other. I remember the trust he had in Chuck and me, when upon reaching the age of 16 years, we were placed on the farm bank account so we could sign checks. We never did write checks to buy personal items, but what a great trust he displayed in us.

What do I remember of his personality? He was a gregarious person, ready to help in any organization or any person. He was involved in the kitchen at every church meal event. He was very outgoing, with almost everything I can think of. By contrast, Mom was the quiet type. His generosity is evidenced by how he treated his fellow men during the worst of the economic depression. In the worst years of the 1930s depression, our home was an attraction to hobos, who would walk the half-mile from Highway 99 to our house to request food for themselves, and feed for their burros. Dad never turned them down, and many times he would invite them inside to sit at our table with us if they arrived at lunchtime. They ate Armenian bread, home made Armenian cheese, and whatever hot meal like rice pilaf, dolma or sarma Mom had prepared. Later in the summer when Mom was working in the vineyard, our lunch was largely watermelon, cheese and bread, and that's all we had to offer hobos. Sometimes, they would be invited to wash their donkeys in the shade of the large eucalyptus tree in the center of the yard, especially during hot weather. We later found out that hobos had a signal system by which they would leave signs along the road to direct other hobos to a friendly family who was a good source for food.

Despite what I have implied about Dad's lack of aggressiveness in money matters instead of his service to church and politics, he did work hard. Then too, he was a great player of pinochle card games and backgammon, both games he enjoyed and was very competitive while playing. He took these intellectual games very seriously and played aggressively.

We'd drive to our church's summer picnics held about twice a year, on the Kings River at Kingsburg, about 12-14 miles from Fowler. Our car was the old 1928 Chevy and we couldn't afford good tires, so sometimes Dad would locate a worn tire and wire it over our bald tire. Invariably, we would have at least one tire blow out on each of these trips, and we would all get out of the car along the highway, while Dad would patch the tube or repair the tire, then he'd use a hand pump to fill air into the tube, and if we were lucky, we'd finally arrive at the picnic, although a bit late.

Once there, Dad was his jovial self again. He would enter every contest and would win nearly all of them—he must have been about 50-54 years old then. I remember once he received a 100-pound sack of sugar for winning the foot race. He would also find a younger person to team with him on a three-legged race, where the left leg of one person and the right leg of the other would be tied together. Then, he once won a wheel barrel race, where someone would hold his legs and he would use his arms to race against the others. And, boy he was the all-time watermelon eating champion for as long as I can remember. He would swallow seeds and all, when others would take time to spit the seeds out. Surely, he was a competitive person in some things.

Dad did like the good life and good things, too. Dad was meant to be flamboyant, but he never had the financial means to live in that manner. Once in the mid 1930s when we were in Fresno, Dad saw a nice large 1929 or 1930 Lincoln sedan that he really would have liked to buy, but George reminded him that he would have to mortgage the farm just to buy tires for the car. Dad didn't buy the car. (I later bought a Lincoln just like it while living in Corvallis, but it had a frozen motor and I never did get it running. I brought it to California with our move, and later sold it.)

He played jokes on friends when he was a young man. One joke was played on a friend who was becoming bald at a very young age. Dad told him to crush a handful of garlic cloves and rub it all over his balding head. To make it work, Dad told him to go to a movie theater for the right environment for the garlic to soak into his scalp and thus nourish the roots of the hair that hadn't fallen out. The man did that, and there were complaints from other theater-goers about a strong garlic smell. Eventually one patron called the manager, who located the source and escorted him out. Dad would tell us about numerous jokes he played on others. But there were no jokes played on Chuck or me by him.

He also knew when not to joke. When things were really tough financially, Dad would join Chuck and me picking peaches for other farms for fresh market where we would be paid a few cents a box. We were hired out as peach pickers and not selling ours, which we did not grow commercially.

I have very fond memories of Dad. He was good to me, and I seldom ever had problems with him. Dad was a great inspiration and I am indebted to him and Mom very much. I wish we could have had more personal time together. There's much that I realize are voids in our relationship: How he felt about being a good communicator but relegated to being a farmer on the constant verge of poverty, his philosophy in general and his generosity. Why didn't he take better care of his health in his last five years? He died following surgery because Dr. Nielson, our family doctor for over 30 years, didn't take precautions about post-operative care; there was no post-surgery intensive care unit in the small Fowler Hospital where he had surgery for a normally minor duodenal ulcer that had plagued him for years. He died because of lack of available blood for transfusion, having been weakened for months prior to surgery. He told Mom who was at his bedside, that he was tired, and he wanted comfort and peace. Ironically, Dad had never been sick in his adult life; he seldom had a cold, had only two filled cavities in his teeth, and had previously never been a patient in a hospital. I often wonder if he thought a patient went to the hospital to die.

Dad was a great inspiration to me in many ways. He shared our sparse depression era table with hobos, who he would invite to sit with us as we ate if they arrived at that time. He gave of his time to our church and to his political beliefs. He taught me responsibilities for obligations and he had a sense of humor that was a pleasure to witness. Amazingly, I am not like him in many ways; I am a joiner as he was. I am also one to spend, as he was but could not afford. He was a perfectionist, as Chuck was, but I am more like Mom: "good enough is good enough". I was fortunate to have had loving parents, and to be the last of five children, which gave me more time with them than my siblings had.

Memories of my dad cannot be complete without additional information from others who knew him and his brother Avak. Their lives were intertwined because both were survivors of the genocide. There was one other male survivor of Garoians, a cousin of Dad's and Uncle Avak, who was living in Soviet Arme-

Dad at the depth of the depression in 1933 and nearing the loss of the farm. Father of five children ranging from ages 21 down to 8 and with no car to drive, he weekly walked 9 miles each way to bring back bread and other food in a burlap sack. Despite these handicaps, Dad has a smile, wears a necktie and jaunty cap, and some would say, he is still a handsome gent.

nia. Although that survivor was deceased by the time I initiated contact, I was able to meet his two sons and his family in Yerevan while I was doing volunteer work as an officer of the Armenian Technology Group after the earthquake of 1988, I was contacted by a man who said we were related. It turned out his grandfather was a survivor of the genocide, and that his grandfather and my father were cousins, from the village of Habousi. I met his father and his uncle who relayed their family experiences as the lone survivors.

INSIGHTS ABOUT MY FATHER RECEIVED FROM OTHERS

In the summer of 2002 while participating in the annual meeting of the Pierce-Arrow Society in New Hampshire, Nina and I made arrangements to visit with Miriam and Victoria Kochakian, relatives living in Methuen, MA. Their mother was a Garoian cousin of my Dad's who grew up with him in their native Habousi. Below, I quote much of the information subsequently sent by Miriam in a letter to me about my Dad.

"My conversation with you about (your) Uncle Avak prodded me to go back to the story in Father Garabed Kalfayian's book "Memories of Yettem, California". (Yettem is considered to be similar to Biblical Eden. It is a small rural town about 50 miles southeast of Fresno where many residents during the 1920s were Armenian immigrants. In present times, it serves the same purpose for Mexican immigrants.)

"Since the introduction concerns your father, I am translating it to share with you, which is an emotional experience for me." From Father Kalfayian's Book:

> "We were at the home of the sheriff of Yetem, Mr. Nishan Tashjian, when we heard that my old friend from Habousen, Levon Garoian, had died on February 9,1953, a Monday morning while he was undergoing surgery. We were very much saddened by this news.

> "Poor Levon", said Tashjian; "in the early days along with his brother, he mixed the sweat of his brow with the earth of Yettem and then moved to Fowler, again working with his shovel and pick axe in order to care for his loved ones."

> "No, there's more than that to his story" said a fellow-member of the Armenian Hnchagan political party. "When I came to California, he was the president of the National Conference Committee; he was a good writer; he was a very devout deacon; and a patriotic Armenian."

> "Oh ho" continued Sheriff Tashjian, "you should have know Levon's brother, Avak—Yes, Avak Garoian, was also an outstanding Armenian, honorable, patriotic, sincere lover of his ancestry and Hnchagan hero".

Miriam Kochakian adds that though her mother never told her this story until she and Victoria discovered it in a book, her mother had generously marked passages in it with her red pencil as was always her practice when she read the story about Avak.

The introduction continues:

> *"You must remember that the Garoian family was a large patriarchal family in Habousi. In keeping with customary ancient practices, forty or fifty Garoian family members lived under one roof- fathers, mothers, grandparents, brothers, sisters, children, and grandchildren. (There were 14 Garoian houses on the street named for the Garoian family.)*

> *"It was an admirable dwelling place—the Garoian hearth. And they say that in that family there lived a most beautiful flower, Avak's wife, Shoushanik; matchless Shoushanik, a beautiful blossom whose reputation of matchless beauty had spread everywhere, even among the Turks and the Kurds.*

> *"During the 1895 massacres, Avak's wife was kidnapped by a marauding gang of Kurdish bandits who had heard of the legendary beauty and had captured and presented her to their chieftain as a wife.*

In another printed story the Chieftain is referred to as a "bey", a rich owner of a large amount of land.

> *"Avak, in disguise as an itinerant beggar, had returned to Haubusen from the U.S." where he was registered in medical school, to visit the farm of the "chieftain". Among other conversation, the Chieftain had boasted to Avak about the beautiful Armenian wife he had "captured" and the two children she had borne. Avak had won the Kurd's confidence with his excellent Turkish speech.*

> *"Weren't you afraid" Avak asked the Kurd "that someday that beautiful lady's husband from America would come and get his revenge?" "Oh ho", laughed the Kurd. "I'm going to be afraid of a giavour (infidel)? Those giavours know only how to pray. They don't know that God is with those who have strength and know how to use the sword".*

> *"You are so right!" answered Avak , and the rest is written history.*

Avak had a 8-inch dagger with a pearl handle concealed on him, and with that dagger he stabbed the Kurd to death and fled. When my father died, he left my brother Chuck a very beautiful hunter's case, 18-karat gold watch adorned on one side with a bouquet of flowers in a tray, with diamonds and rubies as flowers. I received a dagger with a pearl handle. Little did I know the significance of that dagger in inflicting the revenge of a giavour for the kidnapping of Avak Garoian's bride. I have that dagger among the few souvenirs from my Dad.

After he had taken his revenge, Avak fled to Mersin, Turkey to board a ship to return to America. He stopped in Adana to see a close relative, Ovagim Garoian, to get the funds for the trip to his adopted home in America.

I was sent a copy of the above story published in an Armenian book that a friend told me Avak is considered a "hero" among Armenians for his action.

I asked Miriam why Avak didn't retrieve his wife, and she told me he made an attempt, but that his wife could not believe that Avak had killed the Kurd, and that she feared that if she tried to run with Avak with two infants in tow, they would be quickly apprehended with death to all of them. The account says that swarms of Turkish soldiers and police were looking for him for days after the killing.

But, I have jumped many years between the 1900s and even 1925 when I was born and the present time, years filled with growth, sorrows, fears, achievements, and my return to California. It is to these I now return.

TOP LEFT: The Garoian family about 1916 or 17, just before moving to California from Providence, RI. Arpie's wearing the large bow and Isabel is on the right. **TOP RIGHT:** ca. 1950. A relaxed Dad, when all the children were gone, pictured at the house they bought on their second 20-acre farm. **BOTTOM:** The new home had a separate dining room, living room, 2 baths, 4 bedrooms and a fireplace for cozy evening relaxation. It was well earned and deserved, given the hardships endured during the prior 20 years.

CHAPTER FOUR

MOM WAS SPECIAL
...AND A SURVIVOR

Mom was born in 1894 in the populous city of Dikranagerd in south-east Turkey, a region that once was a part of Armenia. Her father was a jeweler, so Mom grew up being a "city" girl. (That's important, and explains why I think she was unhappy living on a small grape ranch in Fresno.) I don't know much about her father, nor of his family. Mom had an older brother and a younger sister, Lucy, whom I had the pleasure of meeting at our farm in Fowler as WWII ended. I don't know much about Mom's own mother, except I have a picture of her sitting in a rowboat on a lake in Providence. She was a very at-tractive lady that I would liked to have cuddled up to and called her "Grandma". Later I met some of Lucy's children, but I have difficulty in thinking of them as "cousins", only because I didn't get to meet them until I was in my 30's. We were all mature people who lived 3000 miles apart, and I suspect both families had grown up poor. I have the idea that "cousins" start "feeling" like cousins during childhood, and you grow up with them and the "aunts" and "uncles".

She would describe their family house in Dikranagerd as a city house with an enclosed backyard where they enjoyed shade from fruit trees during the hot summers. As air temperatures subsided from the heat of the day, they would sleep on the flat roof of their house because the outside night temperatures were always cooler than in the house. I think she felt those were festive occasions for the young girls, and a happy time in their lives.

An oil painting of Mom, probably at age 22-25, likely after the births of Arpie and Isabel.

Mom had a light complexion, blue eyes, and blond hair until she contacted diphtheria, after which her hair turned brown. Lucy also had blue eyes, so I presume their mother did too. Isabel and I inherited our greenish blue eyes from Mom's side of the family, and probably the golden hair of my childhood.

THE DESERT MARCH

What follows is my recollection of Mom's history once she was on the desert march. She spoke very little about that experience, but as a young child of about 6 years, I have no doubts about what she did tell me. I don't know how extensively she discussed this experience with my siblings, because being the youngest, I undoubtedly spent more quality time with her than the older ones did. Mom was a calm person, much as I had found Lucy to be.

The desert march was bewildering to her, because of the uncertainty as to their destination and the mystery of her father and her brother's disappearance. Telling this to me, her youngest child, must have been very difficult. She told of the Turks pulling infants from the breast of their mothers, and tossing them overhead, and then trying to spear them with the bayonets attached to their guns. To the Turks, it was a sport in an otherwise boring job. Babies that didn't get pierced the first time would get tossed in the air until a soldier succeeded. She described mothers and young girls being taken during the night by soldiers, some to return and others being missed. As a child, I had no idea why this would happen. Mom's mother held her and her sister by their hands, day and night, to protect them from harm.

Once they reached the Mediterranean Sea Mom related how the French navy took them aboard their ships and eventually took them to Marseilles, where they were safe. I have no recollection of their life in France, where they lived, and when they left for America. Mom implied the gold coins and jewelry hidden in their clothing was used to provide ship fares to Boston. In later years, when I worked in Europe, I ran across some of Mom's female relatives in Valence, France, and some Garoian women there too. Apparently, the survivors moved north into the Rhone Valley and some settled in Valence and a few in Grenoble.

NEW LIFE IN AMERICA

Mom's mother remarried in Providence, RI to a mean Armenian who made Mom quit school after the fourth grade to work. He charged Mom room and board, and I suspect Lucy too, when she got a few years older. Eventually, Mom went to work in a laundry ironing shirts, where she met a man who also ironed shirts. She thought he was handsome, and though she was shy, they became friends. At the age of 16 she married this man, who was nine years older. She described him as a good dresser, outgoing personality, friendly with everyone, and a "fast" ironer. That was important because they were paid piece-work, by the shirt. Besides, she was still paying room and board to her stepfather, and the opportunity to get married even at 16 was an attractive option. A picture I have of Mom shows her being slim, pretty, and neat. I could see why Dad was attracted to her. Dad courted her and they married in Providence, on July 4, 1910 symbolically independence day for the Nation and for Mom from a mean step-father.

Mom was a devout Christian true to her Armenian faith. This may have been due to Dad's religious commitments too. Of our family, only Mom sat in the pews, because everyone else was involved in the service. Mom worked on the farm as well as taking care of the house: washing (scrubbing) clothes by hand in hot water, cooking for us, mending clothes, making flat Armenian bread once a month with Dad, and canning much of the fruit we grew. In the winter months, Mom would bundle herself in warm clothing, and follow behind Dad who would prune the vines, and she would wrap the canes on wires for next year's crop and tie them with twine. Believe me, this was cold, hard work which I also began to do at age ten. I do not recall seeing other Moms doing this work except Mrs. Yokomi, the Japanese neighbor. In summer, Mom would fix breakfast for us and then go out into the vineyard to harvest the grapes. She was a steady worker at a consistent pace. When I was about 4 years old, she showed me how to spread the fresh grapes on the trays to dry in the sun turning them into raisins. Sometimes Isabel would take over the responsibility of "sitting" me while she also picked grapes, and she would be tough if I lagged behind in spreading the grapes. She thought I was lazy, scold me and on occasions, she would pinch my upper arms. I thought she had a mean pinch.

Being a city girl, Mom enjoyed a clean, city-living condition and relatively decent quality of family life. Living on the farm was not a very happy life for her. She hated the dust, the long hours worked for virtually no income, the worry over meeting our debts, and always, she spoke to us of her expectations that we not grow up to be farmers. Mom was our strongest advocate to do well in school and to get a clean professional career. Dad supported her in this feeling, but Mom made it real for all of us. Constantly.

To earn money, she would help the family harvest and cut fruit for drying. She would be on her knees picking walnuts and removing the green husks that stained her skin black for nearly 10 days or two weeks. She would stir the drying walnuts each day to ensure the kernels would dry from the sun's heat.

And, in the house, she fed us very well. Mom was a great New England-boiled-dinner chef, cooking chicken or meat with vegetables, mainly potatoes, carrots, and onions. She would always have a cake on hand or a fruit pie, either lemon, peach, apricot, or her specialty, "California Sunshine", a mixture of lemon and orange juice, topped with a meringue. The cakes were always a

Mom was 16 when she married Dad. This is the youngest picture we have of Mom. Likely the picture was taken around 1913-14, when she was between 18 and 20.

The only photograph of Mom's attractive mother, taken in Providence. We have no information on her birth date, the year of this photo, or her age at any given date.

plain yellow cake, made with eggs from our hens, and always very tasty, but seldom with frosting. To this day, I prefer a cake without frosting.

Mom had a characteristic about which we all teased her. She would divide remaining cakes or pies into one less piece than we were people. We would ask, "Mom, where is your piece"? She'd say " there wasn't enough for all of us, so I cut enough for the rest of you". We'd all say, "that's not fair, I'll give you some of mine", which we each would do. She'd end up with a larger serving than any of us, and we'd tease her that she was fully aware of what she was doing.

Mom made sure our clothes were always mended and clean. When it was time to wash, Mom would boil water on the stove, pour it in a large wash tub, dilute it with cold water to where she could just stand the temperature, and scrub each garment on the wash board with a crude soap containing lye. Meanwhile, she would have more water heating for the rinse water. Her hands would be red, sore, and tired, and she would spend every Monday morning doing the wash, and drying it outside on the wire clothesline.

By about 1939, we had more acres of grapes in production for raisins, and prices had improved over prices earlier in the decade. We'd also had less rain damage, so our income increased. By this time, three of the children were in college earning money during summer months to meet their needs. One summer day, Dad, Mom and I went to Fresno and spent much of the day in and out of second hand shops, looking at old electric washing machines, with the intention of buying one for Mom. She'd had no warning of this, so any machine that she saw was acceptable to her. The machines we looked at were 15-20 years old, but Mom didn't care, she was surprised that we were even looking, being financially destitute. Dad found fault with every machine and by afternoon, we went home empty-handed. I have no idea what Mom thought as we drove home in our 1928 Chevrolet jalopy, but she talked about what we would be eating that evening. When we got home, Dad wandered around the yard, and Mom and I entered the enclosed back porch and there, in plain sight, was a brand new Maytag washing machine: Dad had purchased and arranged for its delivery while he was parading Mom around the second hand shops. Dad was a prankster whenever he could be, and he pulled the same trick about five years later, this time buying a Bendix front loading machine with spin drying that didn't require placing the clothes in a wringer by hand.

He'd done a similar stunt about 1938 when he replaced the old icebox with our first refrigerator. Actually Arpie paid for the refrigerator in a conspiracy with Dad. You'd think Mom would be on to him, but I do not think she ever did. Dad just liked to play practical jokes, especially on Mom.

After Dad died in 1951, Chuck took Mom to her eye doctor, Dr. Goldman, a very good clinician, but one with very poor bedside manners. Mom had been developing cataracts, and he told her "you are going to go blind". This news depressed Mom and soon she began to feel helpless, even to the point she could not even boil water for coffee. Chuck had served many years in India during the war and recalled that the Indians used an herb called Rauwolfia as a tranquilizer for depression. He took Mom to a Chinese herbalist in Fresno, who knew the healing powers of the plant, and who prescribed it for Mom. Chuck would make a tea of the herb and in time, Mom got over her depression, found another eye doctor who removed the cataracts from her eyes. Soon she was well enough to move into a small apartment in Fowler owned by Mrs. Yavonian.

She lived alone, enjoyed her life in Fowler, where she was a half block away from the grocery store, the post office, the bank, and Roy's drug store, an institution for us all. Roy would send me to Fresno, driving his new car, to get medicines from McKesson wholesale pharmacy. Driving a new car was a real treat for a kid who otherwise rode in an old 1928 Chevrolet. Roy also would ask me to help serve customers at the fountain in his store, with instructions to help myself, too. Roy continued to supply and deliver medicines to Mom until her death. He was a good man.

There were a lot of other Armenian widows who had moved from their farms into town. Twice a day the ladies would congregate under the big apricot tree in the Yavonian yard for coffee and conversation. Mom held court at those sessions and because she was not a gossiper, she had a lot of friends.

Son-in-Law George Kaloostian

When we lived on the ranch, our neighbor was George Kaloostian. I knew him since I was two years old but I didn't realize that he and Isabel were in love. His parents were divorced, so he "adopted" Mom as his mother and in fact, we all loved George like he was family.

After Isabel and George married they lived in Oregon, Washington, Utah, and Georgia before they moved to Riverside. Back in California, George had professional responsibilities in Parlier, near Fowler, where a USDA field research station was located. He always stopped to visit Mom on his trips from Riverside to Parlier. Several years after Mom's move into Fowler, George noticed that Mom had an unvented natural gas heater to keep warm. Knowing the bad effects of natural gas fumes, he immediately went to the local hardware store and bought Mom a small gas heater and vented the fumes to the outside. Little did he know that breathing the fumes had already resulted in lung cancer.

Marian and her husband Karl arranged for Mom to visit Dr. Jones, a highly noted UCLA thoracic surgeon to perform investigative surgery on Mom. To gain access, he cut out a rib, and he found cancer nodules scattered all through her chest cavity and lungs. Dr. Jones just stitched her back up and told Karl to take her home, and to make her comfortable. To ease any pain, Karl gave Mom aspirin and whenever she felt pain thereafter, she would take an aspirin to reduce it. We do not know what threshold of pain she had accepted, but aspirin was the strongest medicine she took. Possibly she would be expected to survive for six months, but Marion never told Mom about having cancer, and provided a special high protein cocktail as a meal supplement. I was working in Oregon at the time, and several times I would visit Mom when she was living with Karl and Marian in Hollywood, and Karl was very gracious to "Grandma" as he referred to her.

Mom told me several times that she was sure happy that they removed the rib, as that seemed to take care of her health problem. Had Mom known about cancer, we think Dr. Jones' prediction would have come true earlier. But, she lived about 9½ years longer before dying of heart failure due to blocked arteries. That was in 1968, but if she had been prescribed one of the early statin medicines, she would likely have survived that problem and lived to a riper age.

Meanwhile, Chuck had gotten married to an Armenian woman born and reared in Jerusalem who was about 45 years old when he met her. How he met her is not clear to me. She turned out to be very difficult, and in short order she was able to turn Chuck away from Mom, Isabel, and to a lesser extent, me.

Talking with Isabel the evening when I wrote this, she mentioned that Mom had given birth to the last three kids in just 6 years and was overwhelmed by the responsibility of the family and work on the farm. Being older, Arpie and Isabel could take care of themselves, but the three younger kids required more attention. Isabel said Mom asked Dad to take care of Marian, who was 5 years old when I was born, and she would take care of Chuck and me. Isabel and I both remember that Dad and Marian had a special bond, possibly starting from this time. Also, Dad's birthday was on March 3, and Marian's was on March 4. Obviously their birthdays were celebrated together.

Mom missed having friends from her native city when she lived in California. She had one friend, Osana, who lived in Fowler and whose husband was unemployed, causing the family to subsist on welfare. Dad didn't enjoy spending time with him because they had nothing in common, so Mom didn't get to see her childhood friend as often as she might have liked. But with each visit, Osana would bake a cake from scratch, which she served warm. Golly, those cakes were enough reason to visit, but Mom just liked to visit with her.

We didn't often see Mom so elegantly dressed as in this photo. She was visiting Marian in Burbank, CA, circa 1960.

CHAPTER FIVE

THE FAMILY'S LIFE ON THE FARM

The family moved frequently during the period of the 1920s; it was an un-settled period in our life. According to the address on my birth certificate our family was living on a farm at Parlier, CA when I was born. Parlier is a small rural town southeast of Fresno, near Selma. They had a rural address out-side the village, suggesting that Dad was a farm laborer at the time.

After arriving in California, the family lived in Yettem, where Dad began work as a laborer on the same farm as Avak. Over a period of five years, they moved frequently. Avak bought a farm in Oleander, south of Fresno, which he lost within a year or two because he could not make the mortgage payments. Avak then bought a farm at Fowler that he lost two years later because he was again unable to make the payments. From the Fowler farm they moved to Parlier, where Dad worked as a laborer. Because the mortgage holder could not find a buyer in 1925 he again sold the Fowler farm back to Avak. I was born while the family lived in Parlier, but they soon moved back to the Fowler ranch.

My family lived with Avak until his death in 1931. Dad and Mom inherited the ranch with a mortgage that proved difficult for them to make the annual debt and interest payments. In about 1932 a Fresno attorney whose surname was Snow had befriended Dad. He drove out to talk with my parents about a new way to refinance the mortgage—the Roosevelt administration had established the Feder-al Land Bank to help small farmers facing loss of their farms to refinance.

Mr. Snow helped fill out and submit the application papers. The result was that the mortgage was refinanced, and extended over a longer period so that our annual payments were reduced. In some earlier years our income had been inadequate because September rains damaged the raisin crop, but with the new financing from the Federal Land Bank, we were able to make ends meet.

When Mr. Snow saved the farm, he wasn't able to save the farming equipment, which was mortgaged through Fresno Agricultural Works, a big farm equipment store in downtown Fresno. While in the second grade—I must have been about 7, they came out to the farm and hauled away our equipment. I don't know where I got the idea, but I feared they would put Mom in jail because we were debtors. For several months during my low period when I would be tired right after lunch, I feared that Mom may have been taken to jail that day, and I would cry softly at my desk. Mrs. Gower, the teacher, would come to comfort me, and want to know what was wrong. I never could tell her, nor did I tell my parents of my fears. We borrowed equipment from the neighbors to do the farming that year. Who knows what similar emotional problems persist in the minds of children today that affect them in school or at any time? Who knows? A child is very sensitive. I know now that a child should not have to be worried about his mother for that reason. We had great admiration for Mr. Snow because of what he did for our family:

- He enabled us to hold on to the farm and pay off the mortgage in 1939,

- we were able to purchase implements again to till the vineyard,

- and for Dad to buy a tractor in 1939 and do away with owning horses as draft animals. We were able to earn money doing custom work.

- In short, he enabled us to remain as a family farm and to achieve what we ultimately accomplished.

THE HOUSE BURNS

Isabel and I have different memories of the family house on the Fowler ranch. I recall it as a two-story house with the bedrooms upstairs. Isabel told me that it was a large one-story house with a veranda on two sides. Isabel is probably correct. One night when we were asleep, Arpie awakened because she smelled smoke, and found the house on fire. She awakened all of us and made sure we had vacated our sleeping rooms. Being young, and probably very sleepy, I went back into the house to find my bed. Making a head count, Arpie noticed I was missing, and correctly thought I had gone back to bed. She came in after me and for the second time, took me out and made sure someone held my hand. The house was completely burned and few of our belongings survived.

The three photos on this page show Mom and Dad in similar backgrounds from early dates to older dates, in succession from top to bottom. Whenever Dad had an occasion to go somewhere off the farm, be it Fowler or Fresno, he would convince Mom to go with him, just to get Mom out for a change of scenery.

After the fire, we needed living quarters, and so Dad converted the large hay wagon into a sleeping room. He surrounded the 8 x 16-foot floor with canvas walls, leaving the "roof" exposed to the stars. He parked the wagon under a large walnut tree near the yard. We also used a nearby small building for storage. That building was 18 x 20 feet, with one window at the rear and opposite the entrance door. We made-do with the hay wagon and the storage building, while the replacement house was being built.

The new house was small for a family our size, about 30 x 36 to 40 feet long with two bedrooms, a connecting bathroom and walk-in closet between them. Opposite these rooms was a large kitchen (which functioned as the community room) and a parlor we seldom used. Several years later a nearby farmer who once had worked as a carpenter, added an enclosed, screened and glassed porch across the back of the house, adding another 200 square feet (20 feet long and 10 feet deep). In the summer months this served as our living room and was where the refrigerator was placed, and later where the laundry facilities were located. The room lacked heat, so we used it for about seven months out of the year as our living and dining area.

Mom and Dad used one of the bedrooms, and Marian, Chuck and I shared the second bedroom that contained two full-sized beds. Of these, Marian had one bed, while Chuck and I shared the second bed. Arpie lived with the Markar family in Fresno when she entered college, but I don't recall where Isabel slept. Within several years Marian left for Berkeley, so Chuck and I then had separate beds.

I don't feel like I ever had much of a childhood. At least I don't recall one. Living on a small farm, with a large poor family may have consumed my childhood. A close family to us was the Shahbazian's who had a daughter named Ida, a contemporary of Arpie and Isabel. They sang in the church choir and Ida was a soloist. The Shahbazian's also took care of their granddaughter, Gloria, who was my age and who had a cupboard full of toys—cars, trucks, and things like that. I played with those when I was somewhere around 3 to 5 years old, but I don't recall any other toys and none that I had. I don't recall Gloria again until we were in high school, but we were in the same classes from first grade upward.

FARM WORK WAS TOUGH

We harvested the grapes ourselves—it was about a 2 to 3 week picking season for us since it was all done with family labor. Being too small to pick, my job beginning at age five, was to spread the grape bunches on the trays when Mom had picked a full bucket. Mom was very nice to me, but when I had to work for Isabel, life was a bit tougher. She picked faster than Mom did, and required me to be available at any time when her pan was full. If I goofed off, Isabel had a mean pinch—she'd pinch my upper arm to a hurt to get me back to work. Lest I leave the impression that Isabel was a ogre, I was very afraid of the dark, and our outhouse was - well, it was an outhouse. Because of the dark I was afraid to use it before going to bed, but Isabel always walked me to it, and stood guard until I was ready to go back to the house. Isabel was driven, but she was kind, too.

1934 and 1935 were wet years, and rains came sometimes while the grapes were still on the ground causing us to lose the crop. I remember one of those years, after selling what crop there was and paying the annual grocery bill at Boyajian's store, we had about $150 left for living expenses and paying farming bills like electricity.

Boyajian's Grocery Store Financed Us When Necessary

When our income was so low that we had trouble paying for groceries, Mr. Boyajian would extend credit for groceries from crop to crop, and in most cases we were able to pay the bill in full annually. There were a few years when credit was extended longer than an annual basis and we could not pay off the bill. In those years, Mom would make cheese and butter to sell to Mr. Boyajian, against our account, and also she would sell eggs to him. In those years, the family had less cheese, butter, and eggs to eat. But the mortgage, taxes, and interest payments were always on time and we no longer faced the annual concern of losing our house and farm.

The Boyajian store was typical of many grocery stores of the era. The shelves of canned goods were stacked behind the counter and you told the grocer what you wanted, and with a special hook he would remove the item from the stacks and place it on the counter. Mr. Boyajian treated all his customers with great respect, whether they were in arrears for a long time or current on their account. He knew his Armenian customers would pay as quickly as they could. When we had transportation, I accompanied my parents to that store frequently; or else Dad would walk the 7 miles to the store.

Eventually Things Got Better

Dad bought a 1923 or 24 Ford model T touring (open) car. It must have been cheap, but he needed a car to go to work. He had been lucky to get on at Sun-Maid Raisin Growers co-op in Fresno, working in the shed lifting field boxes of raisins. Two men would lift the boxes, each weighing about 220 pounds. Dad was known as "shorty" at Sun-Maid, so lifting those boxes with a taller man meant Dad carried more than one-half of the weight. There's no wonder that he developed back pains in later years.

A highlight of the summers was attending the Fowler Armenian Church picnics, usually at Kingsburg along the Kings River, about 15 miles from our ranch.

During the winters, starting the Model T was a real problem. Dad would jack up one rear wheel, pour steaming hot water on the manifold and carburetor, and then hand crank the engine, choking it while doing these things. Sometimes the car was very cantankerous and difficult to start. It would test the patience of Job. Then, one summer Dad overhauled the Model T engine several times. Once, he used old leather from the horse reins as bearing material because he couldn't afford metal bearings. That didn't work well, so Dad bought a 1928 Chevrolet, the least expensive car they made. The tire problem continued with this car too until Dad was able to buy new, cheap tires.

GRADE SCHOOL WAS INTERESTING, BUT …

I was eager for school to start in September because it meant the end of summer farm work. I also really enjoyed being with groups of students. From the second half of the sixth grade through the eighth grade, I was probably the most popular student in my class. During this 2½-year period, my classmates elected me class president each semester. This continued into high school too. I must credit my awareness of different ethnicities, by always balancing nationalities on my appointed committees.

Then in consolidated high school, where our class consisted of over 100 students, I was elected vice president in my freshman year, then president of the sophomore year, president of the junior year, and then vice president of the student body in my senior year. In all of these years, my family (siblings and parents) was very supportive.

THE AROMA OF BAKING BREAD

There is a twist of the embarrassment of taking sandwiches made with Armenian bread to school with the following section that highlights our enjoyment when our parents baked bread.

An important part of any Armenian family's diet is bread. Each month our parents bought 100 pounds of whole wheat flour and made the flat Armenian bread that was a staple in our diet. Using our huge, heavy aluminum tub (about 36 inches wide and 10-12 inches deep), Dad poured in the flour, added warm water, some salt, a bit of olive oil, and a cake of yeast, then mixed it all by hand for as long as necessary. The resulting dough was very heavy and he would cover it with coats and blankets and leave it over night to rise in the kitchen.

The next morning, Mom and Dad would rise early, shape the dough into balls weighing about 1 pound each (slightly bigger than a softball), and set them aside to rise again. They'd cover these with muslin dish towels to keep them from drying and when this job was done, there would be 100 balls, still rising a bit in size while Mom and Dad had a breakfast of coffee, bread and homemade cheese. Meanwhile, the stove was fired up with wood that Chuck and I (depending on our age) had chopped. The oven made the kitchen quite warm and toasty.

Dad would then roll the dough flat (about 1/8 in. thick and 20 in. in diameter), place it on a plywood board, much like a modern pizza peel, and give it to Mom, who would place it on the bottom of the oven until it was partly baked. Bubbles would develop in a few minutes and she would run the plywood under the bread and lift it on to the top rack, where it would finish baking. Meanwhile, Dad would have rolled out another ball of dough and given it to Mom who placed it on the bottom shelf. They continued this routine for several hours until all 100 balls had been baked into bread.

The baked breads would be set aside to cool and when cooled, we would stack them inside a huge wood-staved barrel that looked like it was made of hardwood, because it had no wood or pine pitch odor. The barrel would hold all 100 sheets of bread and we covered the stack with more dishtowels to keep the bread free from dust. A hundred flat breads would last us a month, meaning we ate 3 each day, or one at each meal.

On bread baking day, we kids awakened to the aroma of fresh bread and yeast throughout our small house. Our treat was a piece of the fresh, warm bread, slathered with homemade butter and eaten with homemade cheese. I fondly recall the aroma and taste of these breakfasts on baking day.

The Excitement of the Holidays

Holidays were always pleasant times with our family. In addition to the state and national holidays, we had special Armenian Church holidays and celebrations and we took advantage of them all. Dad's philosophy was that Sunday was the Lord's day, and we did not work for profit. The exception being when we had to irrigate or during harvest. When it was our turn to get water from the irrigation district, we would do the minimum amount of work needed to use our water allotment. Usually we received water for 3 or 4 days at a time, about three times during the summer. When water was available, we had to use it or lose our turn without an opportunity to make it up later. The other exception was during the grape drying season in September. With grapes drying on the ground on paper trays, a rain storm would damage the raisins. Those were workdays on all farms, to reduce the crop loss and to save the raisins. We worked as necessary on Sundays, evenings, and at any time to save the year's crop.

Our big holidays were Christmas and Easter because they were both designated government holidays, based on Christian significance. The Armenian Church, like most Eastern Orthodox faiths, follows the Julian calendar (named for Julius Caesar in 46 B.C. Later came the Gregorian calendar, adopted by other Christian religions.) The Julian calendar is about 2 weeks later than the Gregorian, so Armenians would celebrate Christmas on December 25 because it was the national holiday, but the official Armenian Church celebration of the birth of Christ occurs on January 6. Armenians celebrate the commercial holiday on December 25, as a time to exchange gifts, but the church Christmas is the religious celebration.

I do not remember whether we had a Christmas tree during our very poorest years of the Great Depression. Traditionally, we would have a tree with lots of tinsel streamers (saved from prior years) hanging on the boughs and ornaments on the branches, with an angel on the tree top. We would hang stockings on Christmas Eve, and in the morning we'd rise early to see whether Santa had been to our house. Santa would stuff our stockings with oranges, walnuts, and raisins. We were thrilled to get these special gifts, even though we had them most of the year. Dad was the one who took the role of filling stockings, and all the fruits and nuts would be highly polished, very lovely specimens. Dad was a perfectionist, always seeking for the best in whatever he did.

Regardless of our financial condition, our big feast was held on the religious date of Christmas. Our table would be laden with dishes of stuffed meat balls in broth, one of Mom's specialties, roasted chicken or lamb, mounds of rice pilaf, fresh roasted vegetables and vegetable side dishes. Dessert was either cake or pie, most often lemon pies. When we could afford it, or trade oranges or something from the farm for a turkey, we'd have that as a special treat. Chuck had dibs on the drumsticks, Isabel liked the wings, and I think the rest of us were just happy to have turkey.

Easter was also a very religious holiday-feast day for us, and often the priest would be our guest, since Dad was a deacon and a church trustee, and thus was very good friends with the priest. As with Christmas, the table was laden with savory food, but more often we'd also have lamb roasts with vegetables cooked with the meat, especially after the real poverty years.

We exchanged very few presents, but everyone received something. From the beginnings of our ability to earn money from picking fruit for other farmers, and after we had bought our school clothes, we'd have very little money to buy

Clockwise from upper left: Mom and Dad with their first grandchild, Elaine, 4 years old. Mom and Dad at the back entrance to the Fowler farm house, circa 1948, with my dog Bugs that I left with them. Dad and grandson Leon III, circa 1951. Dad and Mom in 1950 with Grandson Leon III. Lee is about 1 year old. Photo about 1950.

gifts. In those early years, I recall being taken to one of the chain stores known as "5 and dime" stores, such as Kress or Woolworth to do my shopping. When Arpie would come home from Berkeley for Christmas, she would go shopping with me. Arpie was so sweet, and so kind. Often I'd spend about 50 cents for each gift, and then I'd wrap them with Christmas paper saved from prior years. Actually, 50 cents would go quite a long ways; I think a pair of socks only cost 25 cents.

Too soon, as the siblings grew up and developed their own interests, our holidays changed in significance. Arpie died in 1943, and Isabel and George had moved out of state to Spokane. Chuck spent 6 years out-of-country with the military, and I went off to college at San Luis Obispo in 1945. Marian had enrolled at UC Berkeley in 1941. Then, I got married on December 31, 1947, and after graduation, we moved to Oregon. Betty and I would spend Christmas holidays in California, sometimes in Fresno, and sometimes in San Luis Obispo. Having our children around was a special treat for my parents. Dad would lurch around the house until he heard a child awaken, and then he would change the diaper and warm up a bottle. He'd cuddle them, walk around and talk to them; he'd be in an euphoric state. He sure loved having Leon around, because he was the first Garoian grandson, and especially named after him. He'd hoist him on his shoulders and carry him around the yard, always carrying on a conversation, probably making all kinds of promises.

A Close Family

Just as Chuck and I were close in age and did a lot of things together, so did Arpie and Isabel. Arpie and George were in the same years of school and age, while Isabel was George's girl, so the three of them were naturally tossed together as a group.

I was the last of the children to leave home. Coming home one early summer evening, I looked into the house from the driveway as I drove in, and saw Dad and Mom sitting on the bench we called a "sadier", with Dad's arm around Mom's shoulders. I wondered do old folks show affection too? Dad must have been 59 and Mom about 50. I was pleasantly surprised.

Chuck and I joined the Boy Scouts when I was old enough, I think 12 years old, and Chuck was 2-3 years older. Besides the regular Scout meetings, we would go to summer Scout camp with Troop 90 of Fowler. I think Chuck left scouting after a couple of years, and I stayed on. When we went to summer camp, at Camp Oneonta in the mountains east of Fresno, Chuck and I would each take a huge homemade wool comforter as our bedding. Of course, we were the only ones without sleeping bags, and I felt very conspicuous and different. I don't recall how Chuck felt, because he quit going to camp when he was hired by the U.S. Forest Service eradicating gooseberry and wild currant plants in the mountains. These plants were chopped because they were host plants for white pine blister rust, a fatal disease for these pine trees. I was scheduled to go to Scout camp, when I was 14 and I asked the folks if they could buy me a sleeping bag. Though we were still poor, Dad and Mom took me to Gottschalks in Fresno and for $3.99 bought me a sleeping bag so I was not different from the others. I was very spoiled and felt selfish, after I realized Dad spent the last of his $10 cash to get me to "feel better".

Our parents were very supportive of us, at least when I was at home and attending Fowler High School. Dad relied on his children and Mom to work on the farm, since he could not afford to hire anyone. Mom worked during the growing season, harvest, and in the winter pruning and vine-tying season, which were important activities. Arpie and Isabel worked in the cannery in Selma during the summer season cutting and pitting peaches to be canned, I do not recall that Marian worked in the cannery. Isabel was the tomboy of the family, and Dad taught her how to milk the cow, when she was about 14. Later, Marian took over that job until she left home and then the job went to Chuck. It finally became my chore when none of the siblings remained at home. Isabel drove a car when we had one, but Arpie reached driving age in the years we didn't have a car. I doubt whether Arpie ever did drive a car. However, George had a car and when he was available, he would drive us around.

School Sports

Chuck was interested in track as a sport and competed in races such as one and two miles. I also was interested in track, running the 100-yard dash and was the anchor-man for the 440-yard relay. In addition, I went out for football and basketball too, so I had a full-season of after-school sports that kept me from the farm. Dad must have been inconvenienced, but Mom was recruited to help him. He adjusted the farm work with Mom's help to accommodate my sports schedule. Few Armenian dads did that for their sons. Mom was afraid I might get injured, especially from playing football. In my freshman high school year, Isabel brought Mom to watch me play on the junior varsity team in a game with Kingsburg. Mom was on pins and needles the whole time, and I was especially having a great game, but she didn't understand it. Mom was a gentle person, so I am not sure what Isabel could say that would have made Mom be more comfortable about my playing rough sports. When I was a high school junior, I played on the varsity football second team, but I was not good enough to be a starter. That year Mom's fears of my getting hurt came true when I had a painful shoulder separation. I never played football after that, much to Mom's relief. As it was, I was not big enough to be a good football player, but I had "heart" and was competitive, so I was kept on the team. I actually played very little of each game. I am living proof that a youngster can enjoy being on a team for the thrill of the sport and just being with others with similar sports interests.

ACADEMIC ACCOLADES

Despite being dirt poor financially, our family was rich in other ways. First, Dad was a church leader, as well as very popular as a public political speaker. All of my sisters were excellent students, and were on the California State Scholarship merit lists. Marian was also selected by the Fowler High teachers as the outstanding science student of her graduating class, and was presented with the Bausch and Lomb medal and a cash award that she put towards college fees. Arpie and Marian were the most studious of my siblings, and Isabel was next, but Isabel was in love with George, so she was likely diverted from some studies.

Our parents were very proud of their children for their academic achievements. Arpie went on to UC Berkeley and met her requirements for a doctorate, an unheard of achievement for someone from Fowler at the time, and especially from such a poor family. George and Isabel were pretty much a couple throughout their teen years and later George went on to get a degree in entomology. Next he received a master's degree from Oregon State, but I do not recall what Isabel's degree was in. I know she took a lot of science courses, including zoology and botany. Many years later, when George was transferred to Utah State, Isabel went on to get a master's in home economics and nutrition. Marian finished her nursing degree at UC Berkeley and went on to get her Public Health Credential, which is equivalent to a master's degree. Chuck went into forestry, and after his military service, he enrolled and completed a graduate curriculum in international trade at Arizona State. Finally, I earned a bachelor's in plant sciences, and later went on to earn a master's and Ph.D. in economics from the University of Wisconsin.

Mom must have been very pleased that none of her children became farmers. She never liked farm life, but she had no choice for herself. She did everything she could to nurture an interest in education to divert us from farm life, with Dad's blessing, of course. In these ways, we were never rich, but we were a happy family because of these successes of our siblings.

JOYS FROM LIFE ON THE FARM

Today I write these memories and talk about them with my spouse Nina. We each experienced non-economic joys without realizing how fortunate we were to be growing up on a farm, Nina in North Dakota, and me in California. We each remember the nice feeling of walking through warm, wet soil with the mud oozing between our toes, of opportunities to build sand castles with a pet white rat exploring the tunnels we created for it to enjoy its freedom while out of its cage; or the joys of spending a summer without the need to wear shoes unless we were going to town or church; having an opportunity to walk a mile on hot asphalt roads just to jump in a large irrigation ditch for a cooling dip after stripping down to our shorts and not caring who saw us; picking a fresh peach or other fruit from our family orchard to eat with our breakfast; and coming home from school to a snack of dried fruit and walnuts, or in the fall months picking an orange from the trees, feeling the oil from the skins trickling down our small hands, leaving a residue of sweet fragrance. We had no feelings of hunger or fears of where our next meal would come from or when.

Nina and I both were not aware of the character building within our loving families as we were growing up in such a quiet, wholesome environment. As I worked within the grape vines and heard a lone airplane overhead losing altitude as it was preparing to land at the Fresno airport, I did not wonder who was important enough to be a passenger. The thought of some day traveling in an airplane never crossed my mind; the cultural environment I was experiencing did not envision any change in my future from my present. If I thought at all of my existing life, it must have revolved around the undesirable experiences of working with the vines during extremely hot weather, of digging ditches and making furrows among the rows of grapes to help them survive and earn income so we would remain on the farm. I guess some now would call that "building character".

Self Analysis and Soul Searching

There were two conditions to which I was sensitive as a child, but their significance declined over time. In my childhood years I never knew I was from a financially poor family, but now that I have written this memoir, I concede my family was financially poor. We were a rich family in how we respected each other, how we reacted as a nuclear family, in our relations with our church, politics, and treated other people. We worked for everything we ever achieved, and didn't realize some people lived off the earnings of their prior generations and by welfare.

I grew up unaware that I was a member of a second set of circumstances; that of being of Armenian descent and according to some people of influence, I was part of a lower social system. Eventually some social activities were denied me for this reason, as was access to certain employment opportunities while living in the Fresno area. This exposure to such prejudice came as I left my family's sphere of influence and entered into opportunities in which my family ties were unnecessary. The matter of prejudice changed after WWII, and my Armenian peers (who also were first generation-born in the U.S.) enjoyed the result of educational and professional achievements. Education and professional development are significant parts of the social and employment economic ladder, and we took advantage of these opportunities.

From not being aware of being financially poor for the first 10 years of my life while I was under family influences, I began to understand that we were financially handicapped and that my siblings and I worked overtime to reduce this problem. During the period in our life when we were becoming aware of the nationality prejudices that existed, our parents had been guiding us into the solution to this problem through their strong support of education and the professions available to us.

My siblings and I reached national and international prominence because of educational achievements. No one asked what our national origin was. I now reflect back on my siblings, and I see they have had similar professional success: I feel confident they allowed their education and their professional integrity to be recognized and to prevail. I believe my parents' emphasis on education in their children's lives has been successful within a single generation in our family. The wisdom of our parent's guidance may become more evident as the lives of their grandchildren unfold. That is a reflection of our generation's wisdom.

CHAPTER SIX

MOM'S ARMENIAN CUISINE

The complexity of Armenian cuisine reflects the history of the country and its location at the crossroads of east and west, and to a lesser extent, north and south. My travels in the Caucasus Mountain region makes it difficult for me to think in terms of "one Armenian cuisine". From historic Armenia where my ancestors lived for perhaps thousands of years, there remain foods in common with the American Armenians. These are the foods and their preparation also found in Persia, modern Turkey, Georgia, and Lebanon. I grew up with these flavors that were handed down from generation to generation in our family. I believe my mother's cooking essentially reflects a pleasant treat of lovely flavor combinations.

Armenian cuisine is exotic in flavor without being pungent, by relying on the natural exchange of flavors among ingredients. Vegetables and fruits, rice and wheat combined with herbs make sauces and gravies less important to achieve flavors than in many other countries. Lamb is the traditional meat, but when Armenia came under control of the Soviet Union, pork consumption increased to reflect preferences of the Slavic people. Mom never did live under the Russian influence so my mother's cuisine was always true Armenian as it had evolved over thousands of years of influence from neighboring countries and travelers.

As I think back at our family meals on our grape ranch south of Fresno, I visualize the family of five children and two parents sitting around the table in the kitchen, spending time eating a delicious meal and just visiting. That's often when our parents would describe their family life in the old country, sometimes memories of their families, life in their village during peaceful times, and travel distances often measured in hours and days of walking. You can imagine much of their life originated within their families of grandparents, cousins, and close friends. Mealtimes on our vineyard remain a nice memory for me, but we didn't have the aunts, uncles, grandparents, and cousins because they had been killed. The function of eating was more than ingesting sustenance—it was a time for social interaction within the family, except of course, at harvest time.

A typical meal at our house would start with fresh vegetables mostly as a salad with a simple olive oil/vinegar dressing, homemade cheese, flat Armenian bread baked by my parents once a month (the bread never molded or turned rancid), a main dish consisting of vegetables and meat, and nearly always dessert of fresh fruit or dried fruits and nuts when fresh fruits were not in season. My parents enjoyed coffee, while we children drank "tahn", a drink based on diluted homemade yogurt. On Sundays, the main entrée was either roasted chicken, lamb roasted with vegetables, or a New England pot roast that was a specialty of my mother. Armenian coffee, a thick beverage made with powdered (ground) coffee in a special utensil, was served to adults mainly following Sunday meals.

Breakfasts were quite simple and variable depending upon the season. We had home-cured dry olives with cheese and butter. From our flock of 12-18 hens we might have eggs fried in butter. In summer, we'd have Kellogg's corn flakes that we would top with fresh peaches; each morning one of us kids would go into the orchard and pick fruit for our morning cereal. On special occasions we'd have waffles and pancakes. Pancakes and toast were made on the top of the cast iron firebox, so we'd have to stay close to prevent burning. Toasts made on the firebox always seemed to taste better than when made with a toaster, but then, we didn't have the electric toaster. We were encouraged to fix our own breakfasts, which was special for us. We fixed eggs, fried to our preference, and basted the eggs with hot butter.

Many Armenian foods consist of rice and ground meat mixtures, mainly lamb in those days, to have a one-dish hot meal. We added chopped onions, tomatoes, chopped garlic, and parsley, to stuff into tomatoes, peppers, small squash like zucchini, and small eggplant, like Japanese types. These would be dressed with tomato sauce before cooking in the oven or on top of the stove.

Armenians also use a lot of eggplant, prepared in several ways. Mom would roast a large whole eggplant on top of the firebox, turning it frequently so it cooked evenly. Then she would scoop the cooked flesh into a dish, and season it with finely chopped or crushed garlic with olive oil. Sometimes she would cut the eggplant into half-inch slices, and dip the slices in a whipped egg batter, and fry the slices on both sides. Frequently there would be salted sliced cucumbers, hot chili peppers for Dad, and Mom's tourshi (pickled mixed vegetables) too.

To stretch the supply of ground lamb, Armenians often combined fine bulghur wheat with finely chopped onions, parsley, herbs and garlic and prepare the mixture as meat balls cooked in a broth. On special occasions, chopped walnuts would be added to the mixture to make a stuffing for an outside mixture of the meat and bulghur, then boiled in a broth in which they were served as special Kharpet region "stuffed meatballs".

During the depth of the recession of the 1930s, we'd have a rooster or a non-productive hen for our Sunday meal, often stewed. As we got old enough to hold a hatchet, first Chuck, and then I would catch a chicken from the hen house, chop off its head, wing tips, and then the feet, and bleed the fowl before taking it inside for one of our parents to clean and then dip the bird in hot water to pluck the feathers. Rice pilaf with vermicelli was a typical grain to accompany the chicken. Leg of lamb was featured mostly on holidays and special occasions, because of its high cost.

During the grape harvest our meals were simplified to consist of nothing that required cooking, since Mom was picking grapes with us. During the 3 weeks it took to harvest our grapes, a typical lunch was a large watermelon from our garden, Armenian cheese and bread. Sometimes, we would also have Van Camps sardines canned in tomato sauce, with one large sardine for each of us.

Mom and Dad grew a large vegetable garden that supplied us with fresh vegetables used both as meal ingredients and preserved for use in the off-growing season. Globe (round) eggplants were used as ingredients or as a separate dish, and long Japanese eggplant would be used for stuffing. For winter use, the inside seed cavity would be scooped out, and the remainder would be sundried for stuffing in winter months. The dried eggplants would be reconstituted in water, and stuffed with the traditional combination of onions, rice, garlic, chopped tomatoes and ground lamb. We would harvest young grape leaves from our vineyard for use with sarma; non-Armenians such as Greeks call this dish dolmas. It usually is a mixture of rice, chopped onions, tomatoes, ground lamb, and herbs wrapped in young grape leaves, cooked either on top of the stove or in the oven.

Mom and Dad worked together to plant the garden, and enjoyed its harvest, including the preservation of vegetables by sun-drying for off-season use. Okra was another vegetable that was used fresh, prepared with tomatoes, onions, and small pieces of lamb, cooked in a broth as a side dish. Mom would dry the okra for winter use and when needed, she would reconstitute it in water and use it as though fresh from the garden. Tomatoes and Armenian cucumbers, with chopped green onions dressed with olive oil from our trees, and vinegar were typical salads served at least once daily.

We grew every imaginable fruit and nut that could be grown in the Fresno climate. There were navel and Valencia oranges that provided fresh citrus for about 10 months. The Eureka lemon tree bore fruit most of the year; there were blossoms, small fruit, and ripe fruit throughout the year. When the orange supply was consumed, I would eat a fresh lemon I picked from the tree to provide my vitamin C. When fresh tree fruits were in season, we would dry our own supply for the winter.

There were also homemade vegetable pickles made from the garden harvests, and Mom seemed to be able to preserve nearly every vegetable we grew. My favorites were tiny watermelons about the size of a ping pong ball, baby globe eggplant, cut in half, and held together with sewing thread after inserting a slice of garlic between the halves, and pickled cabbage and cauliflower florets. In a separate crock, Mom would keep homemade cheese in a mild brine. I'd like a piece of cheese with fresh bread as a snack after returning from school and doing the chores.

Below are samples of my favorite recipes of Mom's that were passed on to me, then to Lee and Lisa, and now being made by Nina.

SOME GAROYAN FAMILY RECIPES

Most of the recipes that follow have been handed down from Mom Garoyan. Several come from cousins of my Dad who lived in Habousi. These recipes are mainly those that have my Mother's own touch; there are also good recipe books that contain other versions of these same foods.

SALADS

White Bean

This is one of my favorite recipes, especially served chilled during the summer. It is easy to prepare, very flavorful, and complements many dishes. Try adding some chilled shrimp for variety. Goes well with toasted sourdough bread. Serves 4 for lunch or 6 as a side dish.

Ingredients

2 cans (14 ½ oz) white beans (Great Northern, Navy, Cannellini, but not Garbanzo)
¼ c. onions finely chopped
¼ c. parsley, finely chopped
¼ c. green onions, chopped
½ red bell pepper, finely chopped
½ green bell pepper, finely chopped

Combine the ingredients in a serving bowl.

Dressing

¼ c. extra-virgin olive oil
½ tsp. salt
¼ tsp. ground black pepper
½ tsp. ground cumin, or more to taste
Juice of 2 lemons, pulp removed

Wisk the dressing items together until blended. Pour over the beans and ingredients and toss.

Cucumber and Yogurt (Lee's Version)

2 medium cucumbers (I prefer small Persian cucumbers if available)
2 cloves garlic
¼ tsp. salt
1 tbls. dried mint leaves, finely crushed (or dill)
1½ c. unflavored yogurt (not Greek-style)

Peel cucumbers, and slice into rounds about 1/8" thick. Don't use cucumbers with large seeds—they may be bitter even if you remove seeds.

Peel garlic and crush. Then combine salt and crushed garlic in a mortar and with the pestle, grind into a smooth paste. Add the mint to the yogurt and mix well. Stir in the sliced cucumbers and adjust for seasoning.

[Note: you may reduce the amount of garlic, but I don't think it is as flavorful. I choose not to use dill in this version. You may substitute dill for the mint, but do not use both. I sometimes use an additional teaspoon of dried mint, depending on what is being served with the salad. Taste it before adding more. If you use fresh mint, reduce by ½.]

Bulghur Salad

Bulghur is a nutritious dried wheat cereal, high in protein but with little fat when cooked. I can make a lunch meal with cold bulghur alone or with a dollop of yogurt on top. I also like to eat bulghur with pickled peppers on the side. Bulghur is very versatile cooked with small bits of beef or lamb, or even served with chicken breasts. Serve warm or cold as either a main dish or salad.

> ½ c. olive oil
> 4 cloves garlic
> 2 large or 3 medium onions, finely chopped
> 1 15-oz. can chopped tomatoes
> 1 tsp. sugar
> salt and pepper to taste
> ½ c. chopped fresh parsley
> 1/3 c. fresh lemon juice
> 1 c. medium-grained bulghur

Heat olive oil in a large sauce pan. Brown and discard one clove of chopped garlic. Crush remaining garlic and add with onion, sauté until onions are transparent. Add tomatoes, salt, pepper, and sugar. Simmer for 20 minutes. Turn off heat and add bulghur. Blend the mixture well. Cover and let stand for 20 minutes without removing the lid.

Add lemon juice and chopped parsley and mix well. Serve on a bed of lettuce. Garnish with chopped parsley or finely chopped fresh tomatoes.

ONE-DISH MEALS

These recipes are for foods comprised of meat, vegetables, and seasonings that may be served with a salad and other condiments.

Armenian Stuffed Grape Leaves (Sarma)

> 1 lb. lean ground lamb
> ½ c. uncooked long-grain white rice (washed and drained)
> 1 large yellow onion, finely chopped
> ½ c. finely chopped parsley
> 1 ½ cups canned tomatoes, finely chopped
> Salt and pepper to taste (I use 1 tsp. of each)
> ¼ c. freshly squeezed and strained lemon juice

1 pint preserved grape vine leaves (available in a middle-eastern grocery store, or the gourmet section of a large supermarket)

Combine the lamb, rice, onion, parsley, tomatoes, lemon juice, salt and pepper in a bowl and blend well.

Wash and drain the grape leaves to remove salt. Lay several leaves on a flat surface with the stem up (cut the stem off at the leaf and discard) and with the stem end toward you.

Place about 1 tablespoon of the stuffing mixture near the stem end and turn the sides of the leaves toward the center of the leaf and roll firmly away from you toward the tip, making a cylinder.

Cover the bottom of a shallow pan with old, tough grape leaves or several layers of head lettuce to keep the sarma from scorching when being cooked. Layer the sarma around the pan next to each other. After the lower level is filled, place the second layer of sarma on top of the spaces between the sarma on the lower level. When all the sarma are wrapped and placed in the pan, add enough water to nearly reach the top of the sarma on the top layer. Place a flat dish over the sarma, cover the pan, and bring the pan to a boil, then reduce heat to a gentle simmer for about 50-60 minutes on top of the stove. Add more water if needed during cooking.

Serve on a plate. Sometimes Mom would top the hot sarma with plain yogurt as a dressing.

LAMB

Lamb is the traditionally preferred meat in Armenian cuisine. Lamb can be served in many ways: twice ground instead of beef hamburger, legs with shank removed for roasting or butterflied for the barbecue, and various cuts of chops and steaks. I prefer to barbecue over coals that include grape stumps or cuttings for the source of charcoal when possible. Otherwise, I use fruit wood pieces soaked in water for 5 or 6 hours to keep them from flaming. Gas barbecues work well too.

Lee's Lamb Chops

Loin lamb chop that are about 1½" thick (I prefer Costco chops.)

Wash and dry chops. Using a small knife, remove the marrow on the top of the bone and trim any fat on the outside of the chops. I trim all silver skin portions near top bone, so all that remains is meat.

Plan 2 chops for each adult and one for a child. The bones are good to gnaw on too.

I then use the following dry rub over the chops:

Mix:
   1 tsp. granulated garlic
   1 tsp. kosher salt
   ½ tsp. ground cumin
   ½ tsp. chili powder (the pure stuff)
   ½ tsp. coarse ground pepper

Then Mix separately:
   2 large cloves fresh garlic, crushed
   3 tbls. yellow onions, finely chopped

Preparation:
To all of the dry chops, rub in the dry mix and press into the meat. Next apply a coating of the fresh garlic-onion mix and press into the meat. Finally coat each chop with olive oil and red wine from a blend of 1/3 olive oil and 2/3 wine. It will take about a tablespoon of this for each chop, perhaps applied twice. Set aside until you are ready to grill.

Grilling:
Preheat the grill to hot. Sear the chops for about 2 minutes on BOTH sides. Move to indirect heat and continue cooking, about three minutes on each side, for a total of about 4-5 minutes for medium rare (pink center). Remove chops and set them under a foil tent for 5 minutes before serving.

Serve with bulghur pilaf, green beans, asparagus, or whatever vegetables you like. I always serve a fresh green vegetable salad, too, with vinegar/oil dressing.

Shish Kebab

This dish is picturesque, but it takes more effort and personally I enjoy the lamb chops more.

Lamb Shish Kebab (Garoyan Family Version)

Note: Buy an upper portion of a leg of lamb with the bone removed. Wash the leg and dry with paper towels. Remove and discard the layer of external fat. Separate the muscles in their natural layers, and remove the thin layer of silver lining, gristle, and fat deposits remaining on each muscle. The lower leg portion will have tendons that need to be removed, too. I do that by using a sharp knife, and try to skin the tendon and silver lining away from the meat (muscle). The result will be large pieces of meat that you cut into chunks about 1½ inches square. Plan on 4 to 5 pieces of meat for each adult.

Preparation of the meat as described above removes the tough parts that are difficult to chew and may require nearly an hour to do.

Leg of lamb as described above.

After cutting the lamb into pieces, place them in a bowl as you prepare the marinade.

In a small container:
    finely chop a medium sized yellow onion
    3 garlic cloves, crushed or finely chopped
    ¼ of a green bell pepper seeded and finely chopped
    3 tbls. of olive oil
    1 tsp. salt; 1 teaspoon coarse-ground black pepper.
    2 tbls. dry oregano (or Italian seasoning)

Mix these ingredients, and add them to the container of lamb.

Add about 1 cup of dry red wine (Zinfandel or Cab Sauvignon) and ½ c. olive oil over the lamb, and coat the meat and herbs with the wine. If prepared the day before, cover and refrigerate, or allow meat to remain at room temperature if prepared on the day to be cooked. Mix the meat and marinade every several hours.

The preferred way to cook the lamb is over charcoal, using mesquite charcoal or grape stumps if available. Gas burners work okay but do not have the smoke flavor of wood.

About 15 minutes before cooking, place the meat on metal skewers (the kind with flat sides). Try to sort meat of about equal size on each skewer to get uniformity of cooking. Leave about ¼ inch between cubes of meat on the skewers to allow heat to penetrate. It takes about 6-8 minutes for larger pieces of meat to cook medium rare, which will be pink in the center. Place skewers over high heat to sear the meat on at least 2 sides, then lower heat or move coals to a cooler place. Turn the skewers for uniform cooking.

Traditionally, shish kebab appears with alternate pieces of meat and vegetables. This looks very artsy, but the meat and vegetables do not cook at the same rate. I skewer each type of vegetable separately and although I cook vegetables and meat at the same time I watch to remove each when they are finished cooking.

Vegetables to barbecue with the lamb

You can use any vegetable you enjoy cooked over coals. Typically I use the following:

   yellow onions, skinned, and cut into pieces

   bell peppers, seeded and cut into quarters, then in half.

   fresh tomatoes, cut in half or quarters. I sometimes use whole small tomatoes

   summer squash, cut in half lengthwise. (Place directly on grill)

After cleaning and preparation as above, place in a plastic bag and coat with 3-4 tbls. of olive oil and 2-3 tbls. dried Italian seasoning. Set aside as you skewer the meat.

Vegetables take varying amounts of time to cook, so be ready to remove them from the heat at the right time.

To Serve:

Serve the meat and vegetables together on a single plate, or separately depending on how much is prepared.

Serve with bulghur pilaf or rice pilaf with a vegetable salad on the side. A good red wine, similar to the wine used in the meat marinade will be appropriate to serve with the dinner. Leftovers are very good served cold the next day.

Lee's Lima Beans

   1 lb. dried lima beans (I prefer large beans)

   1 large onion (coarsely chopped)

   8 large cloves of garlic (minced)

   2 cans broth, low-sodium, low fat (I use chicken, but vegetarian is okay too)

   1 can finely chopped tomatoes (14 oz.)

   ½ tsp. coarse ground pepper

   salt to taste (I use ½ tsp. or to taste)

   several tbsp. olive oil to sauté vegetables

   2 stalks celery chopped

   2 tbsp. Italian seasoning (or 1 tbsp. Italian plus 1 tbsp. dry Oregano)

Optional

   One smoked ham shank, trimmed of fat, cut into bite-sized pieces. Place the bone in the mixture too. I also add ½ tsp. of Liquid Smoke.

Preparation

Cover beans with water, bring to active boil for 2 minutes, remove from burner and set aside in its water for 1 hour. Option: soak the dry beans overnight in enough water to double volume of beans.

Drain water when beans are fully plump.

In olive oil, sauté chopped onions for 5 minutes over medium heat, add celery and later add garlic until onions are light amber.

To the drained beans, add chicken broth, and enough water to cover the beans. Add pepper, sautéed onions, and tomatoes.

Cover, bring to a boil, and then reduce heat to a simmer. After 30 minutes, add the ham shank if you are using ham, and continue cooking until the beans are cooked. I like the beans thoroughly cooked to where they may be considered mushy.

Additional step if desired: For a thicker sauce, purée and add one can of "butter beans". Or, remove two cups of cooked limas and purée to add as a thickener. Add the puréed beans to the limas during the last 5 minutes of cooking.

To serve, I embellish the cooked beans with pure, crushed horseradish. One half tsp. per dish is about right. I prefer Morehouse Prepared Horseradish (it is the pure stuff).

Enjoy with good, crusty French bread.

Garoyan's Cioppino (For 8)

    8 cloves garlic, chopped or minced
    3 medium onions (each size of tennis ball), coarsely chopped
    1 bell green pepper, seeded and coarsely chopped
    1/2 c. finely chopped celery
    1/3 c. carrots, finely diced
    1/3 c. good quality olive oil

Heat olive oil in a large heavy pan, sauté above ingredients until onions are transparent

Then, add:

    2 cans diced tomatoes (14 ounces each)
    1 c. tomato sauce (optional)
    2 bay leaves
    3 or 4 tbsp. Italian spices
    1 tsp. dried oregano leaves
    medium ground pepper to taste

juice of 1 lemon
salt to taste

Simmer for 2-3 minutes

Then add:
2 bottles clam juice (8 ounce bottles)
2 cups red or dry white wine.

Seafoods
1 1/2 lbs firm fleshed white fish (red snapper, sea bass, rock cod)
1 uncooked crab, broken into pieces and cracked, add 5 minutes before end of simmering
1 dozen fresh mussels
1 lb. shrimp, de-veined
1 lb. clams in shell

Simmer for 12-15 minutes.

If liquid is too much, remove fish if necessary to drain some liquid and reserve. Concentrate the liquid until at your desired consistency. If more liquid is needed, add wine as appropriate

Garnish servings with chopped parsley and lemon wedges. Serve with crusty sour dough bread, preferably not buttered. A green vegetable salad goes well with this.

MENU FOR A FESTIVE DINNER

An example of a festive Armenian meal menu is given below. It was prepared for six guests and Nina and me. The specific menu for the special dinner for guests reflects foods that may be served at a "festive event", but not typically for a daily or even Sunday meal. Even so, the flavors being offered are typical of what we call Western Armenian cuisine.

The Courses

Hors d'oeuvres—an assortment of dried olives, strips of dried New York beef steak seasoned with herbs (Soudjuk from an Armenian or Mediterranean deli), pickled vegetables called tourshi and various cheeses, with Armenian flat bread.

Fresh Vegetable Salad (a typical salad of tomatoes, greens, olives, with olive oil and vinegar dressing flavored with herbs).

Kharpert Keufta: Stuffed meatballs served with yogurt-mint sauce. This is a specialty from the region of my Father, perfected by my Mother. It has been in our family for several generations.

This is a dish of ground lamb and fine bulghur wheat that forms the exterior for the seasoned stuffing. The stuffing mixture consists of onions, chopped walnuts, minced lamb, and herbs. The stuffed meatballs are cooked in a broth, and served with the broth topped with a yogurt sauce. This lovely recipe often makes a meal by itself.

Barbecued Lamb: You may be served butterflied leg of lamb, as selected by your host. The leg of lamb is marinated in a mixture of herbs, onions, vegetables, olive oil, and red wine. The meat is served with vegetables barbecued with the lamb, and served with a choice of rice and wheat (bulghur) pilaf. Do not be surprised if you are offered an additional lamb plate as well.

Dessert and coffee: An assortment of Armenian pastries (baklava). Served with sweetened Armenian coffee.

Armenian Cognac: Armenia was the choice producer of brandy for the Soviet republic. This brandy is from the award winning Armenian Cognac Company located in Yerevan, now owned by Remy of France.

Wines: Appropriate wines before and during the meal should be served.

GRANDSON BEN'S VERSION OF PREPARING SHISH KEBAB

While we were visiting son Lee's family in Scottsdale, we suggested we would prepare a shish kebab meal, with 13-year-old Ben's help, thinking this would be a nice opportunity to acquaint him with preparing Armenian cuisine. His father thought that was a good idea, and told him to observe what we did, and to take notes of the process. After we had enjoyed our meal, I asked Ben if I could review his notes. The following is a typical teenager's version of making a pretty elegant meal:

The gathered materials in order to perform the operation.
olive oil
onion
garlic
pepper
Italian herbs

1. Wash and dry the bloody slaughtered meat.
2. Butcher and hack off the fat and hear the chopped slices scream in pain. (not all meat, not all fat)
3. Also shove the knife into the dead meat just below any gristle and rip it off.

4. When done w/ that put in the thing and RUB (ha ha) olive oil on each. Not too much.
5. Sprinkle garlic and onion on it all, not excessive.
6. Put pepper on too. A little on each slice.
7. Then press it all in with the rounded side of a spoon.
8. Turn each side over and repeat the spicing process. Add Italian seasoning to this side only. A lot.
9. Get 1/3 cup of red wine and spread it evenly.

I was not trained to teach students of this age. I'd hate to be a teacher for a classroom of these students. I'm sure I would not have reached my present age.

Arpie and Dad in the backyard of the Fowler farm, circa 1938. Arpie had finished her Ph.D. requirements and Dad's jaunty look reveals his pride, too.

Left to Right:

Arpie, unidentified, Lee (front), Louise Boyajian (whose husband purchased the first farm we lost), her son Ovan (holding dog), Dad clowning with hands above his head, Isabel, Chuck, Mom and Marian. Circa 1929.

The Kaloostian family: George, Elaine and Isabel, Spokane, WA where George was an entomologist for the U.S. Department of Agriculture. Circa 1944.

Back row, left to right: Isabel, Dad, Mom, Marian.

Kneeling: Chuck and Lee.

Photo taken on the Fowler farm in front of the orange orchard, circa 1935.

PART B

THE LATER YEARS

CHAPTER SEVEN

FEELINGS ABOUT BEING
THE LAST OF THE NUCLEAR FAMILY

This is a tough chapter to write, and I am having a difficult time starting. The loss of loved ones is difficult to think about, even after so many years. It becomes especially personal when you realize how close this family has been. From the family's beginning, we had no close nor nearby relatives, no grandparents, no aunts nor uncles, or cousins. Except for hundreds of family friends, we were like an island to itself. We were virtually alone as for family, so we became very close; we talked around the table at mealtimes, and the haven of the kitchen table was always busy because that was where the heat for the house emanated. The kitchen cook stove provided a cozy place for us to meet; the living room became a vacant room with no central heat. In the summer the living room would be too hot for comfort, so we congregated in the large screened porch or outside under a tree. The "living" room simply served no purpose in our family living.

We became close too, because there were thirteen years between Arpie, the eldest, and me, the youngest, with five children, we relied on each other. Hand-me-down clothes were the norm; when you tired of a garment, there was always another child to hand the garment to, unless you were the youngest by which time it may have been worn out. Even the youngest could wonder when would the next oldest become tired of a garment so I get it as mine—a new item for me.

We also worked together. As a family we all worked at harvesting apricots and peaches from our trees and drying them for sale or winter use, harvesting the grapes to dry into raisins, picking the wine grapes to deliver to the winery, or picking cotton down what seemed like extra-long rows. We rubbed elbows doing this, and it seemed there was no end to our group activities. We relied on each other for help in education too, and in our family, every child kept going to the next level of education available with financial help as was available.

This family togetherness involved George too. He had a science-oriented mind, where some of us were deficient, so he tutored all of us at one time or another, probably with the exception of Arpie, who was his intellectual equal.

Because we were such a close knit family, even an absence, like leaving Fowler to attend Fresno State College (a distance of 10 miles), left a huge void among the siblings. Arpie was the first to leave Fresno for Berkeley, and eventually all of us children moved away. A permanent departure, as from death, leaves an unbelievable void that never seems to heal. I am sure my parents had such devastating experiences when the eldest child, then another die. There must be nothing as devastating as when a parent loses a child who has not had a full life before death. That has been the experience in the Garoyan family. First to die was Arpie, who could be considered the crown jewel of the children, though I am sure my parents did not think in those terms.

THE CHRONOLOGY OF DEATHS AMONG MY SIBLINGS

Arpie (born July 4, 1912; died July 12, 1943)

Arpie died after nearly spending a year as a bed patient at UC Hospital in San Francisco. She was born in Providence, Rhode Island and was the eldest child in the family. She attended elementary and high school in Fowler, and two years at Fresno State College before transferring to UC Berkeley. She received her B.A. and Ph.D. degrees in Social Science in about 1937 and remained on the staff at UC until her death.

During WWII she also worked for the war effort in San Francisco and at the university. She contracted the flu while engaged in both jobs, which eventually turned into a bacterial infection of the blood and heart. Marian was a student nurse at the UC Nursing School and was able to visit Arpie frequently. Arpie wrote letters to our parents almost daily and her will to recover was extremely high. Because of economic conditions and rationing during the war, it was very difficult for our parents to get to San Francisco to visit her and her letters were the main communication during the year. I worked at the Aivasian truck fuel station in Fowler at this time and the Aivasian brothers would arrange for me to get free truck rides to and from Oakland or San Francisco. For some time I was able to visit Arpie several times a month.

Also, I was an out patient of Dr. Evelyn Anderson, a cardiologist at the university hospital where Arpie was a patient. For three or four months my trips to the Bay Area would include visits with Arpie. I was being examined (and x-rayed) for an enlarged heart at the time, a problem related to my pushing beyond my physical abilities in high school athletics. During this period of trips to San Francisco, I would live with Marian at her apartment near the hospital.

Only two years separated Isabel and Arpie, so they were very close in many circumstances. Arpie's academic interests were inclined towards people, and Isabel's led to the sciences, so there was little competition between them.

Marian (Born March 4, 1920 ; died 1970)

Marian died after a lengthy illness of pancreatic cancer. It is difficult to understand the source of this disease. About 10 years later, her husband Karl also died of the same form of pancreatic cancer.

Marian, like Arpie was a scholar. From an early date she was a book worm and voracious reader. I don't recall what she read, but my lingering impression has always been that Marian was not physically involved with the farm, though she must have had some chores as we all did. I don't recall her involved with cooking family meals as I do Isabel, though in later life when I visited her she served very delicious meals. I don't recall her being very active in grape harvests either, (nor do I recall Arpie in the vineyards). Even though she showed no farming tendencies later in life, she took an interest in flower and vegetable gardening in their large yard in Burbank, CA.

Of the siblings, Marian was the most apt to be considered a loner. However she was close to both Dad and Mom, and at times with Chuck, the closest in age of any of the siblings. I recall when her cancer was detected, Chuck returned from farming in South America and hurried to Marian and offered her a blood transfusion. He explained that was a common practice in some parts of the region where he had lived. Marian knew what the effects likely would become, and she refused his kindness. But it does indicate how close they were with each other.

Marian was very pretty. This was a life taken too soon, as was Arpie's. She left three surviving children: Karen, Trudi, and Paula.

Charles (Chuck) (Born September 29, 1922; died 1989)

Chuck was probably the one sibling I was closest to, not only in age, of course, but being a male, in terms of interests and farm work. At the age of 67 Chuck also died of pancreatic cancer, less than six months after being diagnosed with this disease.

Chuck and I were different in many ways, yet we did many activities together. We were thrown together by farm work, both for hire and on the family farm. At a very young age, like 6 or 7, we would turn the trays of drying grapes to make raisins. When we were about 10, we were hired to turn raisin trays for other farmers. This was hot work in the sun, at temperatures ranging from 95 to over 100 degrees. We were paid $1.00 to turn a thousand trays, and on a good day and working fast, we could earn a dollar each. One of our large customers was a skinflint, and not a good farmer so that we would need to cover more acres to turn a thousand trays, but he would pay us only 75 cents a thousand trays. At best we would make about 60 cents each for 8 hours of work.

Another physical difference in our composition became evident when we would haul dried alfalfa hay into the barn for feeding the horses and the cow. These animals needed to be fed daily and not just on those days during which they worked. We would haul the hay on a tall wagon, and when we reached the barn, Dad would throw forks full of hay into the barn, and Chuck and I would distribute it in the loft. This activity created a lot of dust, to which Chuck was not allergic, but I suffered from hay fever. Again, I was considered lazy.

In the spring months, (about late March and April), neighbors Martin Zamenigian, Sam Marootian, Chuck and I would skip school one day a week and take a trip into the foothills and mountains around General Grant National Park, east of Fowler. On these trips we would study animals, landscape, enjoy the warmth of the mountains and the fragrance of the native plants. Then on the next day, we would write excuses signed by us as though written by our parents. One day, Irwin Dann, school principal, asked us "how are the salamander doing these days?" We weren't fooling him at all. I suppose he understood the educational benefits from such trips.

Chuck was a hard worker in everything he undertook. He grew frustrated with school during his senior year and spent the time between classes reading in the school library. He had a temper that could flare, and he was very honest in financial matters. He was intelligent, but like many boys (including me), he was not studious. He was a perfectionist in nearly everything he undertook, and in that respect, he was like Dad. Unlike Dad he was not a joiner, being more like Mom in social matters. He was a good writer, and was able to write some very articulate letters at the request of his raisin farming friends who were angry with USDA policies of the raisin marketing program.

During the last weeks of his hospital care, he refused to take certain medicines to "keep him alive" because he could see no need to prolong a life that was in its last days. He asked me to go into the storage barn on the farm where he kept cyanide and bring him a small supply to close out his life, but I told him morally I could not do that.

I would go to Fresno each week to visit him in the hospital, and I believe he kept himself alive until my last trip. The nurses said he would likely die at anytime during this week's visit. I went to the farm and brought his daughter Adrienne with me for a final visit. We both told him we loved him and Adrienne had other matters to tell him. As quickly as we spoke our comments, the nurse said "he is gone". At that instance, I saw an amorphous cloud of vapor leave his body and rise toward the ceiling and disappear. Was that his soul leaving his body?

Chuck was a very generous person. If I would remark that his shirt looked very nice, he would remove it and say, "I would like you to have it". And, he would mean it. He was very kind to Mom and I credit him for her recovery from the depression after Dad's death. Chuck patiently took care of Mom, cooked her meals, monitored her medicine and brought her out of the depression resulting from her fear of "going blind" as her eye doctor had told her.

George, our family friend (born January 12, 1912; died September 15, 2008)

George was born in north central Turkey and was the eldest of three children. His father immigrated to America, leaving his family in Turkey while he earned enough money to bring them to the U.S. When the Turkish genocide reached their region, his mother placed George in an American orphanage for safe keeping. George told me that one day word reached the orphanage that police were checking every building to find Armenians, so the orphanage hid George in a closet where pots and pans were kept. The young policeman opened the door, saw George huddled among the pots, and closed the door and continued on.

George was 13 years old when I first met him and I loved him as a brother for the next 83 years of his life. In all those years, he was a person I tried to emulate; he personally was calm, reasoning, non-judgmental, and professionally an outstanding researcher who went back to his roots to find solutions for insect control, and technically to the use of the electron microscope to find solutions for complex studies about the genetic composition of an insect species' DNA. He is one to whom the Lord would want to grant perpetual life; in a sense George earned that status with the quality of his research methods and technology that were pioneering efforts that will serve entomological research for years.

During high school George worked hard to earn money; in the beginning he worked with his father buying apricots and peaches, and drying them for sale to packing houses. He hired Chuck and me to harvest the fruit after shaking them from the trees. This represented the first source of money for Chuck and me. A few years later he became an ice delivery man for a Fowler ice and coal retailer, delivering ice during summer months between school vacations. When he had finished his route he would fill our ice box with the ice leftovers.

After finishing his education at Fresno State College, his first job was as an inspector for the Dried Fruit Association, which controlled the quality of dried fruit sold by packing houses to retail stores. Besides earning a very good salary, he was paid mileage for use of his car. He bought a new 1936 Dodge sedan, and our family shared the luxury of that car with George and Isabel.

George attended UC Berkeley for graduate work, then he moved to Oregon State College where he completed his Master's Degree in Entomology, and took employment with the U.S. Department of Agriculture. He was first stationed in Spokane, then Yakima, then Utah State University, then Fort Valley, Georgia, and last at UC Riverside from where he retired. From these locations, USDA also used his research services as needed elsewhere, especially in India and Pakistan. He was elected president of the American Entomological Society, an honor and responsibility he and Isabel both enjoyed.

George, like Arpie, was a life-time member of the California Scholarship Society, in honor of earning A's throughout high school. He also was the catcher on the Fowler High School varsity baseball team.

George died in Riverside at the age of 96. He and Isabel were married in 1935 and they celebrated their 72nd wedding anniversary with family; George ordered fish and chips for this meal, a favorite in his later years.

Isabel (born June 23, 1914- died February 24, 2011)

My remaining sibling, Isabel left me as the last of the Garoyan nuclear family. Isabel's "lack of consideration" for leaving the family with me as the last of the old family leaves me with many mixed feelings.

It seems only proper that I remain after Isabel's death, who was the second oldest sibling. Family deaths have not always occurred in proper chronological order, but that may be due to the genetic diversity of our family. We seem to be unpredictable when we choose to leave this earth or maybe that decision is in hands of a higher authority. But, we have been different and, its more than that, I now feel the responsibility for family members who preceded me, and who mostly are in the Garoyan family burial plot at the Fowler Community Cemetery, only Marian is not in the family plot. I will not be there either. Nina and I purchased burial plots for us and Lisa at the Davis Community Cemetery.

(Let's see, in the rare instance any of the family survivors would like to know, the following are buried in the Fowler cemetery: Dad's brother Avak, Dad, Mom, Arpie, Chuck, Isabel, and George. George's father Hagop (Jake) is in an adjoining plot.)

While Isabel was in charge, she was the Grand Matron of the family's interests. To Isabel fell decisions of funeral sites and keeper of family possessions, though these were actually few. The most significant of these were found in the foot-locker from Mom's apartment in Fowler after her death. Isabel kept this locker without opening it, though Isabel and I knew she had the footlocker, and later so did her daughter Elaine. However none of us had opened the locker until after Isabel's memorial service. The footlocker is now in my possession, with all of Mom's items distributed to family according to their desires.

Isabel took over management of the original farm, and continued to do so after Mom's death. Isabel, Marian, I were joint owners-survivors of the farm estate. Chuck received the newer second farm and house on Adams Avenue, near Cherry Avenue, another 20-acre ranch on which Dad and Mom had moved in about 1946. (For the first time in their life, Mom and Dad had a lovely home, with all of the conveniences they could not afford previously.) As joint survivors of the older Fowler farm along with Marian's three daughters, Isabel kept the books, paid the bills, and at year's end divided the net earnings to all of us according to our shares in the farm.

Income fell off quite a bit during some of the years, and there were no net earnings to distribute, and the young nieces wondered why? It took some explaining, but each eventually decided to sell her interest to either Chuck or to me. Meanwhile, Chuck bought Isabel's one-third interest in the original farm, and Marian's daughters sold theirs to create equal ownership between Chuck and me. Isabel's responsibilities ended when she sold to Chuck, and I suspect she was pleased to end that management chore. (When Chuck died, his daughter Adrianne inherited his share, and within several years it seemed best for me to sell my interest to Adrienne. I no longer had an interest with the old family members gone, and

Adrienne did have an interest in purchasing my shares. Thus ended the family ties of the farm, begun in about 1925, and ending in about 1992.)

KEEPING UP THE FAMILY TIES

Marian's daughters kept in touch with Isabel, but in later years only Paula and her family would visit Isabel and George in Riverside when they would return to Southern California for holidays. That may have been initiated by Paula, whom I suspect viewed Isabel as a surrogate mother. After all, Paula was young when Marian died at age 50, and Isabel lived in Riverside, about an hour's drive for Paula from Burbank. In time, Paula moved to Fort Collins to go to college, married Paige Lunbury and had two daughters. The idea of a close family contact with Paula had special significance. Isabel was very fond of Paula and her two daughters, and George liked to spend time with Paige, Paula's husband.

Isabel was pretty good about keeping in touch with Marian's other children, until her late 80s and 90s. I feel responsibility and the desire to carry on where Isabel left off. I fear I have not done well. Karen and her daughter Felicia now live in North Carolina and we have exchanged Christmas communications. Contacts with Trudi discontinued by her some years ago, probably with others of her siblings, too. I have maintained somewhat cordial contacts with Isabel's daughter Elaine. Elaine has suffered physical pains and undoubtedly has more need for relief than to maintain close contacts with her mother's brother. Rodney, Isabel's son, has not been close with any of his mother's family over the years. He seems content with that relationship.

Then too, there are those relatives living in the east, who were in contact with Mom and Dad, with whom Isabel gradually lost contact, and with some of whom I have been communicating in recent years. The concept of maintaining contact with the Garoyan/Garoian kin has slipped as generations are dispersed. I still maintain contacts with Miriam and Vicky (until her death in 2014) Kochakian, whose mother was a (Garoian) cousin of Dads, and until their deaths, Henry and Marian Manoogian, whose mother's were both a Garoian. Nina and I visited the Manoogians several times, once when Henry was alive, and a second time, after his death. Since then Marian Manoogian has died, so contacts have been lost with their five wonderful children. They do live near each other and have maintained a close relationship that I envy. One daughter who is lovely, as are all of the Manoogian family, lives in Los Angeles, but I do not know how to reach her.

Keeping in touch with Mom's side of the family has been difficult since the death of her sister Lucy. Aunt Lucy had five, maybe 6 children, and gradually we have lost contact with all of them. Several years ago when Nina and I were attending a Pierce-Arrow national meet in New England, we tried to find Lucy's family, without success.

As for the next generation, I am not hopeful there will be familial interactions among us. Isabel's children are Elaine and Rodney; Marian's three daughters are Karen and her daughter Felicia, both now living in North Carolina; Paula now lives in Ft. Collins, CO and her daughter Grace is married and lives in New Zealand; and Anna who lives in Southern California. Very recently Anna visited us in Davis. She is a lovely lady, and we hope to see her more frequently. I fear contacts with Trudi have terminated, but I will send her a copy of this memoir, in case she wishes to respond—the next move is with her.

Chuck left a son, also named Leon Garoyan, who lived in the Sacramento region for a period. I have no knowledge of whether he has a male heir who can carry on the Garoyan name. But recently I learned that Leon lives in Las Vegas. I also had lost contact with Chuck's daughter Adrienne, who owns the original family farm. When driving through Fresno we visited the farm but have been unable to find her there. Very recently I made another attempt to locate her, and found an address for her in Southern California. I am pleased the result is favorable and we have established communications.

There may be one Garoian to carry on the family name, and that is my grandson Ben, son of Leon III. I am not sure that will be much of a burden for him, since our contacts with him are for a few days each year when we go to Phoenix or if he comes to spend a few days with us. The earlier period concept of family clusters seems to be gone with my family.

A family I estimate to have been a vibrant collection of between 100 to 120 in the village of Habousi of Ancient Armenia at the turn of the 20th century is barely holding on. It is down to me, my son Leon III, perhaps his son Ben, and Lisa with no heirs. Unfortunately this number has slipped from 14 households to just three of us individuals. I am presently 91 years old, my son Leon is 67, and grandson Ben is 18. I fear it is too much to expect Ben to repopulate the Garoian name. Do I care? Obviously I do care, since the family has survived over many generations—I like to say we are descendants of Noah's family, who landed on Mt. Ararat.

The line of succession from Leon Jr., left, to Leon III, right and Ben in the center. We wish Ben well.

Bearers of the family name, Leon III and my grandson Ben. This is not a formidable responsibility, but it is important. No fees are earned nor paid for this responsibility. All it takes is a deep regard for the family name, reputation, and a son to carry on the family name. It is not evident if Ben is prepared for this responsibility.

CHAPTER EIGHT

LEE'S AND LISA'S EARLY YEARS

I think back to Lee's and Lisa's birth years, 1949 and 1951 respectively. Here I am in February 2017, age 91, suggesting that I have memories that far back and that I can write about them. Well, lets see.

How do I organize my memories? This suggests my mind has cubicles or files in which I have categorized thoughts about them. Knowing myself, I doubt that to be the case. So, I'll just write and see what comes.

BIRTH OF MY CHILDREN

Lee

Lee was the first heir to carry on the Garoian name and my parents were delighted when he was born. They anxiously wanted a grandson and were so happy when told their wish had come true, and that he was named for his grandfather, Leon, as I was.

Lee was born as a 10-months baby, taking his time to arrive. Betty was in labor for about 28 hours and her doctor, Lee Strickland should probably have delivered him by caesarian. The birth was very tough on both mother and child. The details I recall are that Lee faced the wrong direction, and the doctor spent hours with forceps trying to turn him around. He came out very bruised, tired, and looked pretty beat up. About 4 years later, we found out that a forceps prong had put pressure on his right eye, resulting in serious damage.

Lee in the woods surrounding our house on the shore of Lake Waubesa, near Madison, WI. The children liked to roam the woods and play in the lake.

These were the years of Dr. Spock, whose book was our bible for raising kids. We had a scale, a padded buggy with retractable top, and everything else imaginable. Betty was a very good mother. Lee was weighed every day and his weight recorded. I guess he was measured regularly, too. At the time of his birth, Dr. Strickland announced that Lee would attain a height of 5'6", based on the length of the arm bone from the elbow to the wrist. That proved pretty close to what has happened.

With Dr. Spock's advice, Lee was placed in the sun for a specified number of minutes, something like 10 minutes in any one exposure, and then rotated to another exposure. He was uniformly tanned by the time he was 6 months old. Lee was a model baby, and his delayed birth was really a prediction of his personality. He was a good child, easy going, and well behaved. For the most part, he developed into a model child too, who seldom caused us any problems. He made friends easily, though he was shy; eventually narrowing his close friendships to about five fellow students throughout junior high and high school years.

Lisa

Lisa was born two and a half years after Lee. While Lee was pretty laid back and took his time being born, Lisa was in a hurry and was born a month early. She must have felt confined, and couldn't wait to escape her constraints. Her fingernails were still soft, and it was just evident she jumped the gun. The time it took them to get here pretty much reflects their individual personalities, too. Lee was an easy-going baby, pretty quiet except when put to bed when we had friends over and he wanted to stay up. But in general, he was good about sleeping. Lisa, on the other hand, was a night owl. She still is as an adult. I recall coming home from a meeting at about 11 p.m., and there was Betty sitting up in bed but asleep, holding Lisa in her arms, and Lisa was wide awake and very active. I think that pretty nearly prevails now as far as personality is concerned, too.

Here's Lisa wandering around the woods at Lake Waubesa.
Lee would always be very close, watching after her.

My Children Grow

Lee and Lisa spent a lot of time together and were very close, mainly because we lived in rural areas not near other children. They remained close for most of their lives, even while separated during college years and after.

Of the two, Lee was the shy one (after all, he may have been hiding from exposure to the public, or uncertainty). When they were young, we grew Indian corn in our garden in Corvallis, and around Thanksgiving Lee and Lisa would take the mature ears of corn to sell to neighbors. Lee carried the bag and Lisa was the one who rang the doorbells and made the sales. Lee was very protective of Lisa, holding her hand when they were outside, going to school, or even going to the lake in Wisconsin to play. When we were living on Lake Waubesa, near Madison, there were a lot more kids their age, and Lee always looked after Lisa while ice skating, and when playing games.

During our first move from Oregon to Madison we had just settled into our mobile home in a rural area five miles south of Madison. We bought a new 2-bedroom American (brand) mobile home that was 28 feet long. There was plenty of room in the home, and we came pretty well organized, but as one can expect, we had planned to buy some things after our arrival. Madison had a huge shopping center, with a large Sears store, so we all went to Sears to shop. There was a long entrance hall into the store, with promotion items as we passed by them to find the area we were looking for. Once there, we realized Lisa was not with us. We searched all departments around us without finding her. We feared she had been kidnapped. We went to the nearest Sears security officer and filed a missing child's report, and soon an alert was broadcast throughout the store a number of times, including a very clear description of her clothing—overalls with a blue stocking cap on her head. It would be hard to miss her: We didn't add that her hair was cut off down to the scalp because both kids had a severe case of ringworm from a stray cat Lee had brought home after school several weeks before our scheduled departure for Wisconsin.

Within 15 minutes a store security guard came up to us, carrying Lisa under her arms in a vise grip, and was he mad! He found her riding a mechanical horse in the entranceway. She would just sit on the plastic rocking horse, and people would put a nickel in the slot and she would get free rides. When the security officer tried to lift her off to bring her to us, she was mad as a wet hen—she kicked the guy, beat on his body with her little fists, and otherwise kept screaming for him to let her go. We were very relieved she was safe but she remained mad at everyone, including the security officer. In turn, he was plenty angry, too. Her interests in horses started at this time, perhaps, and continued as her main interest after completing college.

My memories of the two children are heavily oriented to how close they were and how much they enjoyed doing things together. Betty had a regular schedule and she would read to them together, with one huddled on each side of her. She read a lot to them, and that was a highlight of their day. I recall one book was called "The Little Engine That Could", and of course, "Winnie the Pooh" with Pooh bear and I think Eeyore. Obviously, I heard the stories she read to them, too.

She made fabulous clothes for Lisa and dressed Lee up for his trips to church with me. She took very good note of their diets, too. If they lacked contact with a parent, it was with me, since my county agent work often required meetings, sometimes two nights a week. Farmers worked during the day, so we often held

It's 1958 and Spring is in the air in Wisconsin and everyone is smiling, Lisa, Betty and Lee!

educational meetings during evening hours. And that is when the Grange organizations met for their farm meetings; I would have a lot of meetings with
various Grange clubs throughout the county to answer farmer's questions.

When Lee was about five I thought if I bought him an erector set, he would
be inclined to become an engineer. But, he seldom played with it unless one of
us would sit with him and take the lead in making things with the set. Why
did I think he might develop an interest in engineering? Because he was very
good at taking things apart. Lee was about 4 years old when I bought our first
oscillating lawn sprinkler and the next day when I returned for lunch, I found
the sprinkler completely dismantled. I was quite angry, but Betty intervened by
telling Lee that "you can put the sprinkler together tomorrow, can't you?" That
evening when I came home, it was together, with her help. When the first little
transistor radios came out I craved one a lot, and when I got a bit of money
saved up, I bought one that fit into my shirt pocket. Lee somehow got curious
about how it worked, and by golly, it quit working when he took it apart.

Lee and I would attend the Episcopal Church services in Milwaukie, Oregon.
Betty would dress him in nice grey wool slacks, a white shirt with a red bow
tie, and a grey sweater, and off we'd go. Sometimes after church and lunch, Lee
and I would change into work clothes and go fishing on Eagle Creek, a small
river that was a good salmon and winter steelhead fishing river. I'm not sure we
ever hooked a fish but just being on the river and with nature was fun. His span
of attention was pretty short though, and that would put a crimp into fishing.
A few years later when he was 10-12 years old, and we had moved back from
Wisconsin to Corvallis, we'd go out on the Alsea River about 30 minutes away
from home, to fish for steelhead and salmon. I'm not sure we ever caught fish
there either. In time, as Lee developed friends of his own, these fishing excursions became less interesting to him.

In their junior high school years, Lisa became quite shy, and Lee became a bit
more outgoing. He developed strong friendship with about 4 or 5 other fellows,
and that relationship continued throughout high school. Surprisingly, all members of the group were brainy, and at the time, their SAT exam achievements
were the highest of any previous students at Corvallis High School. The two
Thomas boys went on to college, and one got his Ph.D. in theoretical engineering at Stanford University and remained on its faculty. Another was Danny
Doerge, probably Lee's closest friend; when Lee transferred to UCD, so did
Danny. Together they bought a 1957 Cadillac Biarritz convertible that was the
top of the line in its day, and they tooled around Davis in that car, with the top
down. I think Danny did most of the driving, and Lee just sat in the passenger
seat enjoying life. When they graduated from college, they wanted to work out-

Left: Lisa, 4 and Lee, 6 at the Lake Waubesa house. *Right:* Lee in the backyard of our Wisconsin house.

doors; none of this office work for them. So, they both hired on with a roofer, serving as apprentices. I think they planned to spend their lives as roofers and I was prepared to finance their business. Once, Lee was paired up on a roof job with one of the senior roofers, and Lee learned the other fellow was making only 25 cents an hour more than he was, after working as a roofer for 16 years. Lee had been working for 3 years, and then and there, Lee and Danny decided there wasn't much future in working as a roofer.

Lee landed a research job in agricultural economics at the University of Nevada, Reno, and hung his roofer's pouch on the wall as a reminder of his alternative work opportunity. Later he was admitted to the University of Montana for a master's degree, and from there, to Texas A&M to work in research and to work toward his Ph.D. He did these things on his own without any input from me, and I am proud of that. I had a lot of friends in the departments at both universities, and I could have intervened, but Lee did it without my influence.

When he was a roofer, he and Lisa developed an interest in getting a dog. They drove to Elk Grove to look at some Afghan puppies and ending up buying one. That was Lee's dog, but it was something Lee and Lisa did together. I think they invited me along just to keep me aware of their interests.

While in grade school in Oregon, Lisa and Lee would hire out as berry and bean pickers, earning money that they could use for their own discretionary purposes. Lee even had a paper route that got him up about 4:30 a.m. to deliver the *Oregonian* in Corvallis. Picking strawberries and beans was better than delivering papers, since they didn't have to get up until about 6 in the morning. While in junior high and high school, they found work in the Corvallis processing plant owned by Agripac, a cooperative that I had good relations with. Again, they earned money they controlled.

Once, when I returned from a trip to Washington D.C., I came home and Lisa (aged about 15) asked me to go out in the country with her. There I met Tsar, a registered Arabian gelding that she and Betty had gone to Gresham, about 100 miles distant, purchased the horse, and arranged for its delivery while I was away. Tsar was a beautiful horse, and they were best friends for many years. When we moved to Davis, Lisa paid for a stall for Tsar. Management of the stables had boarded a new stallion into Tsar's stable, without authorization. There was a fight between the two stallions the first night, and Tsar suffered a broken knee. There was no option to keep Tsar alive as a result. She took control of it internally, and never did show her emotions, as I know I would, and did, for her. She has become pretty independent and internalizes her feelings, something that remains to this day.

Arabian horses were Lisa's interest, and Afghan dogs were Lee's, but they supported each other completely. Their close relationship and support for each other was remarkable to observe.

After we moved to Davis, Lisa enrolled at UC Davis where she met Jim MacIntosh, either through Jim's working with me on cars, or because Lee and Jim lived in adjoining cottages, or from his boarding a horse where Lisa kept Tsar. In 1982 Lisa and Jim moved to Tacoma to restore cars. I retired from UCD in 1983 to take a job in Ireland, that turned into a seven-year assignment as visiting professor at University College of Cork, and Lisa and Lee came over several times to visit.

It was during their last visit that Lisa learned that Jim had received treatments for kidney stones. On her return she found out he had kidney cancer, and it soon spread to his brain. He lived only several weeks, maybe a month after Lisa's return from Ireland.

IRELAND BECAME MY HOME

On one occasion, my good friend Jean Marie Bouquery of Paris, came to Cork while Lee and Lisa were visiting, and we toured the scenic southwest of Ireland. On the way, we stopped at a restaurant in a small exclusive village of Baltimore. We ordered the seafood special feast that included every type of seafood in existence. We started with a half gallon of shrimp (as a starter). Lee, Lisa and I would pick the shells off each shrimp, and Jean Marie laughed and taught us how to eat shrimp with shells and all. Eating shrimp got easier after that, and faster, too. Several days later, maybe the next weekend, our good Irish friends and fellow car collector Con and Colette O'Sullivan, from Newmarket, a small town north of Cork came to Donnybrook, a suburb of Cork where we lived, and we had a nice feast at home. Colette played the piano, and Con, Jean Marie, and the Garoian's engaged in some beer drinking and a lot of singing. It was an evening to remember, and we do.

Jean Marie Bouquery, a professional associate from Paris (ca. 1985). We worked on many food marketing research projects and remain close friends.

On one of Lee and Lisa's visits, I drove my trusty, old 1971 Audi from Cork to Shannon Airport to take Lisa and Lee to catch their return flight. Before we got to Mallow, a town about 30 miles north of Cork, the car engine started to sputter, and I was not certain we would make it to the airport. The car had failed before, and a local mechanic working from his home had always made it go. This was a different situation, since we had a flight to catch.

I had a friend in Mallow, Dennis Murphy, who was the CEO of one of Ireland's large dairy cooperatives. I drove to his house, explained my problem, introduced Lee and Lisa to his family, and I asked if he would take us all to the airport, which he did. Such kindness and generosity is so typical of the Irish. They are the loveliest people I have lived with, and I miss them immensely since leaving Ireland in about 1987.

LEE'S MOVE TO ENGLAND AND THEN BACK TO PHOENIX

About a year later I moved to Sagy, a little village in France near Cergy-Pontoise, a city 20 miles north of Paris, where I was teaching at an upscale graduate school in engineering and economics. Lee and Lisa came to visit there too, and we took my trusty Audi on a tour of the Loire Valley castle region. We stayed one night at a castle, and enjoyed a lovely formal dinner in the dining room. None of us had stayed at a castle before, nor eaten in one; we had only taken tours of them. It was a pleasant and memorable experience for us.

Backtracking in years to when Lee was a graduate student at Texas A&M, and I had a lot of professor-friends there, I'd manage to visit him in College Station. He took me to an A&M homecoming football weekend, including a huge bonfire of renown, and to see the game. I realized the A&M students, graduates, and faculty were a unique group, a community among themselves. Once an Aggie, you became a former student, not an alumnus, and the Aggie tradition is something hard to get over. Lee had a small apartment, where he and his Afghan dog lived. While we were grocery shopping, Lee introduced me to a pretty female student in Ag. Econ. He said she was quite friendly, but she gave up trying to socialize with him, telling him too much of his social interaction came from dogs and not enough from humans. Grooming an Afghan dog is required daily, and it takes about an hour. With his studies and research, and the dog to take care of, I felt Lee's priorities with the dog were misplaced. In time Lee had several Afghans, Tina and Magic. Lisa ended up with Magic after her return to Davis from Tacoma. I suspect Lee wanted her to have something to take her mind off the problems of Jim's death, and shortly after returning to Davis, having to put Tsar away. In his concerns for Lisa he likely used the excuse of grooming two dogs as a good reason to send one of his dogs home with Lisa.

After Lee earned his Ph.D. at Texas A&M, he accepted a position with American Express in Phoenix. After several years American Express appointed him to its Brighton, England offices, where he purchased a house. While there, I had a short consulting assignment in France. We met in Paris, and drove to the Burgundy wine region, staying in a nice hotel in a small town. While driving on a Saturday, we stumbled on a country event like a local fair in a small town, and sampled Burgundy wines, sausages, and cheeses, ending up buying several bottles of Burgundy wine. That was a great opportunity to learn about Lee's interesting work with American Express, combined with a nice bit of fun, too.

About five years later, he was transferred back to Phoenix, and he bought a house there too. Nina and I visited him, and when he decided to prepare that house for sale, he asked us to supervise the process. Having sold this house he next wanted us to find a new house for him, preferably in the Desert Mountain development where he could live a grand life with access to golf and private club privileges. We agreed to screen houses that met his guidelines, and from these, he selected one that he bought.

Our next assignment was to help find an interior decorator to furnish the house. We interviewed two ladies. One walked through the 3,000 square foot house, and started to tell us what kinds of furniture to buy and where to place them. The second lady walked through too, then sat on one of the plastic outdoor chairs next to a patio table. Then, she asked us to describe Lee: what he liked to do, his life style, and his preferences, and what he was like. Both Nina and I were impressed with this lady, so we took the next step to make an appointment for Pia to meet Lee.

Because of his travel schedules it would have taken over a year for Lee to be available for a complete final plan for furnishing the house. Instead they decided to take the project one room at a time, which gave them ample time to get acquainted. The process extended into a second year, after which they married. Pia had adopted a baby boy at his birth, who by this time was about 5 years old. Lee went through the legal processes and adopted him. Finally the next survivor of the Garoian name has been found, and is now 19 years old. His name is Ben, Lee's adopted son.

Lisa, the CPA and Enrolled Agent

Meanwhile Lisa has completed requirements to become an accredited Certified Public Accountant, and later an Enrolled Agent, a status that qualifies her to represent clients before the Internal Revenue Service tax courts. She is nearly in retired status now, after working on accounting for MRA's (Management Research Associates, my consulting firm) projects destined to expert witness testimony. In many instances she has served as a Forensic Accountant for me personally in several matters, even keeping the books for my car restorations.

In recent years Lisa has helped get my accounts in order. First, she undertook the compilation of 42 years of records to determine the expenditures on a property held for investment to determine the tax liability for a sale. Her skill and knowledge of tax laws came to bear on this time-consuming project. Next she organized records from the accumulation of expenses for a car I have been restoring for four years. Meanwhile she has provided services to other family members. She has remarkable skills and patience.

Lisa remains a private CPA, limiting her activities to analyzing my car restoration projects, including keeping accounting records for my projects.

Lisa took care of her mother's financial concerns for many years, until her mother's death in October 2016 at age 90. Lisa arranged for a trust for her mother's estate and serves as trustee.

CHAPTER NINE

WHAT'S LIFE WITHOUT A DOG?

As long as I can remember, our family had dogs on the farm. After all, what is a farm without a warning system?

The first dog I recall is Fido, a medium-sized female Spitz breed that was an outside dog. Mom thought all dogs were outside dogs and she was not very comfortable letting them into the house, until Mom and Dad were the remaining family at home. Fido was an excellent dog and very protective of the house and yard. She had one person in particular that she did not like, and that was one of the older Kevorkian boys from the farm next door. He must have hurt her some time in the past, because even when we were standing around in the yard talking, Fido would disappear and sneak behind Buck and snap at his ankles. I think Fido had good judgment, because Buck did have a mean disposition. In the spring months when we were about out of raisins from the past harvest, Buck would always have raisins in his pockets, and he would ask me if I wanted some to eat. He would toss a small handful on the asphalt road and I would pick them up, rub them in my hands a bit to clean them, and then eat them. I would liken it to throwing chicken feed to the hens. I never did like Buck, and he was the only one of that family of about 6 kids that I disliked. But then, so did Fido. I believe she was a good dog with wise judgment. She lived a good, long life.

Next, we obtained a male short-haired terrier, another medium-small all black dog, also named Fido, who was also kept outside. Chuck and I were older when we got this dog and as we worked out in the vineyards Fido was a constant companion. He would occasionally chase a jackrabbit, but he'd come back in about a half hour, all tuckered out and lay under the shade of a grape vine near where we were working. Chuck and I would remove suckers growing on the grape vines near the ground and we'd just move down the rows, from vine to vine. Fido would have no problem finding us, because he could see under the vines throughout the vineyard. This Fido was a good watchdog too, but I do not recall if he bit people. By then, Buck had grown up and moved away, so there may not have been a need for this Fido to bite.

Bugs, the Spaniel That Mom Received

Most of these dogs were Chuck's buddies, much more so than mine. If they had to choose, they would go with Chuck rather than me. During my Cal Poly years, I worked at the State Agricultural Inspection station on the Oregon border located on the Redwood Highway, about 40 miles from Crescent City. I bought a black Cocker Spaniel puppy for $20, and it was the cutest little buddy a person would want. Since I lived across the street from the Inspection Station, it was easy for me to take her to work with me. I named her Bugs because I thought that was appropriate for where I worked—our main job was to prevent the importation of insects into California by tourists bringing in infested fruit and plants. I had planned to take Bugs to Cal Poly for my senior year, but because I lived in a dorm, I was not permitted to keep her. So, like most kids, I took Bugs to the ranch to live with my parents. Although Mom was not comfortable with dogs, and certainly not in the house, my parents were reluctant to keep Bugs, but what could they do? So, Bugs stayed on the farm as a house dog, and like all such pets we have taken home to be cared for by our parents, they loved Mom, just as Bugs did. In time, Mom would feel like she had a new admirer. I don't know what happened to Bugs, but she had a pretty nice life with the folks. They would take her with them on trips to town and she became their constant companion.

Like Pound Dogs

In 1947 when Betty and I moved to Oregon, we lived in a small secluded farmhouse in Redlands about 7 miles from Oregon City. I thought a dog would be a good companion. Redlands consisted only of a crossroads store and a Grange Hall. One Sunday I read in the Oregonian about a border collie pup available about 35 miles from our house. So, off I went to look over the pup. It was very cute, and friendly with typical border collie markings, mostly black with a white band around the neck and black socks on her feet. We tried to make a pet of her, but she had just a little different mindset than we did. She grew up, but she was very difficult to train. One day I was visiting a farmer friend who grew thousands of turkeys for the Thanksgiving trade and he complained that he didn't have a dog to train to work the turkeys. We struck up a deal: I swapped the border collie (I have forgotten her name) for a hen turkey, which we ate for Thanksgiving several weeks later. The dog didn't do well with the turkey farmer and he got rid of her. I think I got the best of that deal.

About 6-7months later, someone offered me a Dalmatian bird dog that I thought would make a good hunting dog. Al Parker (my hunting and fishing buddy with whom I worked) and I would take her out to the Oregon State University experiment station near Oregon City and we would try to train her to flush pheasants from the cornfield, but she never got the hang of her job. When she did flush a pheasant, she would chase the bird for a half-mile, never giving us a chance to get within gunshot range of the bird. I gave the dog to Jack McDermitt, the superintendent of the experiment station, who gave it to his sister in Eastern Oregon. It was a handsome dog, but apparently she needed more exercise than she was given; she was not trained as a house dog because she was too high strung and excitable. One afternoon, the dog was left at home while the owners went shopping, and when they returned they found the sofa fabric ripped to shreds. That dog never lasted past that event.

THE AUCTION BARGAIN

The next year we moved from our Redlands house into town. In the first five years when I worked in Clackamas County, we had lived in six houses—remember, this was just after the end of WWII, and housing was scarce and rents were pretty high. I was making $325 a month in those days. We rented a large two-story house in Oregon City that had an upstairs that was made into an apartment, so it became a two family house, with us possessing the basement and the first floor. Lee had been born and was about a year old when I was returning from a farm meeting at night, and I passed the Oregon City Bargain House, an auction house with a live auction going. I went inside, and they were auctioning off some short-haired puppies that looked real cute. I bought one of them for 60 cents, and drove on home with it. Betty was very tolerant, and I thought it would make a nice pet for Lee. I named this one "Bargain", because of where I bought her. Later we rented a small farm of about 7 acres on the Clackamas River that had an old house that was to be our new home. Bargain went along with us, of course, and Lee and Bargain became inseparable. Where Lee wandered, so did Bargain. We had an irrigation pump on the riverbank, where I would spend time while watering my crops, and Lee and Bargain would come along too. Sometimes, Lee would wander out to the pump site while I was not at home, and Bargain would get between Lee and the river and bark wildly and loudly, until Betty realized Lee had wandered too close to the river. That dog really became protective of Lee, and they were very close buddies. When visitors would arrive, Bargain would get between Lee and the visitors, and Bargain would never let a visitor get close to Lee. One Christmas season we left the dog on the farm while we drove to California to visit family, and the neighbor had agreed to take care of the dog. Upon our return, Bargain was not around, and the neighbor didn't know what had happened to her and she was never found. We mourned that loss. That dog loved Lee and Lee reciprocated.

Lisa was born while we were living on "Back Achers", as I called our Oregon farm on the river. The name came in to being when I leased the farm. I bought the sprinkler irrigation system, which was old, and the movable pipes were heavy galvanized steel. The lateral sections to which the sprinklers were attached came in 20-foot lengths, and easily weighed about 100 pounds. Moving this pipe to irrigate the 5 acres I had planted to strawberries was a lot of work, and I would get bad back pains from the effort. Thus, the farm's moniker "Back Achers".

SPARKY JOINS OUR FAMILY

After Lisa's birth, there was a need for a house with better facilities and general condition. We found the right house in Milwaukie, a Portland suburb that was owned by Millard and Millie Reddaway, who lived next door and operated a rhododendron nursery. We were very fortunate to be with such friends, and Lee frequently visited Millie. He was about 4 or 5 years old and was pretty gregarious with our friends. One spring I thought it would be nice to have a small pet for the kids, so I asked the county animal control officer to let me know if he ever came across a small dog. He found a multi-colored cocker spaniel that belonged to an old man who was being hospitalized, so I went to look at it, and thought it would make a nice pet for us. I was assured she had ridden in cars, so I stopped by on my way home and picked up the dog. Her name was "Sparky". During the drive, Sparky just went wild, jumping from the front seat to the back, then back to the front seat again, the entire 6 miles to Milwaukie. It was a wonder I did not crash the car.

Sparky settled down once we reached home, and the kids just smothered her with warm feelings. Sparky became a lovely pet for the kids, and she even became a nice hunting dog for Al Parker and me when we hunted pheasants. She had a lot of stamina, and a good nose, and being a small dog, she could crawl in the bushes and flush out pheasants. About a year later, in 1954, we took off for Madison, Wisconsin, on a sabbatical leave, and Sparky made the trip in good fashion, sitting on the floor at Betty's feet. We brought Sparky back with us when we returned to Oregon City, but she had developed lumps in her breasts, which were malignant. She was euthanized because of the cancer.

It was only a few months after our return that the University of Wisconsin offered me a faculty position with an opportunity to work towards a Ph.D., so we accepted and returned to Madison. If my memory is correct we went a long period without a dog, all during our second return from Madison and our nine years in Corvallis, our move to Davis from Corvallis, and our divorce.

After our divorce I acquired an adult dog, also named Sparky, which I got from the Sacramento pound. He was a cross between a German Shepherd and a Husky, and showed characteristics of both breeds. The head and ears were that of a Shepherd, and the tail was that of a husky, curling back over the spine. Sparky was a powerful watchdog, and would frighten anyone who came up on him unannounced. When I traveled to Europe for several weeks, I asked Warren Johnston to look after Sparky. I had left Sparky in the back yard, and Warren was to stop by mornings and evenings to feed Sparky, and to take him for a walk. Warren lived a block away, and Sparky knew him pretty well. The first night I was to stay in Los Angeles to catch an early flight to Europe, and somehow Warren caught up with me by telephone to tell me when he went to feed Sparky, he found him lying on the sidewalk by the garage, dead. The best Warren could tell, Sparky had knocked the lid off the garbage can, and had found the chicken bones I had discarded in the garbage, and chewed on and swallowed the leg bones. Chicken leg bones are apt to break and be sharp, and the bones had penetrated blood vessels and he died from blood loss. That was a very sad ending to a lovely creature.

Training Gypsy—a Guide Dog

When we moved to Ireland, we missed having a companion so I called the Irish Guide Dog Association to see if we could raise a puppy for them. To our surprise, the president drove out to interview us, to make sure we had adequate facilities in which to keep a dog. We had a large house and yard in a rural setting of about 12 houses that surrounded a golf club, and that pleased her.

The German Shepherd was a puppy from one of her brood dogs, so she took special interest in her. The dog's name was Gypsy, and she had been placed with a family for 4 months, but had been so full of mischief that they could no longer cope with her. By this time, she was a year old, a very beautiful pup, and we agreed to take her on. She arrived late on a Sunday afternoon. We arranged for Gypsy to sleep in an enclosed utility room, with access to the kitchen. Our dinner plan was to cut up a fryer chicken we had bought on Saturday, which we had left on the kitchen counter while we watched the evening news in another room. After the news, we went into the kitchen to prepare dinner, but there was no chicken in sight. Gypsy had pushed open the door between the utility room and the kitchen and the entire chicken had disappeared. The memory of Sparky and the chicken bones flooded my mind, but this was a Sunday evening in Ireland where every store was closed for the day. What to do? Gypsy looked very comfortable, but I was not.

Calling around for help, I located one veterinarian who answered the phone and I explained the dilemma. His advice was to pour a pint of mineral oil down Gypsy's throat and to watch her through the night. Miraculously, a small convenience store was open and it sold mineral oil. Well, I'll tell you what. Having a pint of mineral oil in hand, and getting it down the throat of a one-year old, frisky German Shepherd is some trick. Somehow, I got about a cup down her throat, and locked her in the utility room. Occasionally I would look in on her; she looked fine and she gave me a curious look that said, "What the hell is wrong with you?"

Both Gypsy and I survived the night, she not having vomited. But having pooped in the utility room, there was no evidence of a chicken in the stool. I watched every bowel movement of that dog for three days, and there was no evidence of a chicken in any specimen. I figured Gypsy's digestive system was so acid that it dissolved every bone in that chicken. Well, we survived that experience, without Gypsy being aware of any problem she had created.

But then, I soon came to understand the frustrations of her former trainer. Apparently, she was not housebroken. She needed more training, which we gave her over a year's time, and she was advanced into expert training for another 9 months, during which time we did not see her. After she had completed her training, the search to find her a home, with a young and active male living in a city who also needed a guide dog, was unsuccessful. She was occasionally used as a support dog when another dog became ill. That didn't occur frequently enough and between assignments she became aggressive, so instead of allowing her to become aggressive, they offered her to us to keep. Both Gypsy and we were very happy with this turn of events.

Gypsy liked milk bones that I gave her as a treat between meals. She would go into the back garden in Donnybrook, Douglas, a suburb of Cork, where I

Gypsy, of Ireland. She was trained as a guide dog partly by me, then by professionals. She was properly named; she moved with me to Davis, then six months later to Paris, and after a year, she moved back to Davis where she lived the rest of her life as my buddy. She was a constant companion, and a great friend. In Ireland, the neighborhood children would line up on weekends to take Gypsy for a walk.

planted a vegetable garden, and she would watch me plant the vegetables. Soon I saw several milk bones planted in the soil, with one end in the ground, just as she had seen me plant in the garden. She was growing her own supply of milk bones. The neighborhood children loved Gypsy, and she liked them too. Continuously they would ask if they could exercise her, so on such occasions I had to be with the kids and Gypsy.

Gypsy came home to Davis, in a special container made by a carpenter in Dublin, according to international airlines regulations. From Ireland, the itinerary took us to London, and then non-stop to San Francisco. The problem was that England required a six-months quarantine for any dogs brought into the country, because of its antiquated fear of rabies. England did not accept rabies vaccines as being effective in preventing the disease. But, here was Gypsy requiring an overnight stay; that meant she could not leave the Heathrow terminal. So, I walked her to give her an opportunity to relieve herself before I left the airport for a hotel adjacent to the airport. The container had a big water reservoir to take care of her water needs, and I fed her before leaving for the hotel. In the morning, I walked her again on the airport grounds, outside many buildings, gave her a little food, filled her water container, and left her with the hopes we would be on the same aircraft. She was, and our next visit was at San Francisco, where I let her out of her container, which was not soiled, and I found a way to take her outside. She was not as discriminating, feeling it necessary to use the asphalt instead of searching for grass.

Gypsy was well named, since she crossed the Atlantic Ocean three times in her life. A year later, she took another transoceanic trip, this time destined for Paris, where we lived in the country in a small village named Sagy about 20 miles north of Paris. She had a lovely place to roam and play. And because she was a guide dog in-training, she could go to my office at the University, into the nearby 3-star Michelin restaurant, banks, and virtually everywhere. We would take walks along the country lane adjacent to the property, and into some forest and meadows, where she roamed off-leash. Alas, she had these lovely surrounds for only a year, when she again returned to Davis.

Gypsy had a good life in Davis, with a fenced backyard in which she spent a lot of time. When cancer forced the vets to euthanize her, I think in 1990, she was buried in the backyard, because that was her piece of our property.

Auggie Joins the Family

I did without a companion for a while, but I did get lonesome. One Saturday, I think in 1992, I was casually reading the newspaper ads, and came to an interesting description of a purebred German Shepherd, that was for sale for $10. I was the first to call so I made arrangements to immediately see the dog and I took Lisa too. We got to the address at a little after 10 a.m., and there in the yard was a lanky, thin sable colored German Shepherd and a small terrier, wandering around. The terrier was a yapping dog, but the German Shepherd stood there studying us. As we went to the door, the small dog kept up a barrage of barks, and the big dog just accompanied us. The lady of the house wasn't prepared for us so early, so she asked us to sit on a lounge in the patio—as we did, the Shepherd came and laid at our feet. We didn't realize it then, but we had begun to bond from that moment.

After exchanging information about each other, and talking about why the dog was available, we began to feel a kindness towards this dog—which was Auggie. The dog was available because when she roamed the rural setting in which she lived, she would chase the neighbor's chickens and occasionally, catch one. The chicken owner didn't like that, and on several occasions he fired a shotgun at Auggie, occasionally hitting her. (Later, we were told by a vet that Auggie had numerous lead pellets under her skin.)

Lisa and I decided to buy Auggie for $10, but the owner said she couldn't take money for her pet—she had only set a price to discourage people who had a reputation for pirating stray dogs to eat. On the way home we stopped in Sacramento to buy her some food, a sleeping pad, and water and food dishes.

Auggie went from being a "chicken chaser" to being a "people's pet". She spent the day greeting office visitors at the Center for Cooperatives and would accompany me as I visited clients and business contacts. She adapted well to us.

Auggie turned out to be a loving dog who liked companionship. Going to work with me daily at the university was a new treat, since her former owner left her and the little terrier to roam while at work. Auggie was an intelligent, quick-to-learn, imaginative creature who would become bored without people around her; no wonder she started chasing chickens. On rare occasions when Auggie was left at home alone, she would create a clothes pile in the living room and lie beside it. That was her way of knowing she was not abandoned.

Shortly after she came to live with me, we went to buy sod and as we wandered around the farmyard, she spotted some chickens and before I could stop her she just about nabbed one, but the chicken flew away unharmed. At that point we had a little conversation, and I never put her in a tempting situation again. I think she understood that chasing chickens was taboo. Another time shortly after I had acquired her I was visiting Pat Craig's car shops in Stockton. Auggie came wandering around the shop with me. Soon, Kenny Wilson, the shop manager asked if I smelled something unusual, and I looked around and found Auggie had left a pile in the middle of the shop floor. After I cleaned that mess and washed the floor, Auggie and I had another serious talk, and that was the last time she ever soiled inside a building. Of course, from that time on, I made efforts to take her out at regular hours and at acceptable places for her to do her business. Auggie learned quickly, and so did I. One thing I have learned in raising a dog, is both the owner and the dog learn together; if they do not neither is adequately trained.

When I would interview prospective staff for the Center for Cooperatives, I'd ask if they had problems working in an office where Auggie was present. Those were more liberal days for management decisions, so those interviewed had little option to object to Auggie's presence if they wanted to work in the Center. I had an open door policy to my office, and each visitor would be greeted by Auggie as well as by me. While I served my 5-year term as director, Auggie was a constant part of our operations. Because I was also consulting in the years I had Auggie, she became my frequent companion as I called on my clients, or when I stopped at the restoration shops where my cars were being worked on. On the few occasions when she was not with me, my clients would ask "Where's Auggie" before they would say, "Hi Lee, how are you?" She was always welcomed everywhere I went.

When Nina and I began to date, even casually, we made efforts to introduce Auggie to Nina's dog Sadie, a Doberman. Nina thought that should be done on neutral grounds, instead of on either dog's turf. We introduced them in the two blocks that separated our houses. The dogs seemed to not care much, but soon after, Sadie had to be euthanized due to age-related hip problems. How the dogs related to each other became moot. Sadie was a very gentle dog, but the three Dobermans my brother Chuck had over a 12-year period on the farm, were very mean. That formed my opinion of this breed. I was wrong about Sadie, but we didn't get an opportunity to test out the two dogs as friends for long. Sadie had been Nina's son Tom's dog, until he had to leave Davis for school, yet another example of a son leaving a dog with a parent when he went away to school.

Auggie liked the old cars I owned and riding in them was a special treat. Once when I was bringing the rare Mercedes 300S roadster home from the hangar, Auggie sat on the back bench seat, as regal as she could be by being upright, and looking from side to side as we passed students on campus. She really took to having the air sweep by her as we drove in my open cars. One year I drove the 300S to the Silverado Concourse being held at Mare Island in Vallejo, and since the car was to be judged, Auggie could not ride with me from the storage area to the area for displaying cars. Nina started to walk the nearly one mile with Auggie, until a friend offered them both a ride in his open Pierce-Arrow, and again, she rode elegantly on the rear seat cushion. Another time, she went with us to a Pierce-Arrow weekend tour when I took the 1920 open touring car that had no windows—there were no barriers to keep her from jumping out of car from the back seat, so she sat or stood on the floor of the back seat, and looked out either side depending on what interested her as we drove. Of my three German Shepherds, Auggie was most involved with my cars, and rode in nearly all of them, with pleasure. As with Gypsy, we had to euthanize Auggie for hip problems that prevented her from walking because of the pain; she was about 14 years old when that was necessary.

Auggie had a lovely personality, but different from Gypsy's. Both were companion dogs rather than family dogs, because they developed a very close relationship with one person, especially the one they spent more time with. Basically, Auggie had been brought up by a women, so she tended to bond with Lisa after I got her. But, since Lisa did not live with Auggie and me, she remained close to Lisa, but became my dog. That lasted until Nina and I were married, and then she recalled her days with a woman, and became *our* companion instead of just mine. Auggie liked to play ball, and for her it was a participation game, in which we would have to play as much as she did.

We mourned Auggie for about 2 years, and decided that we could not endure the sorrow of the loss of such a lovely companion again.

Foxy Was Special

In February, Nina flew to Newport Beach for her first visit with Tom and Karen's daughter Je'Anne, who was born in December, 2004. I don't recall how long she was gone, but on the weekend I was feeling sorry that I was alone. I picked up the newspaper and read it from page to page, ending on the section titled "Dogs for Sale". There, I read an ad for a purebred German Shepherd female who was 5 years old with registration papers, and in need of a new home due to illness of its owner. True to form, I called the number in Lodi, a town about 50 miles from Davis. The seller was the dog's breeder, who described the dog as a brood dog that had whelped two litters and then was adopted by an elderly, single man about three years previously. The man and dog bonded, and Foxy Lady was a constant companion to him, riding in his pickup, living in the house, and always beside him. The man had gone into heart surgery, and was unable to take care of Foxy Lady, so his brother arranged for the breeder to find another home for her. Thus, the weekend ad in the Bee.

Again, I was the first to respond. I called Nina to tell her about Foxy, and since we had not discussed getting another dog since Auggie, she said I should go look at the dog. She knew I was at loose ends.

As I entered the fenced property, my first view of Foxy Lady was her running on one side of a fence, barking at another dog on the other side of the fence, both dogs running at full speed—what a beautiful sight to see a lovely Shepherd gracefully running at speed. When the kennel operator, Inga and I had gotten acquainted, she called over the racing Shepherd, and she was Foxy, who responded directly to Inga. At the kennels, Foxy had a large wire cage in the garage that was her home. Since it was February, and being an outside dog here, she had developed a full coat.

My first reaction to seeing Foxy was favorable as she was racing with a lot of poise, her head straight, her ears up, and her tail extending in a straight line from her back. Up close, I was a bit disappointed because she was darker than either Gypsy or Auggie and I had a sable-colored dog in mind. But her docile demeanor and devotion to Inga were evident, and these characteristics outweighed the negative trait I saw in her coloring. I guess her personality overcame any reluctance I had, and she became my dog. With Foxy in the rear of the station wagon, we headed for Davis, and when I left the kennels, I called Nina and told her we had a new pet. Nina was happy to be with her new granddaughter, and didn't sound surprised that I had actually acquired another creature.

Being winter and cold I drove with the windows up. Soon the fact that Foxy had been an outdoor dog while at the kennels became evident. Frank-

Foxy came to us as a five-year-old who had whelped two litters of pups. She was then adopted by an elderly man and when he became ill, we acquired Foxy as our latest dog. She was the most distinct of our German Shepherds and made efforts to be close to both of us.

ly, her smell became overpowering; I drove with my driver-side window rolled down, but the cold was too much, so after about 30 minutes of being cooped up with a stinking dog, I decided to look for a pet shop where I could get Foxy groomed. Finally, I spotted a PetSmart in south Sacramento, and left Foxy in the car while I went in to see if they would bathe her. Fortunately, not many people were having their dogs bathed and I returned in an hour to a cleaned and groomed Foxy.

What a different dog she was—nicely groomed, smelling lovely, and she seemed happy to be with me instead of being abandoned. I think she liked being clean, and I sensed a different demeanor. The only problem was the residual smells that remained in the car while we drove to Davis and when we arrived, I left the windows rolled down to air out the smells. Foxy was home. She came in with no hesitation, and wandered through the house, getting acquainted with new smells, new rooms, and a whole new life. Thus started one of the most remarkable relationships I have ever had with an animal—really a creature is how I came to think of Foxy. And when Nina came home, Foxy extended her feelings to Nina, too.

As lovely as Gypsy and Auggie had been in my life, (and for Nina in her life with Auggie), Foxy was different in ways that distinguished her from the others. Foxy was more docile and self-assured. All of the dogs had liked to chase a tennis ball, but after the first toss, Foxy would take off and play alone with the ball. Gypsy and Auggie would drop the ball in front of you and stare at you until you tossed the ball again. Foxy was content to entertain herself after the first involvement of the game with you. She showed some independence.

Foxy seldom barked except when there was a knock on the front door, or the doorbell rang. After greeting anyone at the door, and smelling them for approval, she would step aside and follow them into the room, and then go off to her favorite sleeping places.

When we were on walks with her and we encountered a friend where we were apt to linger awhile and talk, Foxy would lay down and patiently wait until our conversations had ended. I do not recall any occasion where she would be restless and try to hurry us along. Foxy had great patience.

In time, Foxy became equally close to both Nina and me. This surprised me because in the start of her life with us, she tended to be a man's dog—but then, she had been with a single man for several years before he had to give her up. She just associated with a man and did so in the beginning of her life with us. But that changed. With Nina's computer in the back bedroom of the house, and my computer and office in the front of the house, it was difficult for her to know which of us to follow. She decided that lying in the hall midway between where we were working was a good compromise.

Foxy developed her own preferences too. There are four bedrooms in our house, one being used by Nina as a sewing room, and when Nina was sewing, Foxy laid in that room with Nina nearly all the time. Sometimes, she would go to that room by herself, apparently feeling secure there, or expecting Nina to be returning there soon. One of the bedrooms was truly a guest room in which only overnight guests would sleep, but most of the time none of us entered that room, though the door was always open. When we couldn't find her with us or in one of the rooms we often inhabited, we would find her sleeping or just resting in the spare room. That became know as "Foxy's Room" and her behavior of where she laid in the room pretty much indicated her preference for solitude, or to be available to be petted as we walked down the hall. For solitude, she would sleep along the far wall and the bed, visible only as you fully entered the room. When feeling sociable, she would lay inside her room, but in plain sight of the door.

Even when she was near us, seeming very content to be in close proximity Foxy never seemed to press for attention. Gypsy and Augie would come up and want assurance that we liked them, by placing their head under our hand. Foxy would seldom initiate the need for attention, but would surely respond when we made the approach. I was never sure whether her reluctance was a fear of annoying us, or her preference for us to initiate the petting.

There is great vulnerability when owning a dog; I'm thinking in terms of having such lovely dogs that you think of them as creatures rather than dogs. Each of our German Shepherds was in that category. When their life span ended, the grieving for them was so unbearable that each time we would say, "That's the last one". And twice since the death of Gypsy, we have agreed to live without another pet, and after several years, our pattern has been to get another. This time, I think we are firm; at our age, we cannot suffer another loss. And, we fear what the loss of one of us might have on a surviving dog and how she would cope with that, even with one of us surviving.

You are probably convinced that our lives have been enriched by having the three German Shepherds I have mentioned. Life without them is difficult to imagine, and very sad to not have them as companions.

CHAPTER TEN

Things I Learned About People and Myself from Working

A person doesn't come into life capable of doing anything. I was born through the efforts of someone else, my mother. I presume the doctor who delivered me beat me on the butt to get me to start breathing. Life can be like that as long as you live, with needing someone to beat you on your butt to keep you working and progressing. Alternatively, one can take the initiative and get started with his/her life, often with help or support from others.

I think I took the second option, partly due to genes and mostly by desire. I was also helped by others. I was always small in stature, but the Napoleon complex doesn't seem to be why I did things that led to work or jobs. Maybe it just happened. As a 3-year old I have memories of telling Mom that when I grow up, I was going to buy a yellow bus and take her back east to visit her sister. That suggests to me that I thought our lives would be better if we left the farm; more likely, it boiled down to getting away from Uncle Avak who dominated our family. I do not have alternative explanations. Life was tough, but I am not sure I understood that. But, something compelled me to want to make life better for Mom, so I was determined I could buy a yellow bus and take her elsewhere. Unfortunately, I never did buy the bus. The closest I came was when I was 17 years old, my parents traveled to Boston and Providence for 3 weeks and left me in charge of tending the farm, thus allowing them to go.

Necessity took over as each of my siblings and I became old enough to work on the farm. We were never paid for our work, we just were fed, had a bed to share in a room we shared with our siblings, and I believe we had love and support for each other. We all grew up as a unified family, not just individuals looking out for their own interests. The younger ones picked fruit and the older siblings cut them for drying or at the cannery as Arpie and Isabel did. Our parents were involved with everything else. Soon, we became old enough that we could work for someone else for money, doing the things we were accustomed to doing at home. So, my sisters (all older) worked for the canneries cutting fruit for canning, while my brother and I were too young for such work, so we picked fruit that had been shaken to the ground to be dried. Later, when we were old enough to climb, and move ladders, we picked fruit off the trees, to be packed by others for fresh shipments to eastern markets.

That may have been lesson #1: You can earn more income by doing simple things others cannot do as you became older (and taller).

The last seasonal work my brother Chuck and I could do was to turn the trays on which the grapes were laid to dry into raisins. At the time, we would split $1 for each thousand trays we would turn, and with luck, we would turn about a thousand trays daily, and each earn 50 cents for the day. We did this for about 3 or 4 years until we could do more advanced farm work. Once we met with a very prosperous farmer who had a reputation for being a cheapskate. He wanted us to turn trays for him, but he would pay us only 75 cents a thousand trays, so we were each earning 37.5 cents a day for our efforts. We worked harder (faster) to earn the 50 cents we could have earned elsewhere. After two days, we decided that just wasn't possible for us, so we devised a system of turning the trays that enabled us to earn the 50 cents each. However, the system we used resulted in some of the raisins flying off the trays, which would create more work for the farmer who had to retrieve the raisins lying on the ground. We earned our usual income, but it cost the farmer more money to salvage the raisins that flew off the trays as we turned them. This wasn't a good solution for either of us.

I think that was lesson #2: If you try to pay someone below a prevailing wage, it may cost you more in the long run by them taking shortcuts that can mean lost money for you. Pay people for an honest job and don't try to make your profits by beating up those who work hard for you.

When I was about 14 or 15 years old, the prospect of getting a car by doing farm work was pretty slim. First, farm work was seasonal so it wasn't always available when you needed money, or a large sum of money with which to buy a car. Then, I realized that more money could be earned from off-farm work than from farm work. But, I had no skills that I could trade for more money from a job. I just didn't know how to get such a job. But, walking the 2 miles from home to school and another 2 miles back in the afternoon, I would pass a gas station that sold "economy" gas, and though I didn't know the owner, we would wave to each other as I walked by. I think I was the first to start waving, and then he responded, and that continued for several months.

After much thought, I decided that if I could learn how to serve a gas customer, perhaps I could earn money year around, more than I could from farm work. So, one day I got the courage to walk up to the owner, Mr. Larry Thorson, and asked him if he would let me work for him free so I could get experience enough to where a gas station on the other side of town on Highway 99 would hire me. He thought it over a few minutes, and he asked when I wanted to start. I told him that now would be okay, so I was shown how to greet the customer, how to pump the number of gallons wanted, to check the oil without being asked, how to wash the windshields, how to wipe the bugs off the lights, and to offer to check tire air pressure. In a few days I was taught how to collect money and to make correct change. I apparently mastered all of that in two days, because Mr. Thorson decided that on the second day, he was going to pay me 25 cents an hour. On weekends, I could make $2 a day, compared to the 50 cents I received for turning grape trays. I owe a great deal to Mr. Thorson, who soon told me his first name was Lawrence, (and for me to call him Larry) for giving me a shot at earning real money. During the first summer, Larry opened another gas station, this one in Fresno. He hired me to work there on my own and for 10 hours each day, I would make $2.50, and $5 on the weekend. Larry also taught me what the word "service" meant in terms of a customer. He sure was good with his customers and I wanted to be the same as Larry.

Lesson #3: If you do not care what your starting salary is, and even if it is free, you could learn what it takes to move from a lower to a higher paying job. Learn what the owner feels is important for his customers and duplicate that behavior.

In time, I moved up the wage scale. In 1939 Dad bought a Ford Ferguson tractor, and so we no longer kept horses. That of itself left us more time, because we no longer had to feed the horses. Additionally, it opened up more land to grow grapes, since we didn't need to grow alfalfa for animal feed. Being a kid deprived of a car of my own, I took every opportunity to do tractor work on our farm. Soon, neighbors would ask Dad if I would disc their vineyards or plow a field. We always obliged, and the money I was paid was given to Dad. In about a year, I must have been 15 or 16, Dad bought a Messinger crop duster that mounted on the back of the tractor, and I didn't have to sulfur the grape vines to control mildew by walking every row with a back pack duster any longer. I could use the tractor to do that, and I could do 3 to 5 acres an hour, and sometimes it may have been as many as 8 acres an hour. The tractor not only made farm work more fun but it was a good way to earn money by working for other farmers. And, after the second year, I was asked to dust vineyards with cyanide, a very poisonous insecticide used on grapes for control of leafhoppers. When there was no wind movement I was able to earn $100 for 3 hours work, mostly from 4 a.m. to 7 a.m. I would turn that money over to Dad, too, and I felt good about contributing to the family finances. We took no safety precautions such as wearing a gas mask because there was little information available for applicators. But the dusting of cyanide was very dangerous work.

Lesson #4: Farm work (interpret that as hard work) can be fun and also profitable when using good equipment. People will pay you good money in return for doing a dangerous (to life) job for them.

In college at Cal Poly, all agricultural students were required to have a farm related project. Most students would plant a crop and then sell it or feed it to an animal in their project. I learned that most students could grow a good crop, like tomatoes, and then not know what to do with the fruit. For my project, I bought field-run tomatoes from students, packaged them by size in new or clean boxes, hauled them to Fresno every Friday afternoon for sale to hamburger joints and the smaller tomatoes to grocery stores. I'd pay students a dollar a box, and sell them for $5 a box, taking about 20 boxes in my car. For the return trip, I'd take grapes from our farm and sell them to the Cal Poly cafeteria and two grocers in town. Later I'd take oranges from the farm and sell them to the same grocers in town. Needless to say, I made good money, and even considered buying a pickup truck and starting a business after graduation.

Lesson #5: There are opportunities to start a business all around us. We need to be observant, perform a service to suppliers and to customers, and to take a risk. The lesson really was that I had developed opportunities but was attracted to a salary instead of being a business owner, and I think I was unable to see beyond risk far enough to start my own business. I have passed up opportunities for self-employment that perhaps I should not have.

After graduating with a B.S., my first job offer was at Oregon State University. My brother-in-law, George, (married to Isabel), told me about an opening for a horticulturist at the Hood River Experiment Station, so I applied. About a week later I received a letter telling me the job had been filled, but there was an opening for a horticulturist in the Willamette Valley in Clackamas County (just 10 miles south of Portland). If I were interested, he would arrange for me to be given a tour of the county so I could see the horticultural farms first hand. Arrangements were made, we hauled everything we owned in the car, (expecting to be offered the job), and drove to Oregon City for the tour. It turned out that the tour was really for a couple of farm management economists to look at pastures, and I was taken along for the convenience. All I saw were strawberry, raspberry, and blackberry fields, but no tree fruits. At that time, my understanding was that only trees produced horticultural fruit crops.

As we drove along a strawberry field I recall one of the economists asked me what variety of strawberries we were looking at, and I told him I did not know. I didn't tell him I didn't know strawberries had varieties, and that all I knew about the crop was stealing them at night from our farm neighbors in Fowler. Aside from that, I knew nothing about berry crops.

The next day I drove into Portland to meet Charles Smith, who was a lovely, wonderful guy and whom I always admired while I was at OSU. He asked me about my tour and interest. I told him that there were no tree fruits, only strawberries, and I didn't know anything about strawberry farming. His response threw me: "Well, I can understand that but if your letters of recommendation are true, you can learn, can't you?" I sat there a bit puzzled and told him "If you want to hire me under that condition, I will be happy to accept". So, he arranged for me to drive to Corvallis, take care of all paper work and then go back to Oregon City to meet my new associates.

Charley asked me what salary I expected, and I said I understood the starting salary was $2500 a year. He said he would start me out at $3000, just to keep me in line with others. So, I received my first raise before I even went to work.

On the job, I spent hours reading the bulletins about berry crops, their culture, diseases and insect pests, etc. One of the first telephone questions I got was "How much pressure should be used for spraying walnut trees?" I said, "I do not know" and hung up. I had sprayed trees before but did not know anything about the machines. I soon learned from one of the other men in the office who overheard my response was that I should have told the caller that I would look up the information and call him back. But then, I really didn't have a clear understanding of what I was expected to do on the job.

Lesson #6: Learn something about the company you are going to work for before applying for the job. That makes you more attractive at an interview. OSU must have been very impressed with my letters of recommendation, enough that they did not question the curricula I took. But, I did start to become a risk taker, a bit, anyway.

I learned rapidly on the job by asking many questions of the horticulturalists at OSU. I also did a lot of critical thinking on my own. A major problem of strawberry plants was a weevil that laid eggs on the plants and when the eggs hatched, the worms burrowed down and ate the roots. The standard control was not working well. I asked my friend Bob Every, the Extension Entomologist, whether an application of an insecticide spread on the soil and disked in before planting might give the desired control. He encouraged me to run an experiment, gave me the chemicals and supervised the experiment. (This topic is described in greater detail beginning on page 142 in order to not duplicate this research achievement.)

Lesson #7: If you are awed by someone's title but not his work, don't spend time cottoning up to that person. He's asleep on the job, and associating with him will get you nowhere. Instead, do the work he was supposed to do for you and do it well to cover your tracks, and the truth will prevail with those who are important in your career.

I have progressed into jobs for which I would not have considered myself qualified, and not been offered several jobs which I have felt I could do well. The former is professional while the latter is political.

I was offered and accepted the job at OSU though I was not sure I was qualified. But, I have letters from the editor of the daily Oregon City newspaper and an editorial praising my contributions as a farm advisor. So, I learned quickly on the job and apparently I did well.

I was granted an assistantship at the University of Wisconsin in Agricultural Economics by Prof. Ray Penn, who saw something in me that I did not know. Later I became an assistant professor in that department. After my Ph.D. and back at Oregon, I took leave to serve as one of four economic advisors (staff economists) with Secretary of Agriculture Orville Freeman during the Kennedy administration. I also served on President Carter's Presidential Government Reorganization Program. While still at Oregon, my major professor at Wisconsin, Dr. Fritz Mueller, had become Chief Economist with the Federal Trade Commission, and invited me to work with him in Washington, but I felt I had to gain status at OSU because of the political aspects of such work. After I came to UCD, Dr. Mueller, now back at Wisconsin, offered me the job as director of a national research project on "Organization of Food Marketing", which I did not accept because of personal interests here at UCD. Had I accepted, that was a second major crossroads with Fritz that would have greatly changed my life.

Lesson #8: People create their own limitations by having a low estimation of their potential. I have experienced confidence by others regarding my abilities, which I have apparently lived up to, though I did not have that same confidence in myself.

I have always benefited by hiring the best people I can, even when they exceed my abilities, because their work will carry me along with them. I have never been afraid of hiring the best, and have fortunately been able to do so. The same is true with graduate students. Work with the best you can get, and they will never forget you, and they will always carry you along. Paul Mohn, of USDA was one example of a professional colleague. Al Spina, a senior executive of Tri Valley Growers, and later an associate in MRA, is an example of a very talented business executive who contributed greatly to my career. And, we remain good friends.

Lesson #9. Good people are worth searching for, and associating with. Never give up that opportunity.

Most of us will work for others who will supervise our performance and results. Sometimes, we will have supervisory responsibilities over others too. In either case, it is important that everyone understand in advance what is expected in terms of results. Measuring performance without having information in advance about what is expected is unfair and bad management. And, if you are self-employed, it is important to establish quality standards for your work that are acceptable to your clients. I have found that establishing reasonable but high standards for your own work is good for your own satisfaction and keeps your client base happy.

Lesson # 10. Establish result expectations for your work that will give you satisfaction from your job. If you work for someone who does not do this, set them yourself and get acceptance in advance from your supervisor and expect to be evaluated on achieving your performance and goals. Everyone is entitled to know in advance what is expected, and to be evaluated periodically on that basis.

CHAPTER ELEVEN

PEOPLE WHO HAVE
INFLUENCED MY LIFE, AND HOW

This is a tough assignment mainly because it involves such a long period of life—91 years at this writing (I am clawing my way up to 92 in May 2015 if God's plan remains on target.). As I live longer, I have found more people become influential, for different reasons. It's not easy, either, because one's near-term memory is apt to be better than your earlier memories. You owe gratitude to more people.

For this section I have thought back to those people who I recall have left something in my life that has lingered over time. I could say that nearly all contacts have had an influence on me, and that would likely be true. But to do that would be impossible and probably of limited interest. I've narrowed the list to those who have so influenced me that I can feel it within my bones, my mind, and my soul. These people left a lasting mark on me, and carried me through the *muck* of life to have meaningfully changed my life. I could easily mention my many graduate students, but I just cannot list them all. But to them I say, "Being absent is not an indication of being left out". Each would need a chapter, including Walt Armbruster, Gail Cramer, Stavros Kouroukalis, Stan Thompson and Roland Wentzel.

MY PARENTS

My list starts with my parents, Leon and Beatrice, who have been extremely influential in my life. Dad was determined to become an American, so much so that he stowed away on a ship to the U.S. from Liverpool, England, *twice.* He had been returned to England by immigration authorities. He had a problem with his eyes that was apparent to immigration authorities who refused him an entry visa. Before the third trip he had his eyes treated and he made the trip legally. *That taught me determination.* All of this took place about 1897-1901.

Dad had a college education in journalism, from Euphrates University, a college run by American Protestant missionaries in East-Central Turkey, who arranged his transfer to England to continue his education. *This suggests to me that there are people out there who will help you if you allow them, and to be a loner is not necessarily a good thing.* Don't be unwilling to receive assistance, though Dad's pride did prevent our family from receiving welfare assistance during the Great Depression of the 1930s, when we were as poor as church mice. Still, life worked out well for us all.

For example, when my sisters' shoe soles wore out, Dad would find old machine shop drive belts that were being thrown out because they had broken. He would bring home pieces that he would measure and cut for shoes and then he would nail them on. I recall Isabel telling about how embarrassed she was to wear her shoes, because the center of the belting was white, and she would take black or brown crayons to color the white fiber on the edges of the soles. Of course, the belting lasted much longer than the original soles, so the coloring was a continuous job. *I'm not sure what lesson I learned from this. Was it that being too proud is sometimes bad?*

Dad and Mom were very religious, and brought us up in the Armenian Church. Of course, Mom was very devout. Every Sunday was a day of faith, and I do not recall our family working on Sundays except during harvest or only to save the year's crop. Many years later, while I lived in Ireland, I saw a small-scale farmer strolling among his piles of hay on a bright Sunday afternoon, and I asked him if he was working in the hay? His response was "No. What man does on Sunday, the Lord scatters on Monday." Same philosophy; same devout belief.

Then too, comes my exposures to honesty and faith in family. Mom and Dad had received financial help from relatives in New England, who loaned them money to take the train to move the family across country to California. Although my parents' expectations were to repay the loan, they were unable to immediately do so. By 1940 Dad had finally paid off the farm debt and there was a bit of money left over. Dad went to the local Bank of America manager and asked him to figure his debt to these relatives from 1916 or 17 to 1940. Then Dad sent checks to them with principle and interest for all of these years.

I feel I have a rich heritage in family integrity and honesty, a moral code that I have tried to live by throughout my years. I doubt I have done as well as my parents did. However, my son Lee is carrying on from where I may have left off.

Recently daughter Lisa reminded me of years in Oregon when we would meet the Parker Hinckley family at the Oregon State Fair in Salem; the Hinckleys would drive from Oregon City, and we from Corvallis. Because Hinckley was in charge of a 4-H display, he received reserved car parking. While I was telling the parking attendant that I was a member of the Hinckley party, Lisa and Lee both remarked loudly, "Dad, we are not with **the** 4-H group, we are just going to meet Hinckley." I was beginning to learn of children's integrity. About 10 years later, after we had moved to California, I was told Lee needed a pair of orthopedic shoes, which were available in San Francisco. I parked the car and we started walking towards the store located on the other side of the street. With no car traffic, *I told Lee we would jay-walk. He refused, saying "Dad, if you break that law, how do you decide which law you will not break?"* I still recall that remark to this day; his integrity still prevails.

Several years ago we spent a few weeks at his house in Scottsdale, and I was working on some papers I had taken with me, and I needed some paper fasteners. I asked if he had any, and he said "No, I don't use them". So then I asked if he had any from the office, and he responded, "Dad, I don't take things that belong to the office for my personal use".

VERA ROBB

Anyone alive who knows me also knows who Vera Robb is and how she influenced my life. She was my 8th grade teacher at Fowler Elementary School, and she was one of the strictest teachers I have ever had. She maintained tight control of her classes, which over time, included Marian and Chuck before I came along. By the time I got there, she was quite familiar with the Garoian kids and had a good idea of what to expect.

Our little town of Fowler had more outstanding teachers than we were entitled to, and they all were influential. It wasn't until I went to Fowler High that I had some teachers who were probably just as good, but who didn't have as much influence on me. I would consider Ruth Sneed, Pop and Mom Kellogg (as they were known) among my Fowler High School's outstanding teachers. So, what set Miss Robb apart from these other good teachers?

I think it was a combination of good writing attributes, but specifically Miss Robb instilled in me the importance of proper grammar and sentence structure for better composition for communication that leads to better understanding. She had a no-nonsense approach to her teaching—but she was also warm and friendly in a way that didn't allow her to have teacher's pets. She was patient with all of us, not just the smarter or quicker to learn students. I don't know how she did that, without the smart students getting bored—I was one of the smart ones, but not the smartest—that was Floyd Wilkins. But I was on a par with George Toyama, and together the three of us high achievers were not bored. She kept our attention even when things were going well for us—Floyd was a brilliant student, and everything came easily for him except humility. He had a problem with that. George and I enjoyed working together on tough assignments; George being better in arithmetic and algebra than I was, but I was better in the social sciences than he was. We remained close friends throughout 12 years of schooling, but when the Japanese families were evacuated during WWII, we lost touch with each other.

As I was writing this, I wondered what happened to George, so I "Googled" him, and with some effort, found his name and telephone number on the internet. He was very surprised to hear my name, after 68 years; we had a nice visit. He became an engineer employed by Cal Trans (his math strengths sure came through). He never married, and is the oldest living of his family.

Professor Raymond Penn

While I was still a county agent for horticultural crops (farm advisor) in Oregon, I learned that farmers had many places to go for information about growing crops, disease and pest control recommendations, and fertilization. Increasingly, I realized that farmers needed more help in the business and economic side of farming, and I spent nearly equal time with the economists at Oregon State as I did with the horticulturalists. I learned more about farmer cooperatives' programs to promote Oregon fruit products, mainly strawberries, and farm management questions. It was in 1953 that the American Agricultural Economics Association held its annual summer meetings in Corvallis, and my economist friends at OSU asked me to attend the meetings. That sounded like a good idea, I ran into Vernon Shahbazian, a fellow classmate from Cal Poly, and one who had gone to school with Chuck before the war. Vernon was from Reedley, about 15 miles from Fowler, and he was a "farm boy" as I was. Vernon had been working on his Ph.D. in Agricultural Economics at the University of Wisconsin (Madison), but had recently taken a job with the California Department of Agriculture, Marketing Division. He invited me to "The" Wisconsin Party that night, so I went along. He introduced me to a lot of professors from Wisconsin, and some grad students. One person I liked immediately, was Ray Penn, who was the Chairman of the Ag. Econ. Department at Wisconsin.

We did a lot of visiting and socializing that evening, and the next day we met again, and Ray asked about my activities as farm advisor, educational interests, and general topics like farm problems of my clientele. I told him I was eligible for a sabbatical leave from OSU, and was thinking about going to Michigan State for graduate work in horticulture.

The next day we had another visit, and he asked if I would be interested in graduate work in agricultural economics at Wisconsin, and if so, he would offer me an assistantship in his department, on the spot. He said some nice things about me and how I would fit in well in "the Wisconsin idea" that prevailed at the University. I agreed to his offer on the spot, subject to approval of my sabbatical leave by OSU.

Once I was at Wisconsin, Ray took me under his wing, and whenever my classes permitted, he took me with him throughout the state for meetings where he met with farmers to discuss dairy and agricultural policy issues. He helped develop my class program, and supervised my master's thesis topic. From Ray, I learned how he discussed controversial topics without becoming argumentative. Farmers could sometimes get heated regarding government programs that affected their income or farming practices. But in all my experiences with Ray, he took an educational role with these farmers, and never an adversarial role. Ray was a real inspiration for me, and I have tried to be like Ray when dealing with controversial issues.

I was asked to conduct a study of the benefits of a merger between two farmer dairy cooperatives that were competing in Saskatchewan, Canada. Our study showed substantial savings could be made that would increase prices paid to dairymen, but to achieve those savings, the number of milk receiving stations would need to be reduced from 42 to 18. At the final meeting with the two boards of directors, we heard a lot of criticism about this reduction in numbers of the stations, because the board members didn't want to face their neighbors if they proposed cutting out the neighborhood delivery station. I thought of Ray Penn, and responded, "okay, tell me which stations can not be closed because of public relation problems, and I will tell you how much less you will be able to pay for milk". We went through quite a number of such delivery stations that "MUST" be retained, and when the data showing the lower prices to farmers became evident, the boards went along with our original economic recommendations. That is the way that I felt Ray would have handled a potentially divisive issue.

About 5 months after I returned to my job as farm advisor, Ray called again with another "offer that was too good to refuse". He said the department wanted to hire me full time on the faculty as a fruit and vegetable marketing economist, with an opportunity to work on a doctorate within the department. It really was a wonderful opportunity, so again, we moved back to Wisconsin, this time having resigned from OSU, a state and university we loved very much. Once there, Ray had me assigned to Professor Robert Clodius as advisor for my graduate program, another wonderful act by Ray. *When Bob Clodius saw my grades from the first semester, (all A's), he thought I could take more courses and still work full time. His plan for me included taking courses during summer session on a full time basis by using my vacation time. The only problem was this was against policies of the graduate school. So, he said, "The dean is the one who wrote that policy, and someone with that authority might like to be asked to change the policy on an individual basis".* So Bob arranged for a meeting with Dr. Connie (Conrad) Elviam, dean, who listened to Bob's proposal, and on the spot agreed to the change for me. That meant I could complete my doctorate in 2 ½ years), which was about normal for full time students, while I was drawing full pay for my work within the department.

Ray Penn not only influenced how I viewed education of controversial public policy matters, but he changed the direction of my entire professional life. He and other members of the faculty of the Department opened up vistas in national agricultural policy levels of government that I would never have been able to achieve.

Willard "Fritz" Mueller And Robert Clodius

Fritz came to the University of Wisconsin, Madison, several months after I was employed. He was a Wisconsin native who got his bachelor's degree in economics from Wisconsin and who earned his doctorate at Vanderbilt (in Tennessee). He studied with Professor George Stocking, a noted economist whose reputation was earned for the research that led to the "Cellophane" antitrust case; this set the standards for controlling non-competitive practices by large companies that resulted in higher consumer prices. As a student in Industrial Organization and Public Policy, Fritz went on to the University of California, Davis, as an assistant professor in agricultural marketing. His stay at Davis was pretty short; so short that some of the professors who are still at Davis do not remember Fritz' brief tenure. When UW offered him an opportunity to return to Wisconsin, the decision was very easy for him.

Fritz and I are the same age. While I was getting my start as a farm advisor, he was getting his advanced degrees. Before Fritz joined the faculty at UW, Professor Robert Clodius was my mentor within the department. Bob was a brilliant economist, and one of the best university lecturers I have ever known. His freshman class in introductory agricultural economics was jam-packed with students—over 300 each time it was offered. Every doctoral candidate in the department would also attend his introductory classes, because not to was tantamount to failing the general written exam of doctoral candidates about agricultural economics. *To this day, I recall the finesse of Bob's lectures in which he explained complicated economic problems in theoretical terms that were understandable. Bob was assigned as my mentor when I was hired, and I was very fortunate.*

When Fritz joined the faculty, I worked jointly with Bob and Fritz on my academic program for the doctorate, and with Fritz on the professional topics of my educational programs and research.

I soon found I was being drawn into close research affiliations with Fritz; he offered an opportunity to engage in public policy education and research interests that Ray Penn had stirred up in me while I was working on my masters. You can probably figure out where this part of my story is going; the University of Wisconsin as an institution captured my naivety, developed my interests, and opened up professional channels that I had never expected possible. I was completely engrossed in "The Wisconsin Idea", the great concept of a wonderful university administration and faculty developed over its first 100 years, in which its motto was "The boundaries of the State are the boundaries of the campus". The faculty of this great university was involved with nearly every aspect of social and economic problems faced by its citizens: land use planning; unemployment insurance; worker's compensation; worker job safety; agricultural policies; and many more.

It was here, in this environment, that I was offered the opportunities of a lifetime: the development of a native son of immigrants, to expand knowledge and gain understanding of the major problems of agriculture and the development of policies that provide solutions to these problems. The little farm boy of Armenian descent from Fowler, California, a town of less than 1000 people, who had observed and experienced racial discrimination, was becoming able to speak out on a national level; whose opinions were asked and often put to practice, and who met with senators and congressmen seeking to find policy solutions. That is what Ray Penn, Fritz Mueller, Bob Clodius, and the University of Wisconsin enabled me to become.

My work with Fritz was probably the result of the influence of Ray Penn and Bob Clodius. But Fritz gave me opportunities to work with him, to ride along on his coat tails, so to speak, and to gain a reputation as a result of my close association with him.

George Kaloostian

George was my brother-in-law married to my sister Isabel, but he was more like a mature brother to me, especially as an icon in many ways. We met when I was 3 years old, as someone on whose lap I would crawl when our families would get together. Of course, I didn't know at the time that he was actually courting Isabel; courting in those days (in 1928) was done discreetly and often with the family around.

Throughout his 96 years of life, George was non-judgmental about people. In reality, I never heard him speak unkindly about anyone, whether about our elected officials, those he worked with professionally, and personally those he could have hated. Tolerance and patience were virtues that George had learned. I hope a bit of it rubbed off on me.

Professionally, George had opportunities to use his intelligence and research methods to find causes for the spread of virus diseases on fruit trees. He found such sources of disease spread from unlikely host plants to fruit trees, including viruses in pears, apples, citrus, and other fruits. Farmers benefited considerably from his research findings that led to control methods that kept the farmers in business, and at the same time the U.S. Department of Agriculture received recognition for George's work. George received recognition from his research reports in professional journals, and was elected president of the American Entomological Society. Consumers benefited from his research by enjoying the greater abundance of fruits he worked on. Being saved by a decision of a young Turkish soldier (see pg. 83) who let George live was a great benefit to world society.

He had an interest in cars, too, and he influenced my purchase of 1955 and 1956 Ford Thunderbird sports cars.

Arnold Haseley

I recognize that at any specific moment it is difficult to be aware that someone is engaging you in experiences that will influence later life and have an effect on where that life will take you. I hired an associate at Oregon State University, Arnold Haseley, who is one of those people who taught me much in the two years he was with me. I was greatly impressed with Arnie and he became a partner in a consulting business I was authorized to develop while a professor at OSU. Arnie's life was cut short when a car in which he was a passenger hit a bridge abutment on I-5 near Salem. Arnie was killed instantly, and I was called by a mutual attorney friend of ours to inform Arnie's wife Pinky, and sisters in New York of the disaster. Arnie's influence on me was of the magnitude of those I have discussed above had we had more time together.

KIRBY MOULTON

Kirby was appointed at UC Berkeley shortly after I was hired by UC Davis, and we quickly became colleagues. We worked as teammates on research projects; we taught courses together at UC Davis, we traveled to foreign countries to engage in studies of interregional competition from production of specific crops on California's farm industries. We published as joint-authors on many of these research studies. We even shared leisure time with our families. After my retirement, Kirby and I continued to collaborate on crop marketing problems. Gradually Kirby became an authority on wine marketing, receiving international acclaim for his independent work, and I retired and moved to foreign locations for long-time assignments.

PAUL MOHN

Of those named, my work with Paul Mohn persisted the longest. Our friendship began at Oregon where Paul served as an Extension Agricultural Economist and I was a county agent (farm advisor) who would call on him to help find ways to improve marketing of fruits and vegetables for Clackamas County farmers. Forty years later we were still working together to find methods to improve farmers income.

While I was in the graduate programs at the University of Wisconsin, Paul moved to Washington, D.C. (Department of Agriculture) to work on the development of cooperatives. Soon Paul offered me funds for research and teaching projects for cooperative development. I believe I received funding for four, maybe five of these research projects over time. Several became projects that were national in scope, meaning that we would be available to introduce the teaching plans to economists in all states.

After my retirement from the University of California, I was employed at University College, Cork, Ireland, where it became possible to obtain funds from the Bank of Ireland to expand cooperative teaching and research for dairy cooperatives. I was able to hire Paul Mohn on a part-time basis as a visiting professor to work with me for about five years.

Paul and I provided assistance to other organizations interested in education programs for cooperative members. Truly, the results of this working relationship left a marked influence at other universities and the cooperatives with which we worked, internationally.

AL SPINA

When I became employed by the UC Berkeley, several of my colleagues were surprised I didn't know Al Spina, the V.P. of Operations for Tri Valley Cooperative, the world's largest (and at the time, the most successful) fruit and vegetable cooperative, with seven operating plants, all within California. I made an appointment as quickly as possible to meet Al; I had known the cooperative, some members of its board of directors, and Bill Allewelt, the CEO for many years through my national connections with cooperatives.

It wasn't difficult to become friends with Al. In short order, Al had me conducting meetings with groups of TVC's operating management on various economic and business management topics.

Often these meetings were held at Tri Valley's largest factory in Modesto, so it was only natural for me to become acquainted with Al's parents, Frank and Lucy, who were local farmers. In time, Lucy began inviting me for Italian dinners and then I would be expected to stay overnight. As my friendship with the family developed, I would often make the Spina ranch my overnight headquarters when I traveled around the valley. It wasn't necessary to coordinate these stays with Al; it was a standing invitation from Frank and Lucy, which sometimes included meals with Al's Uncle Tony and Al's Grandmother Ciccerelli, who would host us to dinner at the nearby Ciccerelli house.

Grandmother reminded me of my own mother, both in appearance and in graciousness. Tony was a cordial host, and sometimes we would imbibe more Galliano than prudent. Once I was expected to help Al and Frank fertilize a young walnut orchard the morning after one such night of a large Italian meal and too much Galliano. I am surprised I didn't die as I worked in that orchard, with a big hangover.

With Bill Allewelt's approval, I would ask Al to work with MRA (Management Research Associates, my consulting company) on specific projects where his expertise was needed. Tri Valley would benefit from Al's experience with problems in other companies that exposed him to industry and company issues outside his immediate TVC responsibilities. He never was asked to serve as a consultant to a company that was a TVC competitor.

When Al retired from Tri Valley, he became an associate for MRA, and these activities led us on international assignments to Thailand, Vietnam, and Singapore, besides domestically within California and Washington.

Al's ability to dissect operating problems of companies in the food industry was very instructive to me. The MRA assignment with Jack Woolf's family farm organization at Huron, CA led MRA to make a feasibility analysis, help design a tomato processing company at their ranch headquarters, and in finding their general manager for the plant was a project that gave us much satisfaction. And, it proved to be a successful venture that led to other feasibility analyses.

Al became a personal as well as professional friend; essentially we considered me a member of the Spina family.

THOSE NOT NAMED ABOVE

Some of those named were (or became) friends for longer periods than the time of our joint collaborative activities. I have worked closely with many more people than these and my professional career and personal life has been strengthened as a result of these relationships. I have been fortunate with the closeness of the results, and regret I have not mentioned others who have contributed to my life but this list would be extensive.

Richard Howitt would be one I would include. Richard and I have been colleagues since 1970, and share our interest in economics as well as our car hobby. Richard is perhaps the closest person I have known whom I consider to be a genius; there is nothing we have encountered that he cannot sit down and reason how it works, and how it can be repaired, though he may not have seen the object before. Then, **Greg Wood**, son of my mentor Dr. Burt Wood, who carries on the role of his dad with me. From my car activities, would be **Ken McMurphy**, whose soul I remember each Sunday in my prayers, and whose virtues I recall constantly. Included in that category is **Larry Munson** who also restored several fabulous cars for me.

In another role are the following people who taught me things of a professional nature that made it possible for me to serve agricultural cooperatives and help them to achieve their main economic mission on behalf of farmers: **Attorney Robert Kerr** of Portland, Oregon. (Incidentally, he served as a Judge at the Nuremberg War Trials at the end of WWII.) Working with Robert while I was an agricultural economist at Oregon State University enabled me to gain skills in numerous mergers involving 46 cooperatives in the United States and Canada. From **James Morris**, an attorney from Stockton, California, whose practice embodied integrity personified, I learned much about farmers' needs for protection from unscrupulous practices by companies serving farmers. Over a 20-year period I probably served as expert witness on 20 legal cases for Jim and his clients.

No person can serve as major professor for research of graduate students without learning more about economics than previously existed; after all, that is the purpose of professional research, especially for a graduate dissertation. I learned much from the research by **Walter Armbruster, Gail Cramer, Stanley Thompson, and Roland Wentzel**, all of whom not only became outstanding in their professions, but all became heads of their departments. Roland became head of the USDA Crop Insurance program after which he became owner (with his wife Barbara) of a group of high level home furnishing stores in the San Francisco Bay area. (With time, I could have learned more from Roland.)

John J. Inskeep, head of the Oregon State University Agricultural Extension Service in Clackamas County, Oregon, with whom I worked on my first professional position after graduating from Cal Poly, became the first of the professional mentors who influenced my career. He taught me the importance of promptly communicating to clientele information on matters affecting their livelihood, of keeping administrators informed, and engaging in research to solve problems when needed. Without his support, I might have been reluctant to engage in research to find better farm practices than those widely used. John also encouraged me to be active in statewide agricultural organizations when it would help my work within my county area. In a way, John served as a father image, not only professionally, but as a fellow hunting, fishing, and camping partner. Through John, **Al Parker**, a state forester became my close friend too, who not only was my best friend socially, and professionally, but also with whom I established a wholesale nursery business to grow ornamental plants. Both were very helpful in guiding my professional development without being aware of their influence.

I don't know how to comment about three individuals who gave international exposure to me at almost the same time. One is **Dr. Professor Denis Lucy**, of University College, Cork, Ireland. It was Denis who came to Davis to encourage me to become a visiting professor in his department. He provided me with professional contacts and guidance, opened his mind and heart to us to make us comfortable as residents of Ireland, and made us his family's guest until we could find housing. We became good friends with his entire family, starting with his equally capable spouse Sheila.

Next, is **Jean Marie Bouquery**, an agricultural economist with wide industrial contacts in France and elsewhere. We shared contacts in many countries, and helped each other with critical assistance to strengthen each other's research. We hosted each other's family in our respective homes, and otherwise became friends with his parents and his children, and he with mine. His father was a rural (farm) appraiser in Chartres, as a member of the resistance movement to protect the Chartres Cathedral during the German occupation. He worked with others to remove all of the colored glass windows from the

Cathedral, to number them sequentially in anticipation they would be alive to replace them, to package them in protective containers that were hidden underground to protect them. Fortunately, they succeeded, and today, you would not be aware of this dangerous and gigantic effort to protect such valuable, art and religious edifices; to engage in dangerous efforts for such a historic, valuable monument. We remain in close and frequent communications to this day.

I have worked with **John Pike**, CPA and investment banker for over 20 years, first while at the University of California during the effort to finance the acquisition of Del Monte by California cooperatives. John obtained the intent of a major Swiss bank to provide $4.3 billion to finance the acquisition. The concept did not proceed because of one cooperative's attempt to circumvent the draft agreement.

Later John retained resources of MRA staff for recommendations on the investment of $50 million in South East Asian food marketing companies. This led to participating in a feasibility analysis for a huge food-oriented industrial park project on the Haw River in the Mekong Delta of Vietnam. The huge development offered sound economic potential to proceed, but then the world recession of 2006 brought its halt. John has been an amazing individual that helped finance major development projects.

I've had the pleasure to work with a wide array of top-level professionals in economics (both academic and consultants), finance, and law. I am told I have contributed to their projects in my capacities; it is I who has found the opportunities to work with these outstanding professionals a privilege. I am indebted to them for these opportunities. I regret some of those mentioned are no longer with me; they contributed so much to my development.

CHAPTER TWELVE

PROFESSIONAL ACCOMPLISHMENTS

Some of my career accomplishments have had a lasting effect long after the events were completed. Whether my family and others will be aware of these is doubtful because some may not realize my involvement or may have forgotten they were accomplished. I especially think this to be true within the University of California, which is so huge that one's work is often not evident- that may be another way of saying that a person may be unproductive but retain his job. I have worked under both tenured and nontenured positions within a faculty, and I prefer the nontenured status if institutional productivity is important to the university.

I make no claim that the projects I was involved with were only of my doing, since with most activities I have not worked in a vacuum. Many projects were so complex that working as a loner would not have been practical. I have nearly always received support from others, sometimes directly and sometimes indirectly by receiving an impulse that led to my attention and interests.

What do I consider an accomplishment? It's a contribution that changes the way things are done or how people view something tangible that results in more satisfaction or an improvement in thinking that leads to better results.

Another question is what has been my profession within which my accomplishments have been made? I consider myself to be a "man of the earth". By that I mean that my rural background has been an important ingredient of how

139

I approach a situation, a problem, or an opportunity. Does that affect a person differently than if that person had grown up in the city? I do not know because I've not had that exposure. I mostly work with nature instead of against it. I approach problems or opportunities by asking could results be more meaningful for those involved? Sometimes this leads to frustrations and impatience for me because those affected may not have the same values and experiences I have and it takes time to bring them along to what I have in my mind. It's not equivalent to "I am not arguing; I am just speaking to get you to agree I am right". Having said all of this, the reader has no concept of my profession.

For most of my developing years I planned to be an attorney. As history reveals, even after I had a degree in horticulture and worked as a horticulturist, I still gave serious consideration to attending law school in Portland by attending night classes. But an option of becoming an economist by attending the University of Wisconsin over-ruled my interest in law, but only after seven successful years working as a horticultural farm advisor.

MY FIRST ACCOMPLISHMENTS WERE IN HORTICULTURE

It is ironic that I was destined to be successful working with berry farmers. Having taken no courses in berry production, the growing of these fruits became a self-taught project. Farmers asked for help in insect and disease control, and it was my responsibility to provide them with the answers they needed. I fulfilled this need.

Fungus Disease Control

A common problem for growers of bramble and cane berry crops in Oregon was low yields and crumbly berries. With the help of Dr. Ed Vaughn, an OSU plant pathologist, we outlined a spray program for control of anthracnose, a fungus disease that affects many varieties of cane fruits by damaging the outer bark of the canes and preventing them from allowing movement of soil moisture and nutrition to the plant's upper branches.

The solution was simple. Using a number of demonstration plots on farmers' fields, we educated them when the proper time was to spray to prevent the fungus infections. The results were amazing and farmers experienced higher yields. This educational project left a good feeling with farmers, processors, and strong support for my work.

Root Weevil Control

Lack of adequate control of the strawberry root weevil was a serious problem in all berry crops grown in Oregon's Willamette Valley. The problem was that the female adult weevil would lay eggs on the crowns of berry plants, After the eggs hatched the larvae would crawl to the roots and with their voracious appetites and their large numbers, would destroy the plant. The damage occurs by the larvae feeding on the roots below the soil. Controlling the adults with bait as recommended by OSU did not provide sufficient control.

I wondered if there might be a better control system. Bob Every, the Extension Service entomologist from OSU and I were good friends, and one day after completing our work for the day, and sitting with a cool glass of beer, we pondered the problem bothering me. We wondered if we could mix an insecticide into the soil before planting the strawberry field that would give protection for the life of the plants. Together we made plans for an experiment, and I then discussed the idea with Glen Schaeffer, a graduate of OSU who with his father was a prominent berry grower. He was intrigued, and offered us an acre of a new, larger planting for our trials.

The results were significant; for a period of three years there was no weevil damage within our experimental acre, while there was damage in the remainder of the field where traditional weevil control methods were applied. Each year, I harvested fruit from both the treated and the field on which traditional baits were used. The fruit from both areas were frozen by Glen's processing company to determine whether the treatments affected fruit flavors. Next the frozen berries from both fields were made into jam by one of the nation's largest preserve manufacturing companies to determine whether any differences in flavor developed as a result of making jam from the frozen berries. Also, OSU Experiment Station chemists tested tissue from plants from the two plots, to see whether residual chemical toxicity effects had developed from the treatments. Then, the products from each year's analysis were tested over time to see if any adverse effects were detected as a result of aging as in inventory. The new method of insect control had been tested and the results were excellent. I published the results in a bulletin from our County Extension office.

Then all hell broke loose, originating from the office of the researcher who I had asked to conduct the research and whose response had been, "It couldn't be done, and it wasn't safe". He asked the fruit processor to which Glen delivered all of his fruit, and who had professionally frozen the fruit for our research, to complain to Dean of Agriculture Earl Price, with a request that I be fired. In due time Dean Price asked for an appointment with me to explain what I had been doing. At the meeting I explained the need for research, the procedures followed, and the results. Dean Price placed his arm around my shoulders and thanked me for my research work. The practice was adopted throughout the

Valley; farmers' costs were reduced, and control of the weevil was as we predicted. And, I did not get fired.

Achievements as an Agricultural Economist

Director Education

Farmer cooperatives have helped many family farmers stay in business by giving them a voice in the marketing of their products that ultimately affects their income. The purpose of these cooperatives is to increase income by taking on some of the middlemen services and their profits. For many years, the Garoyans have been a member of Sunkist, Diamond Walnut, Raisin Bargaining Association, and the Farm Credit Association. In the mid-1930s we had also been members of Sun-Maid Raisin Growers.

Cooperatives not only offer farmers a voice in marketing, but also in the major decisions made by their co-op. In my opinion, the biggest decision of members is the election of members of the board of directors, who have the ultimate responsibility for the key decisions for the cooperative.

In 1961 Paul Mohn, an USDA Extension Service economist asked my interest in developing an educational program for directors of cooperatives, as a pilot program which, if satisfactory, would serve as a model for the extension services in all states. Paul also recommended I hire Arnold Haseley, a graduate student completing requirements for the doctorate at Purdue University to work with me on the project.

The short version of this story is that we took on the project at OSU, hired Arnie, and for two years did research and completed a program to make more effective decision makers of farmers. Upon completion we needed to test the program to see how farmers serving on a very strong cooperative board would respond. We invited Pendleton Grain Growers of Oregon to be our cooperators for a two-day forum; while we knew the CEO, we did not know the board members. We found they were cautious decision makers—they offered to come to a half-day program, but reserved the right to suspend the event if it did not meet their interests. We accepted their challenge. After our half-day session the board voted to continue for the full two-day session we had requested. Upon completion they asked us to conduct research on their business operations. This was a pleasing response from a very strong board, and a relationship that continued for many years. We now felt confident in our ability to offer a good educational program on a national scale.

It turned out we were correct. All states but Alaska offered cooperatives the educational program we developed. Canada, through its Cooperative College at Saskatoon introduced it to cooperatives (including credit unions) and provincial government agencies from Manitoba west. The text book we wrote that every participating director received, was the first comprehensive book for cooperative boards of directors anywhere, and was printed 18 times by Oregon State University, and upon my employment by UC Davis, an additional seven times in California.

What is significant is that directors became more focused in asking discerning questions and specific performance results, especially about budgets and performance goals. The work of CEOs became more precise, and both management and the board members felt more confident.

MERGERS AMONG COOPERATIVES

Research on cooperatives and education about cooperatives were a major part of my professional responsibilities. We developed close rapport with directors, CEOs, attorneys who specialized in cooperative law, and accountants who served cooperatives. Robert Kerr was an Oregon attorney with whom I worked most closely, and to a lesser extent with Gerson Goldsmith. Both were very competent, nationally recognized authorities on cooperative legal matters. After moving to the University of California I worked closely with cooperative attorneys Robert Taylor, and Seth Huffstetler, both of Los Angeles.

Research by my graduate students showed that a very few number of large proprietary companies controlled much of the food processing and marketing sector of agriculture. Most farmers' cooperatives were not effectively competing with these giant firms, and many were too small to be effective in selling to the large grocery food store buyers. I undertook an educational program for cooperatives to recognize these problems, and how to improve their declining influence with large market organizations.

I was aware that the effectiveness of cooperatives in the increasingly concentrated food distribution system had become difficult. The doctorate research by Gail Cramer, a graduate student working with me, indicated that many companies that had merged for at least 10 years or longer had not achieved their pre-merger objectives. Based on Gail's research, my associate Dr. Clinton Reeder and I studied how to improve the results of mergers, since industry concentration data convinced us that many of the cooperatives in the west would need to combine, or were destined to fail. We developed a procedure by which we could apply our organization of merger arrangements on an actual merger in Oregon. The results were successful; within six months the merger had achieved normal operations, and the new company began to achieve its merger objectives. Normally it required two years to reach this status. Following these procedures, word was out that OSU had a system to merge companies that worked well.

Many decisions are required for the complex legal, financial, marketing, operational, member or investor communications processes and personnel matters involved in a merger. There is a hierarchy of decisions, and timing becomes vital to achieve results as quickly as possible to consummate the needed modifications. Research by Roland Wentzel, another of my graduate students, enabled us to adapt a PERT (Project Evaluation and Review Technique) mathematical program to bring time, finances, activities, personnel and other critical decisions into a time network by which to establish a critical path. PERT is a planning system developed by military engineers during WWII, and subsequently used by civilians for the planning of complex building projects.

Over a ten-year period, I participated with mergers that involved 44 cooperatives in the Pacific Northwest and Saskatchewan in Canada. For each of these, we planned the process using the PERT procedure. Each worked out successfully as projected whereas most mergers in prior years had failed to achieve desired results in many years, if at all.

RUSSIAN MINISTER OF AGRICULTURE ASKS ABOUT POTATOES

As a researcher interested in agricultural policy, I began to observe that U.S. farm policies were moving towards more government regulations, controls, and influence in markets and crop production. What I had been reading of Soviet farm policies, it seemed they were moving closer to the U.S. model. I wondered at what point and on what practices and policies the U.S. model and the Russian models might converge. Starting in 1975 I wrote my thoughts in a paper that came to the attention of several U.S. federal agencies. One of these agencies was the CIA, and the other was the Voice of America. We developed interests that resulted in my researching developments in agriculture policies in eastern European countries of Poland, Hungary, Romania, Yugoslavia, and sometimes in the USSR and Bulgaria. This relationship lasted until 1987.

This research enabled me to visit each communist country every second year and to develop ties with government agencies, usually the agricultural ministries. In each country I would give lectures on marketing and the operation of a privately based market system, explaining how individual farmers make farm decisions they considered to be in their best interests. Representatives of the country would take me to state or cooperative farms, and processing plants, and to state-operated food stores. I would visit the same farms or food processing plants in successive years, so I was able to make comparisons over time about changes in crop outlook, or technology. Over time, I observed a declining state of technology and crop outlook, due mainly to communist systems of centralized decision making rather than natural and environmental conditions.

In 1978 I was invited to visit Moscow, and was asked to make a 10-minute courtesy visit with Mikhail Gorbachev, who had recently been appointed to the Office of Party Secretary of Agricultures at the age of 47. In the 1960s he had been a rising star as administrator of Agriculture and a regional party leader. With the courtesy introduction, he asked me how is it that in the U.S. we have fresh potatoes available all year long, when the Soviet Union had more geographic (and climatic) regions than the U.S. has for potato production. This discussion took nearly two hours, far in excess of the 10 minutes allocated. He was very cordial and obviously found our discussion very useful. As I left his office, I encountered six very angry officials who had been kept waiting to see Gorbachev. Their anger was apparent as they glared at me as the secretary accompanied me out to the waiting room and bid me goodbye.

PRIVATIZING COMMUNIST FARMS

Upon the breakup of the USSR, the question of how to establish a system of private ownership of farms in communist Russia was of interest to the U.S. government. The governor of Nizhny Novgorod (the former Gorki) had expressed an interest in some form of conversion from communist ownership for certain industries, including farms, within his state of Russia. This was a region of limited entry to Russians because it was the center for war materiel and aircraft manufacturing. In about 1990 I was retained as a World Bank-financed team member to consider ways to privatize both communes and collective farms.

I developed six distinct models for conversion, hoping that one of the systems would appeal to members of the communes for converting to private ownership. Interviews with the peasants and the farm leaders indicated they really did not want to bear the risks and responsibilities of being an independent farmer. Over 80 years of communism had taken away their incentives and encouraged them to avoid risks. Many had no concept of how to make farming decisions despite my efforts to explain this responsibility. I am not aware of the results of the extent of privatization of Russian farms, but I fear it was not accomplished.

PRIVATIZING FARMS IN ARMENIA

The next year I had the opportunity to advise the new Parliament of Armenia (a former Republic within the USSR) about land reform and privatization. I spent several months talking with farmworkers, state ministry of agriculture officials, and members of the parliament in drafting privatization policies and procedures for the country. The parliament modified, adopted, and put into practice, generally as proposed, the concepts developed with them. I urged the parliament to establish a system of private farms that were considered to be of efficient size instead of subsistence farms. Parliament took the opposite model of small, family sustaining farms. I thought the parliament made a mistake, but the economic blockade by Turkey and Azerbaijan virtually crippled the Armenian economy in the early years. The blockade prevented fuel for tractors and machinery from being imported, but the small-scale farms were able to use manpower rather than machines. Farm output was higher than it would be under my model, primarily because of the Turkish blockade.

Helping Karabagh

A few years later I was asked to help the government of Karabagh develop a privatization plan for the country. Following the Armenian model, we were able to design a privatization program for Karabagh that was adopted by its parliament.

While this was going on, I was asked by the International Monetary Fund to go to Moldova to work on a privatization system for the wine industry that involved a few government officials who wanted to buy certain wineries and storage facilities for themselves, and to team up with a U.S. marketing company to market Moldovan wines. I discouraged this project because it would not have helped farmers, but instead, would have made former communist officials wealthy.

Overall, the privatization of farmlands in Armenia and Karabagh has given me much satisfaction. The procedures worked, and could some day become a model for other countries, possibly Cuba.

Achievements Described in UC Davis Emeriti Oral History

On May 13, 2010, my long-time friend, Professor Richard Howitt engaged me in a UC Davis Emeriti Association oral history project dealing with my personal family history, and my professional activities and accomplishments. The interview discussed many topics that are consistent with the tone of this chapter, especially relating to work accomplished in California of which even my direct supervisors within the university had little awareness.

For over 100 years California farmers have organized cooperatives to improve their crop returns. Sunkist, Cal Cot, Diamond Walnuts, Sun-Maid, Blue Diamond, and hundreds of similar cooperatives have become highly successful in improving farmers' incomes. Tri Valley became the world's largest fruit and vegetable farmer processor cooperative. A good friend, Bill Allewelt served as the CEO that made much of this success possible. Al Spina was his second-in-command during these years, and after retiring from Tri Valley he became an associate with Management Research Associates (MRA), my research organization.

Another tree fruit processing cooperative became organized when several privately owned processors found it difficult to survive. Ralph Bunge, who was president of the California Cling Peach Association helped bring together a number of these small private canners by organizing them into California Canners and Growers, a cooperative. For a while Tri Valley and California Canners and Growers were able to increase returns to their farmers. Because much of their canned products were for private label buyers like the major retail grocery companies, the two cooperatives soon began to directly compete by reducing prices to buyers. It didn't take long for these two formerly successful cooperatives to reduce canned fruit prices enough to lose money, which meant lower returns to their members. Soon cling peach growing and canning was not profitable, and the industry used a market order agreement to pay farmers to remove trees to reduce future production.

Meanwhile, retailers were concerned that the downward trend in prices at which they had been buying would be offered to their competition at even lower prices. The retailers reduced long-term purchase commitments for fear a competing retailer would negotiate lower prices, putting further pressure on the selling prices of the two cooperatives.

This was a serious downward spiral when low prices offended everyone within the industry. I was close to both cooperatives, but closer with Tri Valley. With Bill Kinney, a UCD graduate student, we analyzed price trends that showed after one co-op lowered prices, the other followed within several days. Bill Allewelt showed interest in ending the pricing-loss of sales spiral and agreed to two things we proposed, if I could get Cal Can to agree:

- organize a new cooperative called California Valley Exports for international sales. The purpose was to have one sales organization offering products of both co-ops to foreign buyers to remove surplus supplies from domestic markets.

- organize "one-desk" (joint selling) for private label buyers to eliminate one seller from the domestic market.

The results were evident almost overnight. The industry was brought into a profitable position in a matter of weeks.

Unfortunately, the results were short lived. Behind the scenes were powerful forces that were trying to convince the two major banks financing the two cooperatives that there was need for only one cooperative to survive. Bank of America was a lead bank financing Cal Can, (and influenced by pricing practices during the pre-organization of the One-Desk Selling cooperative), and had made it known that Cal Can would likely not be financed for the next year. That was during the early weeks of Governor George Deukmejian's election, and relying on his popularity in being elected, I asked UC Davis Dean of Agriculture Kinsella if he would be willing to explain the role of the new selling organization to the governor as a means to restore stability in the industry. Governor Deukmejian made that approach but BofA would not reverse its position. Cal Can was forced to go into liquidation, at substantial loss to members. I believe it need not have happened—Is this another indication of the complacency and arrogance of large scale financial institutions?

In about 1969-70, Stokely Van Camp was also feeling the pressures of the canning industry along with several smaller private companies, and I received a telephone call from Robert "Bob" Collins, president of the California Pear Growers Association, asking me to attend a meeting in San Francisco to talk about the acquisition of these private canners and converting them into a cooperative. The short version of this episode is that following meetings extending over months, growers accepted the challenge of entering the canning business by organizing Pacific Coast Producers and to become owners of Stokely. PCP had a different management financial involvement (than other cooperatives) from its start that gave management an incentive to succeed. The founding board of directors came from farmers who had little previous interest in the cooperative form of organization. I suspect the management team made decisions differently from other cooperatives. Significantly, it is the only one of the three canning cooperatives remaining, and even expanding by its acquisition of Carnation's Contadina Woodland tomato processing facilities.

Fresh Fruit Growers

California farmers growing fruit for canning were not the only ones suffering from low prices. In the early 1970s there was a surplus of stone fruits grown for fresh consumption that resulted in low returns to farmers. One day while attending a meeting in Fresno, a grower concerned about the low prices and the poor financial condition of the fresh fruit industry asked if the university could help. Further discussions continued, and I suggested a solution could be the formation of a farmers' cooperative to exchange marketing information daily among *grower-shippers*. Loaded with information, sample organizational paperwork, and references for legal assistance, the cooperative was organized and is still operating. This special exemption for farmer cooperatives from the antitrust laws had been tested and cleared by the U.S. Supreme Court a few years earlier, by legal action involving lettuce growers in the Salinas area.

Other Farmer Cooperatives

Virtually every commodity grown in California has one or more farmer cooperative that provides some sort of service to its members, most often the marketing of farmers' crops. An earlier call from Bob Collins (founder of Pacific Coast Producers Cooperative) informed me of a need to improve the marketing of wheat from California farmers. We organized the California Wheat Growers Association.

One of the first groups I worked with when I returned to California in 1969 was a group of San Francisco Bay herring fishermen, a loosely existing group with no well defined objectives. I assisted that group to organize and function as a fishermen's' cooperative, which is granted the same privileges as organized farmer cooperatives.

Much later, Delta fishermen were assisted in organizing the California Crayfish Producers Association, for the orderly processing and marketing of crayfish to Sweden's markets. A processing facility was started for uniform quality of packaging frozen crayfish for the developing European markets.

The Central Valley has a group of dairy cooperatives dating back to the 1920s when farm storage and farm-to-dairy plant transportation was difficult. Meanwhile as these conditions improved, comparable improvements in technology occurred; and the marketing of processed dairy products became more competitive. The need for dairy plant consolidations arose, and with Dick Johnsen, president of the Agricultural Council of California, we held numerous meetings with the cooperatives during the 1970s to improve cooperatives' performance. The sum of these years of discussions resulted in the combination of two cooperatives in Merced County, reflecting the non-economic problems of merging farmer cooperatives. Our ability to merge 44 cooperatives in the Pacific Northwest and in Saskatchewan within a 10-year period is amazing. Chief executives of California cooperatives have great control of cooperatives, mainly by exercising power over their boards of directors. Executives with strong personalities make mergers very difficult, despite such needs.

Meanwhile, operational problems existing with some cooperatives were amenable to being solved. In Glenn County we helped the Dairy Cooperative determine whether to invest in a continuous butter churn to replace the obsolete batch churn then employed. The result was a lower cost operation and more consistent butter quality. This enabled the local cooperative to maintain its operations in an isolated but growing region for milk production.

Del Monte Acquisition by Cooperatives: A Missed Opportunity

When Del Monte, the giant international food company with a San Francisco base ran into financial problems and proceeded for sale, as director of the Center for Cooperatives, I thought the opportunity for cooperatives to acquire this huge business as a subsidiary was worth discussion. With Dick Johnsen we invited chief executives from Blue Diamond, Diamond Walnut, Tri Valley Growers, and Sunkist to a meeting in Sacramento to discuss this idea. They asked for information, so additional professionals were brought in, and a source of financing was tentatively arranged. After several meetings, Blue Diamond and Diamond Walnut executives decided the project was not consistent with their normal nut businesses, so they withdrew, leaving only Tri Valley and Sunkist. The representative of Tri Valley tried to make an end run to acquire the canned operations of Del Monte and failed; the Sunkist board decided their main objects were to market the citrus fruit of their members. Thus, though the needed capital in the range of $3.4 billion for acquiring Del Monte was pledged from United Bank of Switzerland, through efforts of John Pike, an investment banker, the concept failed. The result would have been that Sunkist would have acquired sales of about one-third of the U.S. banana business, a large part of the pineapple, and other tropical fresh fruit, while Tri Valley would have obtained facilities and the valuable Del Monte label, the premier national label for canned fruits and vegetables.

These forward-looking opportunities would have provided substantial benefits to farmers who owned these cooperatives. But as with all organizations, there are vested interests (such as CEOs) who seek personal gains and suffer from excessive egos. Had the cooperatives continued their initial interests the cooperative structure would have transformed the concept of cooperatives in the arena with large corporations.

The years as director of the Center for Cooperatives gave me a stronger platform for furthering farmers' involvement in the market system to enable them to gain higher incomes. In fact, my involvement with cooperatives began during my years as a county agent (farm advisor) in Oregon when cooperatives were important for marketing the crops of farmers. Then, after I became a faculty member of the University of Wisconsin, my involvement with cooperatives increased, and I assisted county agents to organize farmer cooperatives—the Antigo Potato Growers Association was an example. Professor Marvin Schaars told me later that he had tried several times over a 30-year period to organize a cooperative of potato growers, without success. We did it.

When I returned to Oregon State University, this time within the Agricultural Economics Department, one of my assignments was to serve as the secretary of the Agricultural Cooperative Council of Oregon, with which the university carried on research and educational projects. That relationship led to my serving on the board of directors of the National Council of Farmer Cooperatives, and also to being elected to the board of trustees of the America Institute of Cooperation, both located in Washington, D.C. Through these 12-year involvements, I was a member of the powerful Legal and Tax Committee of the National Council. In addition, because of my interests in antitrust laws and their partial exemptions for farmer cooperatives, becoming involved with large-scale organizational cooperation among cooperatives during my academic years at UC Davis was a natural development.

Center for Cooperatives

A legislative mandate originating from the leadership of California cooperatives (from Dick Johnsen and Lee Ruth with the Agricultural Cooperative Council of California), and supporters of consumer cooperatives (through efforts of David Thompson) established a research and educational program about and for cooperatives of all forms. I was asked by Ken Farrell, vice president of agriculture of the university, to serve as the founding director of the Center for Cooperatives. I left my retirement and consulting activities for a five-year commitment. I proceeded to:

- organize a governing board,
- hire a staff representing all sectors of cooperative interests,
- establish criteria for soliciting interdisciplinary research grants from private and public university scholars and a review system to evaluate proposals, and
- seek private sources of funds to support research grants that would supplement state funds.

In total, 12 research and educational projects were started in the first year, financed mainly from private funds.

A series of publications called *Working Papers* and *Research Reports* was established for public distribution. By the end of my five-year commitment as director, the center was established with permanent staff, cooperation among farmer and consumer cooperatives had become established and trust developed between these two types of cooperatives, with a strong framework established for the center's success. Initially the chair of the Department of Agricultural and Resource Economics at UC Davis had not supported the establishment of the center, but we still developed working relations between the department and the center.

During the next six years, a replacement director appointed from a large mid-western cooperative, isolated the center from its supporters, and he was terminated after much of the first 5-year achievements had been set back, including relationships within the department. After an attempt to maintain the center with a part-time director from the department, all attempts were stopped and the center was abolished. This is an interesting situation in which a center established by the state legislature and located at the University of California was terminated by the university and not by legislative action.

PRICE ANALYSIS FOR PROCESSING TOMATOES

Pricing analysis for California canning tomatoes began many years ago by Professor Sidney Hoos of UC Berkeley's Giannini Foundation. The problem of equitable prices to be paid to tomato growers by processors was a critical ingredient to maintain fair prices between processors and farmers. When Dr. Hoos retired and I had been employed within the Agricultural Economics Department, I was asked by the California Tomato Growers Association, a farmer's cooperative, to continue these pricing studies. The information was made available to both growers and processors to provide economic information around which prices would be negotiated. The process provided stability to a growing industry that became the largest source of processed tomato products worldwide.

Upon my retirement from UC Davis, I was asked to continue this service, which I did through MRA, until I left to work in Ireland.

CHAPTER THIRTEEN

Lee the "Sportsman"

I'd like to say I grew into becoming a sportsman from experiences with Dad or because I grew up on a farm, but that's a big stretch of nonsense. Our sporting events on the farm consisted of shooting rabbits that ate young grape vines we would plant either to start a new vineyard, or to replace a vine that had died. Sometimes, Dad would spray or sprinkle blood on the young vines, something he had been told was repulsive to rabbits. But, I don't know where he would get the blood to do that, and as the vines grew, the new leaves would not be coated with blood and the rabbits would eat those leaves. So we practiced rabbit control by shooting them; the neighboring Gonsales family would help us by hunting on our land and eating the rabbits. We didn't eat rabbits because they were carriers of tularemia, a disease transmittable to humans that didn't seem to bother the Gonsales family.

Occasionally we would get big infestations of worms that would start from eggs deposited by the pretty yellow and orange butterflies that soared over the alfalfa fields. Once the worms ate the alfalfa leaves, they would be attracted to the nearby grape vines, and they would then eat the grape leaves. After all, grapes were our livelihood, though not too good a life for us, so we'd have to go after the worms.

Dad would plow a deep furrow around the alfalfa field, and the worms would fall into the trench, but would have trouble crawling up the crumbling side to get to the grape vines. There would be several thousands in the bottom of the furrow. Then, Dad would plow a second furrow that buried the worms that had accumulated in the first furrow, and they would suffocate. Well, that didn't sound like giving wild creatures a sporting chance either, but it was a natural method of insect control that worked. It would be considered "organic" pest control in these modern times. For us, it implied we lacked the money to buy commercial insecticides.

My first memory of becoming a "real" sportsman was going fishing with my high school friend, Bull Moose. His name was really Al Clement, a huge guy whose parents spoke French as their first language. Al was the star fullback on the varsity football team at Fowler High, and also the shot putt thrower on the track team. We were like the comic characters Mutt and Jeff, because Al was 6'4" and I was lucky to stretch to 5'6" on a warm day.

Al knew about a pond near Selma that contained fish. He borrowed a small rowboat and brought tackle and worms for both of us. We were prepared to go fishing for "sun" fish, which consisted of Bluegills and Crappies, both very nice eating fish. And, no state fishing license was required at this pond.

We caught a lot of fish and I know my folks were very happy. We didn't eat fish too often because it cost too much money. On the other hand, chicken was free because we raised them on the farm and there was always one hen that had slacked off laying eggs and she would end up on the dinner table.

THE BIG BUCK

Later that year, which might have been in 1941, Al and I went deer hunting in the coastal mountains of San Benito County. It was in late September, after the raisin harvest, but the weather was still quite warm. We hunted ravines on the eastern slope of the foothills, one of us going on one side and the one on the other side. We would come across small patches of low shrubs at the bottoms of the ravines, which provided deer with good shelter from the hot sun. We expected they would be bedded down as we hunted, and if there were deer, our movement would startle them and they would flush out of their hiding.

It had been a tough hunt, and we had seen no sign of deer. Normally you would expect to see tracks of deer movement, and sometimes their droppings. We were thirsty, hot, and tired as we were about to give up the hunt and head home. But we came across a big patch of shrubs, and just as we got near it, we heard a loud crashing through the shrubs. About 50 yards ahead, there stood the largest buck deer we had ever seen. The deer was close enough that either of us could have taken a shot, but we were so startled, and then so impressed with its size, that we both yelled to the other "hey, look at that giant buck". Neither of us raised our guns. We just stood there and gawked. Later we talked a lot about the huge size of the buck, and the fact that it had a single antler on each side, with no forks. We decided it was an old critter, as Al told me old deer will revert back to a single antler that could be 3 or 4 feet on each side of the head, and as large as a teenager's wrist. We were glad we didn't even try a shot, and proud we were able to brag about the huge buck we saw.

Later, someone told us we were lucky we had not taken a shot—it could have been an elk, which did live in the area. Had we shot an elk, we would have broken the law, first because it was not elk hunting season, and second, we did not have elk tags. So, we were happy to have been just "sportsmen" on that day.

Vistas to Embrace, Opportunities Galore

Moving to Oregon for my first job after Cal Poly gave me more opportunities to develop my sporting interests. Oregon abounded with forests and an abundance of rivers. Fishing for salmon and steelhead were close by, camping more enjoyable and big-game hunting more exciting. I soon learned that Oregon's outdoors had plentiful opportunities to live from the land, and if you didn't take advantage of that, you were losing out on the great potential of life. This was an exciting time for a young Californian.

In 1947, I became an agricultural agent in Clackamas County. My territory covered the area south of Portland, east near Mt. Hood, west by the mighty Willamette River and south about equidistant between Portland and Salem.

Within this region, my work involved many opportunities for a "sportsman's" life close to heaven—I was:

- conducting experiments on farms,
- on call by farmers who had problems with their fruit crops that needed help,
- conducting educational meetings for farmers,
- taking care of home garden problems of city people to the extent I could fit it in.

It was a good life, and one of the most enjoyable jobs I have had. I had a state car that I would keep all the time, and drive to and from the office, and often, just work until day's end and then drive home from my field visits.

Hunting with the Parker's

Al Parker and I were very close friends, and with his wife Mae, we adopted each other as family. Al was a generation older, and had grown up in the Scappoose area west of Portland. His dad was the first white child born in the region, and he remained there all his life. Dad Parker was a man of the woods, and in those days, one was expected to live off the land. He was an excellent deer hunter, and could track a deer for miles and then sneak up on it. That night his family would enjoy deer liver and onions, a rare treat. I was fortunate to hunt with Dad Parker, Al, and Mae for about 10 years, and I learned a lot about deer hunting and the care of game.

Around the camp fire, after we had taken care of the day's kill and while Mae, who had been hunting all day with us would be fixing a lovely meal, sometimes deer liver and onions, Dad would be asked to have a drink of whiskey. He'd always decline, but as we insisted, he'd take the bottle by the neck, tilt it to his mouth, and take a drink—we'd watch the whiskey go down his throat, gurgle, gurgle, gurgle, gurgle, gurgle, and then he'd pass the bottle on to one of us. Dad only took one drink a day, but boy, what a long drink! (For any reader who thinks my reference to Mae being the only one fixing dinner, fear not, Al and I took our turns to cook and clean up. Later as John Inskeep joined our group, he would also take his turn with meals).

Trout Fishing on the Deschutes River

Al Parker, John Inskeep, (my boss at the office) and I often would drive east over the mountains to fish one of the nicest trout and steelhead rivers of central Oregon. The Deschutes River emerges from the ground as a full–sized river and flows north into the Columbia River at The Dalles. John had friends who owned a cattle ranch on the river and whose gate was open only for friends they allowed to fish on their property. We camped on a sandy beach, with good fishing for a half mile of our campsite. We were very fortunate to be able to fish such lovely waters. We had to be careful because rattlesnakes came down to the river about a quarter mile south of our camp to cool off during the heat of the day. Fortunately, we never encountered any near our camp, but we would keep alert for their presence. We'd go fishing at this spot for a three-day trip several times each year, always the three of us, and we always had fun. We had been told that pouring whiskey on a snakebite was good therapy, so after the evening fishing, one of us would wander around with a whiskey bottle pointing out facetious rattlesnakes and offer us all a drink from the bottle. We controlled many snakebites each night in that fashion.

I learned a lot about the outdoors from Al and John. We'd also go clamming on the Oregon beaches during low tides that were good for digging.

Al had a great deal of patience, something that I have lacked. On a hunt to Muddy Ranch on the John Day River, where we hunted each year, we saw a huge buck on a distant ridge, silhouetted by the sunrise. The antlers would glisten as the buck moved its head, and it was evident it was a trophy set of antlers. We had no thought of shooting it, because of the long distance away, but we just stood admiring the creature, and hoping the animal would decide to wander down the ridge towards us to feed on the alfalfa fields. Well, that didn't happen, so Al asked, "should I take a shot at it to get it moving?" I said "sure, why don't you try that, but will your gun reach that far?"

Al thought it over, and we decided the distance to be about a half-mile from where we were on another ridge. Al put his rifle scope on the animal, and said the deer had 6 points on one side and 7 points on the other. Then, we talked about the distance, and how high above the deer's back he should aim. Should it be 7 feet? 8 feet? The longer the distance, the higher the trajectory needed. Finally, Al decided 9 feet was about right. So he stood there, bracing his gun against the trunk of a pine tree, threatening to shoot. I thought he would never do it. He held his breath, took a final aim, and fired. The whole process seemed like a half hour, but it was less time. I watched the animal crumple and fall, and remain down. Al had felled a deer at a great distance. It took us nearly an hour to go down our ridge and to climb the deer's ridge, and when we got there, we found the deer had fallen in such a position that it had nearly bled out. Needless to say, we had to skin the animal in its place, and quarter the carcass, and pack it out on foot. Al and I made two trips that day, Dad brought the head and antlers, and Mae carried out the liver and other organs. Our hunt for the day was over, and that evening we had fresh deer liver and onions, and a bit of Old Grand-Dad whiskey.

One of the rewards of deer hunting was the deer hide (skin) that we would have tanned by people who did this for a living. One hide was not large enough to make a jacket, so we would give or take a hide from our hunting partners to have jackets made. Deer hides would tan in natural rich colors, and are extremely soft and comfortable to wear. I have two jackets remaining that are probably too small for me now, but they hang in the closet, as reminders of an interesting time of my life.

FISHING THE MADISON RIVER

On our first trip from Oregon City to Madison, Wisconsin, where I had been accepted as a graduate student for my master's, we decided to camp and see Yellowstone, the Grand Tetons, the Badlands, and that famous drug store in Wall, South Dakota. We bought a tear-drop trailer, that was about 12 feet in length, and had a full-sized mattress on the main floor, and two bunk beds at each end of the main crawl space. Lisa called hers "her bumper". At the back was a lid that covered a small gas burner, an insulated ice chest, and cupboards for dishes and utensils, and a small sink. We were pretty well self-contained and the cooking and sleeping en route went pretty well.

I had planned to fish whenever we were in trout country, so we stopped in a small campground in West Yellowstone along the Madison River. After setting up the trailer, I got my fishing equipment and wandered the 50 yards to what appeared to be good fish country. There were plenty of others with the same thought, so finding a spot to enter the river was difficult. The Madison was open only for fly fishing, and live bait and salmon eggs were illegal. I left my jar of salmon eggs in the trailer, and decided to use a small mosquito fly pattern I had used on the Deschutes. I was not a good fly fisherman, so I placed the fly on a bubble to get enough weight to toss the fly about 25 feet from me. Normally, I would want the fly to be dry, meaning it would float on the surface, and resemble an insect that had just settled on the water, but the bubble pulled the fly just under the surface, like 2 or 3 inches. BAM, I had a fish on, and it gave me a lot of fight, but in about 8 minutes I landed it in my net. It was a beauty, 20 inches long, and very fat. Since the limit was 2 fish a day, I moved down stream a bit, and started fishing again. Within 10 minutes, I had hooked another trout on the same fly, and fought it for awhile and landed it too. It was a perfect mate in size and weight to the first fish I had caught. Working my way back to shore I was greeted by a game warden, who admired (examined) the fish, then looked into my creel for salmon eggs. The warden was doubtful that my small, bitty dry fly could be so lethal. He commented that other folks were using fancy dry flies and had not caught any fish that afternoon. The next morning before we left, I went back with the same equipment and caught two more nice fish. Each fish was enough for the four of us, so we had fish four nights straight.

Although Wisconsin had a good reputation for trout fishing and even big game fish like Muskies, I never had time to fish. But, during our second move to Wisconsin, we lived on Lake Waubesa, in a summer cottage that had been winterized. Young Lee decided he wanted to fish off the pier from our shore. On his first attempt he caught several catfish, and proudly brought them into the house, wanting them for his breakfast. We told him cleaning his own fish was a part of fishing, and showed him how to do that. Thereafter, he cleaned his own fish.

Lisa, on the other hand was not interested in fishing, but she was always with Lee. There was a Mallard duck that had nested and hatched 6 ducklings, and Lisa would attract them to the pier to be fed. Lee and Lisa would feed them small pieces of bread, and they would come swimming whenever the kids approached the pier. It was apparent that one duckling was not a favorite of the mother or the other babies, because it would always be about two feet behind the others. Lisa called that duck "lonesome Joe", and the kids would always make sure it got more than its share of bread. Lisa had become a sportsman, too.

In the winter, the lake would freeze over, and Lee and Lisa would borrow ice skates and join the neighborhood kids in skating. Both became proficient on skates, and enjoyed their winters on Lake Waubesa.

After I had finished my studies and we returned to Oregon I did not develop sporting interests with the kids. However, I did get in some salmon fishing with fellows in the Ag. Econ. Department, and we'd do a lot of crabbing too. I never did fish again after I left Oregon for California in 1969, nor did I do any deer hunting. But I have many photos of hunting and fishing with my buddies Al, Mae and John, and many memories that I revere to this day, over 60 years ago. What a lovely way to live.

CHAPTER FOURTEEN

THE CARS IN MY LIFE

Cars have always fascinated me, at least since I was 6 years old and Marian, Chuck, and I walked 2 miles to school along Highway 99 south of Fresno. It was a choice between walking along the highway facing the cars or walking the railroad tracks that paralleled the highway. During the dense foggy weather common to the San Joaquin Valley, we would walk the railroad tracks because there was less rail traffic. While walking along the highway, we were not sure if a car might drift from the lane when drivers were not able to see clearly.

Some of the cars I would see on the highway were spectacular. Most unique were the cars I learned were called Pierce-Arrow, luxury cars with headlights incorporated into the front fenders. I vowed some day I would own a Pierce; eventually I owned four.

All told, I have owned at least 150 cars since those days, many of which are not significant today, but owning any car in the 1930s was a reflection of one's financial condition and priorities. Most of these cars are listed in three tables that comprise the phases of my life and the types of cars I acquired.

- The Early Years, when acquiring a car was equivalent to gaining mobility and "stature"

- The Sporty Cars

- True Classics, for engineering qualities, prestige and pride.

THE EARLY YEARS

In 1939, (I was 14) Chuck left me his 1930 Model A Ford convertible with rumble seat when he was called for active duty by the California National Guard. At that time my parents owned a 1928 Chevrolet 2-door, not a very pretty car, but this was the car in which I learned to drive. In 1941 I bought a 1935 Ford 3-window coupe for $150, a very pretty and rare body that brought me up to date. But, the next year I traded it for a 1936 Ford V-8 coupe. My tendency to gather cars had begun to be evident as shown in Table 1. In all, there were seven cars in progression from the 1931 Ford to the 1953 Ford Country Squire station wagon.

CARS IN MY LIFE—EARLY YEARS

Model Yr	Make/Model/Body Style	Years Owned	Comments
1928	Chevy 2-door sedan	1936-39	Parents' car
1931	Ford A roadster w/windows	1939	Gift from Chuck
1935	Ford V-8 coupe, 3 windows	1941	Paid $150
1936	Ford V-8 coupe	1942-45	Paid $200
1941	Ford V-8 coupe, 4 passenger	1945-49	
1947	Plymouth, 4 passenger coupe	1949-51	
1947	Chrysler Windsor, 4-door	1952-54	
1953	Ford Country Squire dlx	1955-59	3-spd, overdrive

FROM UTILITY TO SPORTIER CARS

By the time we were in this stage I had spent four years in Wisconsin, either as a graduate student or as a faculty member, and faced the harrowing question of whether to remain on the Wisconsin faculty, or return to Oregon in a new position at OSU. In four years at Wisconsin, I had shifted my professional interests from horticulture to economics, and in doing so, shifted my influence and scope of activities from the local to the national scene. We truly faced a difficult decision that in reality made a fundamental, irrevocable change in the direction of my subsequent years. I feel either position would have been professionally successful, but our personal life would have been substantially different. It also changed the car collection opportunities, because I would have had less time for cars if I had remained in Wisconsin. Also, I would not have had the influence of Dr. Burton Wood, my mentor in professional as well as automotive interests.

Burt Wood directed me towards interesting cars by guiding my collecting passion through 10 Mercedes and seven Rolls-Royces. The next two tables reflect this influence in the list of cars I owned during the years I was under his professional tutoring. The Pierce-Arrows were remnants of my interests that developed during my grade school era.

Some people collect items to hoard them. I purchased cars because:

- I appreciate their designs and performance,

- they enabled me to earn money from their sales to finance additional purchases, and

- I can bring the most desirable of my cars to competitive show condition.

Highlights of this era are described below.

In about 1971 or '72, Richard Howitt, a colleague at UCD and I became interested in selling older cars imported from Chile and Argentina. This was intended to be a purely monetary interest. We bought a small rural lot outside Davis and built a shop where Mark Milton, a young friend and several of his friends worked to get the cars to run. We brought in about 15 cars over a 2-year period and sold them, sometimes just as quickly as we could get them running. We didn't make any money, and perhaps we got our investments back when we sold the land and building. For sure, we didn't make any money to buy any keeper cars for ourselves. Jeri Howitt, now Richard's wife, helped us clear the cars from customs in Oakland and San Francisco.

Richard and I had an opportunity to buy a rather rare 1950s Bentley 3 position coupe from Neal Kirkham, thinking we would restore it. Neal's bottom price was $12,000, and our top price was $11,500, so Neal kept the car. Many years later he restored the car and sold it for a ridiculously high price, showing Richard and me that we could be somewhat too cheap for cars of value.

SPORTY CARS IN MY LIFE

Model Yr	Make/Model/Body Style	Years Owned	Comments
1960	Chrysler Newport Sedan	1960-69	My first new car
1964	Chrysler Newport Sedan 300	1964-72	
1968	Chrysler Imperial 4-pass. convert.	1967-73	
1957	Mercedes 220 S coupe	1964	
1958	Mercedes 220 S coupe	1965	
1957	Plymouth Barracuda 4-pass. coupe	1965-68	
1953	Kaiser Henry J 4-pass. coupe	1966-68	
1955	Ford T-Bird convert.	1960-74	
1956	Ford T-Bird convert.	1972-74	Porthole top
1947	International ½ ton pick-up		
1917	Jordan Sport Marine touring	1965-73	Last one surviving
1958	Ford T-Bird 4-pass. coupe	1967-69	
1954	Jaguar Mark 4 or 5	1967-70	
1955	Mercedes 300 S Roadster	1962-2004	
1930	Lincoln V-8 4-door sedan	1965-72	
1955	Mercedes 300 SC Roadster	1962-95	
1971	Mercedes 280 SEC 3.5	1986-95	
1959	Rolls-Royce SC-1	2000-11	

HIGHLIGHTS OF THE COLLECTION AND RESTORATION OF TRUE CLASSICS

Classic cars have a specific definition for serious car collectors that I will not identify herein because it is not germane to this memoir. What is relevant though is that they are often expensive luxury cars, made from 1925-1948. However I include a wider range of my cars in the loosely defined list of classic cars in the table below.

True Classics—The Ultimate Cars 1971–Present

Model Yr	Make/Model/Body Style	Years Owned	Comments
1947	Rolls-Royce Silver Wraith	1972-80	
1948	Rolls-Royce Silver Wraith	1973-74	
1930	Pierce-Arrow DCP	1971-97	
1930	Rolls-Royce PII All-weather	1971-2004	Hooper
1958	Mercedes 300 SL Roadster		
1957	Studebaker Golden Hawk	1978-98	
1933	Rolls-Royce PII Open Touring	1970-71	
1934	Pierce-Arrow 1203 Convert. coupe	1989-2005	12-cylinder
1962	Mercedes 300 SL	1995-99	
1959	Mercedes 230 SL Roadster	1965	
1957	Mercedes 250 S 4-door	1965-89	
1956-59	Mercedes 280 SE Convert. 4-pass.		3 cars owned
1952	Bentley Mark VI Convert.	2010-17	
1954	Bentley R-Type Saloon	2009-17	

1930 Pierce Arrow

This was the first one of the real classic cars I restored, and it should have taught me a lesson about being more careful selecting the restorer—I cut my eye teeth with this car—one of four remaining, dual-cowl bodied Pierce-Arrow cars out of about 25 that were originally built. Its rarity made the car a candidate for a full restoration.

Before WWII the car and its owner were sent to England where the owner represented the family flour mill business. I don't know if the man remained in England, but the car did and it survived the bombings of London. While there the car's steering had been converted to right-hand drive and a trunk had been professionally added, modified from a '36 Buick. In 1945, the car was purchased by a U.S. military member and shipped to San Francisco. Shortly afterward, it was bought by Len Olson, the retail lumberyard owner in Lolita, a small town about 20 miles south of Eureka, in northern California. (I bought the Pierce and the 1930 Rolls-Royce from Len Olson as a pair in 1971).

After several bad starts with incompetent restorers, I located Ken McMurphy from Martinez, CA to complete the restoration. In subsequent years Ken restored three other cars for me.

1930 Pierce-Arrow. The '30 Pierce-Arrow made it big time at Pebble Beach—First in Class and Most Elegant Open Car. This was the first classic car restored professionally for me by Ken McMurphy.

Lee, left, making the presentation of the '30 Pierce-Arrow to two judges at Pebble Beach. On the right is Ken McMurphy with a sly smile, as Lee responds to another question from the judges.

The Pierce-Arrow was first shown at the Pierce-Arrow Society's 1988 annual meet held in Michigan, where it won the Vandeveer Trophy for the best restoration. The next year it was shown at Pebble Beach, where it won First in its Class and the Most Elegant Open Car award. About 20 years later it won the Vandeveer Award again for its new owner, without any effort except for an occasional polishing.

1930 Rolls-Royce Phantom II

The Rolls-Royce was another lovely, rare car, built by Hooper, a noted English coach builder. The original owner was Count bon de Souza, a Brazilian with European financial connections, who maintained a London address at the Claridges Hotel. Over the years he was a frequent customer for Hooper-designed and -built bodies for his Rolls-Royce cars.

It was logical for this to be the second car I had restored, since it was a mate to the Pierce-Arrow, and equally distinctive. That was the start of my friendship with Steve Galdrige of Carmichael, a good mechanic with many useful skills. The first effort was to replace the badly deteriorated wiring, followed by finding a new engine head. After all of the mechanical work had been completed I next

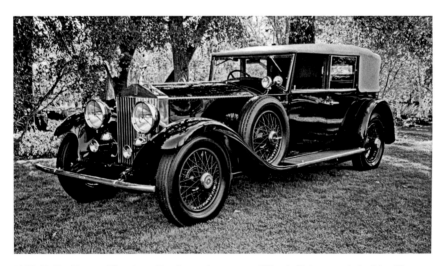

1930 Rolls-Royce Phantom II, all-weather convertible, built by coach builder Hooper. The car was originally painted black, but after restoration, it was painted an aubergine color copied from an eggplant. It has a highlight of Burgundy color on the wire wheels and the body at the door-top level, called "Wentzel Cabernet Sauvignon" because it matches the color of the wines made by Lee and Roland Wentzel from Roland's grapes.

decided to complete the restoration by replacing the upholstering, the top, and a new paint scheme by Roy Dryer and the painting by Ken McMurphy. We achieved our objective to make the car "elegantly sporty".

Its first showing was at the prestigious Silverado Concours d'Elegance, where it won a ribbon for First in Class. In August, 1991 the car was shown at Pebble Beach where it received the Hooper Award, one of the RROC's major awards. Ken Karger, noted Rolls-Royce and Bentley authority (and Hooper expert) who checked us in at the RROC (Rolls-Royce Owners Club) meet, remarked "Hooper's would be very pleased."

1934 Pierce-Arrow Convertible

People often ask how I found the cars on which I am working, as though I have a secret communication system. The truth is that I am a joiner, so I have been a member of many car clubs. If you have been active in these clubs, you make contacts with many people. I remind myself, "to have a friend, be a friend". It is that simple.

The 1934 Pierce-Arrow 12-cylinder convertible was another rare find. I was told about it by Eric Rosenau, who had been asked to restore the car for its

1934 Pierce-Arrow Model 1302, convertible coupe, one of five remaining. This car was restored for me by Larry Munson of Turlock. Note the Burgundy paint trim is the same as on the Rolls-Royce Phantom II, "Wentzel Cabernet Sauvignon", also used on many of my other cars, such as the 1937 Pierce on the following page.

owner who lived in So. Carolina. Eric lived in Ramona, CA and until his death in 2012, was the best authority of Pierce-Arrow cars in the country. Even after his death, he may be considered the best authority, based on his technical articles written. Eric had forgotten more than most "new" authorities have learned and it was fun to work with him.

I trailered my 1937 Pierce-Arrow to Ramona to have him make final adjustments on the transmission-overdrive unit, and when there, I was graciously given room and board with Eric and Molly. It was obvious Molly kept Eric on schedule. Eric showed me the 1934 Pierce, and I fell in love with it when I found it could be purchased.

My relationship with my son is strong and I value his opinions. I nearly always discuss a car's availability with him, and we usually agree, though we live thousands of miles apart. That's why telephones exist, and even at age of 91, I feel the urgency to call and talk with Lee on a weekly basis. With his encouragement I bought the 1934 Pierce, of which there are only about 5 remaining.

The car required a total restoration; the engine did not run, it needed bodywork, new upholstery, and a new paint scheme. Eric rebuilt the engine and

1937 Pierce-Arrow Model 8, one of four remaining. The car was restored at my house garage in Davis. Mark Milton, Richard Howitt, Richard Bowley and I all worked on it. Anne and Richard Bowley lived with me for a year to finish the mechanics and painting. The car has a 4-speed transmission with factory overdrive.

1920 Pierce-Arrow Series 51, a rare body fitted with a California top. I sold the 1934 Pierce-Arrow convertible to buy this car. The windows slid back to make an open-touring sedan and slid forward to make the body of an enclosed car. The 6-cylinder engine was very powerful and fast, beating race cars of the era. The engine had been rebuilt by Allan Schmidt when it was owned by Willis Boyd.

transmission. My friend Roy Dryer, helped select the color and paint scheme, as he has on most of my classic cars. Together we selected a lightly pinkish cream color, with maroon highlights. It was a Sikkens paint of German origin, called "Juvenile Flesche", which I shortened to "virgin titty pink".

This car won its class in each show where it competed. It was shown at most California concourses, including Pebble Beach. The '34 Pierce was a favorite of Nina's, but alas, I sold it to take on other projects.

1962 Mercedes Benz 300 SL

I've had great respect for Mercedes Benz cars since 1962, when I bought my first one. Again, it was my mentor, Burt Wood who introduced me to these lovely cars.

I have owned many of these cars, including several 220 S coupes, a 230 SL roadster, a 1957 250 S sedan, about three 280 S cabriolet 4-passenger convertibles, a 1971 280 SE 3.5 coupe and a 280 SE 3.5 convertible, a 300 S roadster

1962 Mercedes Benz 300 SL Roadster, with son, Lee. When acquired, it was a "basket case" and was restored by Larry Munson of Turlock to a 100-point car.

and a 1952 300 S cabriolet, both very rare, and an even more rare 300 SEC roadster. Also, Dick Howitt and I owned a 1968 300 SL roadster for several years. Then, son Lee was sold a 1962 300 SL roadster by a Stockton collector, without running this by me, and it turned out to be a badly rusted, high-mileage car with disguised mileage because the odometer had been rolled back. It was later that I received a file folder of the condition report of this car, which I still retain.

There was not much that could be done with the car. Even so, to help us, Larry Munson, a car restorer in Turlock accepted the project to restore the car, which he completed in about two years. I would go down weekly to work with Larry and his crew, and I would stay in Larry's house while I worked on the car. Eventually the restoration was completed, and the result was a perfect restoration, known as a 100-point car. I lost $100,000 on the car when it was sold at the highest price in several years for a 300 SL roadster in recent auctions. Today it would be worth in excess of $1 million. This truly is a hobby!

1955 Mercedes 300 S Roadster

One afternoon at the office, Burt Wood dropped in to tell me Lawson Robertson, a friend of ours, had been killed while returning to Portland from Albany, Oregon. He had worked the day with another friend, Sam Suklis, who was a car enthusiast like Burt and me. Working until midnight, Lawson drove north on I-5 from Albany heading to Portland. He dozed off near Salem, and when the freeway made a slight curve, the car continued on a straight path and hit a huge oak tree. Lawson died instantly.

Lawson had a collection of 12 very desirable Mercedes, which he left to the mortuary owners where he worked. Not being car enthusiasts, but wanting Lawson's friends to share in the ownership of the cars, they offered them to a group of us.

Burt had recently added a car to his collection, so he wondered if I wanted to see the cars that remained, thinking I may be ripe for a good car. I ended up buying the '55 300 S roadster, one of about 105 made. The car ran beautifully. About 20 years after buying the car I had a new roadster top installed, and had the car repainted its original factory color. I kept this car for 46 years, before selling it to another Mercedes collector, Pat Mathew who has a private Mercedes museum in Glen Ellen, in the Napa wine producing region.

1952 Mercedes 300 S Cabriolet

This was another of Lawson's Mercedes, acquired by Sam Suklis, but with a cabriolet body. There were a few more of this body design made than of the roadster, but both are very desirable cars, even to this date. The 300 S engines were used eventually in the 300 SL series that followed, but the engines were installed in a slanted fashion to lower the configuration of the 300 SLs. I don't recall how many years I kept this car, but I would guess it might have been at least 18 years. It was in equally very good condition as the roadster.

1959 Rolls-Royce SC1

In my opinion there have been three outstanding models of Rolls-Royce, of which I have owned two. My criteria is the engineering that went into the model's suspension, engine and drive train, steering, design, and reliability. The P II Rolls were made from 1928 through 1936; my P II was 143 GN, described a bit in a previous page.

The next model I like is the 1957-60 Silver Cloud 1, with the 6-cylinder engine, and a lot of comfort features built into the car. These cars continued the reliable performance of the P II; many for export had factory air conditioning, power steering, a very quiet operation and a smooth ride. I bought my 1959-60 SC-I on eBay, one of the first items I bought over the internet. I goofed many times while bidding on the car, trying to get the last bid of the remaining seconds. In the last 30 seconds my bid rose from $50,251 to $3,500,251, which was ridiculous. So I tried to cancel, without success. Then, with 10 seconds left, I tried to telephone eBay but there is no way I could find how to do that. I had a business meeting downtown to which I arrived late, and my mind was not on the subject of the meeting, but on my foolish bid. Arriving home after the meeting, I went immediately to eBay to find the result of this huge bid, and I received a message "Congratulations, your bid bought the car". Then, I found that I had to pay only $52,251 for the car. I had lucked out. Can you imagine paying $3.5 million for such a car, especially when you do not have that amount of money?

The car was original, having been driven less than 25,000 miles from new. The owner drove the car mainly to go for coffee on a weekend morning. After my purchase I drove the car whenever we wanted to impress people, because that is what such a car is for. This car was a keeper, but I needed funds to complete the restoration of a 1952 Bentley, so I sold it to Bob and Bernice La Mar, my friends who have thoroughly enjoyed the car, even to the point of competing in car shows and winning trophies.

1952 Bentley Mark VI Convertible

I acquired the last of my cars in 2010 as a "basket case". Its restoration began immediately and was completed four years later. It is a 1952 Bentley Mark VI with an interesting history. The model was Bentley's first production model following WWII, but its manufacturing process was different from the new system put into effect for post-war production.

Before the war, Rolls would sell the chassis and running gear for a car, with a forward delivery date that could take several years to be completed and delivered to the buyer. In the meantime, the buyer and the factory would find a coachbuilder who would help the new buyer decide the type of body to be built and installed on the chassis. In time the buyer would get delivery of his car. You did not go to a Rolls-Royce or Bentley dealer, look over the inventory, and drive home with a new car.

After the war, the factory decided to become more involved in the process of designing, building and installing the bodies on the chassis. This resulted in tighter control of the cars and closer exposure to buyers. It also provided cars to buyers in a shorter time, because the car would have been built at the facto-

1952 Bentley Mark VI, Original "Basket Case" condition. This is the best view I had of the convertible coupe before I purchased it. I was unsure whether to go through the ordeal, so I had a professional examine the car. The rarity of "Sir John" (as we named the car), and his personal history made us believe the car worthy of being preserved for posterity. Time will tell.

ry, and conceivably it could be available from inventory as a standard factory production.

The 1952 Bentley that I bought was not factory built, but in the older tradition of being built by a professional coachbuilder for a special buyer.

B342NZ was commissioned by Sir John Black, managing director of Standard Motor Company, the largest traditional car manufacturing company in England. At the time Standard produced seven makes of cars, so in a sense, it was a smaller image of General Motors of the U.S.

Following the victory of WWII, Sir John wanted to introduce a sports car to appeal to car buyers in America as well as in England. Stuart Peck was hired to design the convertible, which was the only car he designed from stem to stern. Sir John ordered a Bentley Mark VI chassis, and in conjunction with Mulliner of Birmingham, a coachbuilder, Stuart Peck designed the body that would serve as the prototype for the car they wished to produce for the export market. They eventually built certain features from the Bentley design on the body of

1952 Bentley Mark VI, Restored. Four years after we began the preservation of "Sir John", the car was accepted for the 2014 Pebble Beach Concourse d'Elegance. We opted to show the car with its top down, believing the contours of the car showed best in that manner.

For the next two shows, we decided to keep the top up with better results. At Ironstone, "Sir John" was awarded the trophy for the "Most Elegant Open Car." The next show at Neillo's Concourse in Serrano, we again displayed "Sir John" with its top up and here it was selected as "Best of Show". Of course, "Sir John" won the "Best in its Class" at both events.

the Triumph TR-3, a company that they had purchased before the war. That served the purpose for Sir John's designing of B342NZ. After keeping this car for 14 months as the "prototype" model, Sir John sold the B342NZ after the successful launch of the TR-3.

In 1962 the Bentley was sold to C. J. Gelber of Encino in southern California, and after 2 intermediary owners, I acquired the car. It had been in storage for 38 years, left partially dismantled, and badly rusted in areas that were not visible. This Bentley is also unique because it was owned by Sir John Black, an industrialist who was knighted by King George V for his military services to the UK in two world wars. Furthermore, it was the only Bentley (or Rolls-Royce) body made by Mulliner of Birmingham after the war.

My objective was to preserve this car as it was when Sir John took possession. In August 2014 the Bentley was shown at Pebble Beach Concours d'Elegance, a world-class car show and was accepted largely based on my prior reputation for car restorations.

In September 2014 the car was also shown at Ironstone Concours d'Elegance, a very large event with over 400 cars in competition, that is hosted by long-time friends John and Gail Kautz. It won the Best in Class and the Most Elegant Open Car awards.

Then, in early October, 2014 the Bentley was shown at the prestigious Niello Concours at Serrano in Northern California, where it was awarded the Best in Class and the Best of Show.

Awards

Overall, the following cars have won Best of Show or equivalent awards:

- 1930 Pierce-Arrow dual cowl phaeton at the National Pierce-Arrow Society meet AND Pebble Beach
- 1930 Rolls-Royce P II Hooper All-Weather Sedan at Rolls-Royce Owners Club national meet
- 1934 Pierce-Arrow Model 1702 Convertible Coupe at Silverado Concours d'Elegance
- 1952 Bentley Convertible Coupe at Ironstone Concours d'Elegance AND Niello Concours at Serrano

The moral of this experience is: Have a good friend as an advisor who does not compete with you as a collector. Also, be on good terms with a banker or source of money to help with the financial requirements of being a serious collector. I had Burt Wood as the former and George Campbell as the latter, and I went on from there.

I owe a very special thanks to Roy Dryer, a nationally recognized car and classic wood boat artist for the assistance in establishing the spectacular colors and paint designs for these cars. Roy is a professional of wide renown and a gentleman of the first order. Each of my cars reflects his knowledge and paint color skills.

1934 Pierce-Arrow. This was Nina's favorite of my cars, but to her regret, I sold it to purchase the 1920 Pierce-Arrow. Auggie was allowed to ride in the 1920 Pierce and had the back seat all to herself.

CHAPTER FIFTEEN

TOO YOUNG TO MARRY

We were young and inexperienced when we married, I at age 21, and
Betty age 20. In many ways I thought I was mature, but that was hard-
ly true when it came to marriage. I haven't discussed this topic before, but in
retrospect that may have been true for Betty, too. I can't say. But then, that
may just be a symptom of my immaturity for a personal relationship as close as
marriage.

We met after I left Fresno State College and transferred as a junior to Cal
Poly in San Luis Obispo. I was selected to be editor of the student newspaper,
El Mustang, which we mocked up and printed at the San Luis Obispo *Telegraph
Tribune* plant. Betty worked at the Tribune and was in charge of classified
advertising and keeping the financial books for that part of the newspaper. She
was attractive and friendly, and I was egotistical enough to think she might find
me attractive too. After all, I was a student leader on campus, first as editor, and
that spring, elected president of the student body, with my term beginning July
1946. But aside from those weekly meetings at the Tribune office, we never dated.

During the summer between my junior and senior year, in 1946, I took a job
as a border inspector for the California Department of Agriculture, stationed
at the coastal Redwood Highway entry point between Oregon and California.

That fall, I returned from the summer job and settled into class schedule
preparation in order to qualify for graduation in June 1947. I also had to

start my leadership of the student government. I had run my campaign on an aggressive platform that I had won handily and thus I had to follow through on. I had strong feelings about supporting Cal Poly athletic programs and attended most intercollegiate activities. But being nearly broke, I moved to free off-campus housing at Dr. Mc Capes veterinary hospital in town. My responsibilities were to answer telephone calls on Monday-Friday nights and I had to be at the hospital every weekday evening. There was little time for social life with me working there and consequently there was very little time for Betty and me to get to know one another well. But we persevered and looking back, I now realize how immature we were to undertake the next big step.

By December we had decided to marry, so I took her to Fowler and introduced her to Dad and Mom, told them of our intentions, and they asked if we would be married in the Armenian Church in Fresno. On January 4, 1947 we were married, with my parents and Mom's cousin Leo Kerbajian and his wife Esther also attending. We had a group lunch to celebrate, then we left for our honeymoon in Yosemite to begin life as husband and wife.

Without making prior reservations, we drove to the Ahwahnee Hotel and asked for a room. They had a vacancy, for $400. Confused, I proceeded to ask what the rate was for just one night, and I was told that $400 was the one-night rate. Well, we decided to leave Yosemite and drive to Bass Lake and find a less expensive motel. It was dusk as we neared Bass Lake and an oncoming car veered into our lane, struck the left side of my car and failed to stop.

I promptly turned around, followed him to his house, took the license number from his car and drove to the sheriff's office to report a hit and run accident. The sheriff said, "That is John's car", and that I must be mistaken because John is a good driver and would not do such a thing. In those years I had a sheriff's permit to carry a concealed pistol, and wearing my pistol, I considered visiting old John and having a talk with him about this incident, but I never did. Betty must have wondered who she had gotten herself involved with and what type of pistol-packing idiot she had married.

Job Search

We made it back safely to San Luis Obispo but had no place to stay, so Betty arranged for us to move in with her family. We moved out when I found a small, one bedroom cottage a few miles out of town and we lived there until I graduated. Then we left for Fowler to live with my family while searching for my next job.

Betty, 1952.

We stayed in Fowler through July, with little prospects for my employment. Then, my brother-in-law, George, wrote to me about a research opening at the Hood River Experiment Station of Oregon State University in Corvallis. I applied but the job had been filled. Next, I received a letter from Charlie Smith, assistant director of the Agricultural Extension Service at OSU telling me of a position in horticulture open in Oregon City and wondering if I was interested. I responded, received an invitation to visit the area to look over the county, and for the county staff to look me over. Betty and I packed all our clothes, and other personal items into my 1941 Ford coupe, and drove to Oregon City.

We stayed in a small motel in Oregon City overlooking the waterfalls on the Willamette River and I was given an agricultural tour of the farmlands. The next day I drove to the Imperial Hotel in downtown Portland and was offered the job. I accepted on the spot. The first day on the job, John Inskeep's (my boss) wife Bea invited Betty over for the day while I was touring the county. Their dog had recently given birth to 8 pedigreed Golden Retrievers and the local newspaper reporter had come over to write a story and take pictures of the litter and their mom. Consequently, Betty's picture was taken with the pups instead of John's wife—that's like beating your boss in a golf game on your first day of work—not a good way to start out. Needless to say, the picture was a front-page story in the local paper, along with a brief story about my job appointment. The Inskeeps got very little mention.

OUR FIRST HOME IN REDLANDS

Our first task was to find a place to stay—housing right after the war was very scarce, and quite expensive. John Inskeep found a house in a little country crossroads town of Redlands, about 7 miles from Oregon City. It was a 2-bedroom house, with a bathroom, and 2 additional rooms, on a 20-acre farm, with garden space, hen house, and small barn. We rented it for a bargain price of $25 a month! I think we lived at Redlands for nearly 2 years, growing a large vegetable garden, harvesting blackberries, raising chickens, and 25 turkeys. We also raised a pig for meat.

Just as quickly as they were able to fly, the turkeys became a nuisance. Somehow, they knew which bedroom was ours and at sunrise, all 25 would fly to our window and gobble to awaken us to be fed. We raised them to about 20 pounds weight and then sold many to co-workers for Thanksgiving dinners. Parker Hinckley, a co-worker helped kill them and pluck their feathers to make the turkeys oven–ready. His price? One turkey for their own dinner.

The pig was something else. From a 60-pound piglet, we fed it a diet of corn and buttermilk that I brought back with me from the local creamery in Oregon

Lee and Betty, 1947.

City—it cost me 10 cents a gallon, in a 5-gallon milk can. That pig grew to about 200 pounds and I arranged for a portable slaughter truck to come on a Thursday morning to butcher our fat hog. When the truck arrived, and we went to drive the hog to the area near the garden for slaughter, we found the hog dead. We couldn't believe it, but an autopsy showed it had died of a heart attack the night before.

One time we drove about 50 miles to buy an Australian sheep dog puppy to keep Betty company. It was a pretty black and white pup, but she was difficult to train so I traded her for a turkey to a farmer-friend who intended to train her as a herder for his 10,000-bird flock. Can you imagine I traded the dog for a live turkey? I thought we got the best of the deal.

Life in the country was pretty boring for Betty, so we moved into Oregon City. She was expecting her first child, and with me traveling a lot throughout the county, it just felt like the best move would be into town. Before our move, Betty had taken a job as bookkeeper at the Gladstone Plymouth dealership, so she had learned to drive our car to get to work.

Due to a shortage in housing, we made 6 moves in 5 years, nearly always moving upscale a bit with each move. With each move, we had to fix the kitchen counters and lay new linoleum on the kitchen floors. I became very good at both tasks.

Several years after Lee's birth in Oregon City, I decided to raise certified disease-free strawberry plants while still employed as a farm advisor, so I found a 7 acre farm along the Clackamas river, about 4 miles from Oregon City. It had been used for growing fresh vegetables for sale at the Portland wholesale market, and I thought it would be a good place for my venture. The problem was we were now back in the most primitive house of our marriage, with a son about 2 years old. Not only did I have to do the linoleum jobs, but we had a well that tested positive for contaminates. Under supervision of the county health officer, we treated the well with chlorine and cleared the problem.

I bought a Ford tractor with tools to farm with, and the heavy portable galvanized sprinkler irrigation system from the former farm owner. I haven't said that our farm bordered on the bank of the large Clackamas River. By this time, baby Lee was about 3 years old, and as a very active child, he must have driven Betty to worry about his safety all day.

To complicate the matter of names, I had an employee working in the strawberry nursery and his name was also Lee. Son Lee would go out and spend hours with my farmworker Lee. One day the nursery worker looked up and saw the Ford tractor coming up the driveway, with young Lee at the controls. Somehow, he had started the tractor, shifted into gear, and was slowly driving towards the nursery plants. Young Lee had four guardians: Betty, Bargain, nursery-worker Lee, and the Lord.

Next came our daughter Lisa, who was born while we lived at "Back Achers". Life became more complicated and harrowing for Betty after Lisa arrived. Our friends, Millard and Elsie Reddaway had recently bought a house with about ½ acre of land on which to expand their rhododendron nursery and they suggested we move into it. It was a nice move, close to friends, near school and stores, and finally, to a nice house. We moved, and for once, life for Betty had become pleasant.

Betty had always hovered over the kids, but now she could devote time to make lovely clothes for Lisa and outfit Lee in nice clothes to wear for school and when he and I went to church. I do believe those were the happiest times for Betty. Elsie was a good neighbor and friend to us all as well.

Soon I became eligible for a sabbatical leave from Oregon State, and we started planning for me to attend the University of Wisconsin, in Madison. From the nice house and friends in Oregon, we were to move again. This time, we bought a 28-foot mobile home that reduced our living space from a 5-room house with a yard to a 280-square-foot mobile home that slept our family quite snugly.

The year passed quickly, and we traded the mobile home for a smaller, older one that we hauled across the country back to Oregon City, where I returned to my job. Five months later, Wisconsin offered me full time employment with the privilege of taking courses on a half-load basis to earn a Ph.D. in Agricultural Economics. This required me to resign from Oregon State, which was a difficult decision because we were successful with University administration and my farmer clientele. And for once, I thought Betty was very happy with our situation. Back to Wisconsin we went, arriving in Madison during Thanksgiving week. We made the trip with our cocker spaniel Sparky again at Betty's feet for the entire drive, pulling a 20-foot enclosed trailer carrying our washer, refrigerator, mattresses and all our other possessions inside. The trip went well until we came to a ground blizzard in the plains of Wyoming that obliterated the boundaries of the highway. In Iowa we encountered ice on the highway that slowed our speed considerably because the trailer had a mind of its own. We finally made it safely to Madison, but Betty had to keep the children entertained while I fought nasty road conditions.

Betty was not a dog person, but she had Sparky all of the way, with no complaints. In fact she did not complain about any of the decisions made during our marriage, despite how much they disrupted her life. She was a good trooper and I had been fortunate, and the kids had enjoyed having an excellent mother.

I don't think Betty made friends quickly at any of the locations where we lived. At Oregon City, she was very close with the Hinckley's; Parker Hinckley was in charge of 4-H programs for the county. His wife June, was a very warm person and she and Betty became close friends. The Hinckley's had two children who were about the same ages of Lee and Lisa, and they became good friends. Also, I worked with Al Parker, the state forester in our office, with whom I developed a son-father relationship in many ways, but in all ways we were together professionally nearly every day. Al's wife, Mae, became a loving friend of our family. The Parkers became the ones we did many activities with—fishing, trips to the beaches, hunting in which Mae would be a partner when John Inskeep, the boss, and Al, and his father, and I would camp out in the woods, or along a river bank for as many as four days. During these occasions, Mae never asked for any favored treatment, and really was "one of the boys". Betty and Mae were very close, and I suspect that Mae took on a friendship that partly involved a mother role with Betty, but more likely, she was a true friend of Betty's. Our second move to Wisconsin must have been a severe hardship on Betty as we left her very close friends on what was expected to be a "permanent" move to Wisconsin.

WISCONSIN LIFE

We lived on Lake Waubesa, one of a chain of four lakes around Madison, living in what had once been a summer home and was now winterized. Anyone who has lived in the Midwest and North Central states will understand the true description of the meaning of a "winterized summer home". This house had a detached garage along the road, with a concrete walk from the house to the lake shore. The house was small, with 4 rooms of which 2 were bedrooms. The only source of heat was a large oil heater in the "living" room. The coldest temperature we experienced was -37 degrees. In such really cold temperatures, we would place a 12-inch fan on top of the stove, pushing heat down over the heat chamber and distributing the warmth from the ceiling to the floor. In that manner, we were fairly comfortable. Without that addition, our feet were very cold, ice would form on the inside of the window glass and we would not be comfortable.

The university offered free classes for professors' spouses and I encouraged Betty to take advantage of this opportunity at a great university. She took several courses during our second year (of our permanent stay). She opted to take courses in logic, which surprised me, since she was quite logical by nature. In fact, with her near genius intellect, logic classes came quite easily for her.

When three years of Wisconsin winters had passed, and friends at the University of Wisconsin had an expectation that we would buy a house in Madison and settle in, memories of our life with close friends in Oregon and of our families in California began to come alive again. Oregon State offered me a job as associate professor of Agricultural Economics in Corvallis. I felt I owed my colleagues in the department at Madison a huge debt, but our family ties, life style, and the better weather prevailed—we packed up and became Oregonians for another 10 years.

Corvallis Life

The move to Corvallis was a good choice for us all. Being a town of about 35,000 residents (besides about 12,000 students), and the university having such a proud reputation throughout the state, life took on a brighter potential. Lee and Lisa got settled in school easily. Betty was invited to join the women's group called Farm Circle that engaged in many volunteer and social activities. For the first time in 12 years, we owned a new home with a half-acre lot, and much room for gardening. Yet, to me it seemed like Betty never developed the close friendships she had when we lived near Oregon City. Of course, the children were now in their teens and required a lot of her time.

She took comfort from her sewing abilities, and made very handsome clothes for Lisa and occasionally very dressy suits for herself. Still, I am not sure how much of these activities contribute to one's social life or communications with others. I suspected she was not getting enough involvement to keep her challenged.

To give her some outside activities, we discussed the possibility that she propagate plants, given that we had a huge lot. She showed interest, so I contacted Glen Schaeffer, my close friend in Clackamas County whom I had encouraged into growing nursery plants while I had been county agent. Glen expressed interest in establishing a source of heathers, a plant easily propagated from cuttings and not requiring much land to grow to a size where they could be grown for several years for sale. I had propagated heathers with Al Parker while we operated Greenever Nursery so it was an easy venture to get back into. This interested Betty, so I found a Quonset building frame measuring 20 x 40 feet, and constructed it in the back of our gardening lot. We covered the frame with low-cost clear plastic, which worked well. Betty grew thousands of small heather plants for Glen, but lost interest after a year or so. It wasn't much of an intellectual challenge, I suspect.

One of my university responsibilities was to serve as secretary to the Agricultural Cooperative Council of Oregon, including arranging and holding educational meetings for farmers, farm directors, and managers of farm cooperatives. Also, Mary Holthouse, the administrative assistant to OSU's Dean of Agriculture Earl Price served as treasurer for the group, but needed to resign. Betty was experienced in accounting, having kept books before our marriage, and for about a year after we first moved to Oregon City. The board of directors appointed Betty as treasurer and she kept accurate records for the Cooperative Council. She was not comfortable in making public reports at the large annual meetings, so I agreed to present the annual financial reports to the membership, if she kept the records. That didn't work out well and she resigned.

Meanwhile, opportunities for me to become involved professionally on the national and international scenes grew substantially, in some quite prestigious roles. The nature of the opportunities required I spend months at a time away from home.

As I was gaining in stature with national activities subject to White House and Congressional approval, duties at home were thrust more on Betty, probably an unfair role for her. When the opportunity for an appointment as a full professor at UC Berkeley was presented to me, I accepted. Betty and the family remained living in Corvallis for a year, with visits of one or the other for the year. We made the move to Davis by mutual agreement, but our relationship stuttered and then broke down between us. We were divorced within a year of our move after nearly 26 years of marriage.

Betty remained in Davis, and after Jim's death in Tacoma, Lisa returned to Davis and lived with her.

CHAPTER SIXTEEN

———— ✦ ————

THOUGHTS ON LIFE, DEATH AND LIVING

In earlier years, I don't recall I had much interest in the above subjects and I suspect I gave them little consideration. My uncle Avak died when I was about 5; actually, we lived with him instead of the reverse. As the elder brother, he pretty much dominated my father, who was about 13 years younger. It was traditional in the old country that the eldest son took the role of the father upon the father's death. To this day I thought he was cruel to my mother, and surprisingly, I recall telling Mom that everything would be okay after he died because Avak would not bother us anymore. By dominating my father, he dominated our family as well.

As a youngster, life was good and so was living. It had to have been, because I had no reason to think about it and it took a few years for me to understand that we were poor. If a child *thinks* life is good, does it matter that the child does not know it is not good? Should the child be told life is bad because the parents are poor? Our's was a caring family, with many good friends, and as the youngest of five, I knew my family was kind. Our visitors would make a great fuss over me and I was probably spoiled as a result. No one has told me so, but it was probably true; I didn't need to know life was difficult, too.

Arpie, my first recollection of death

My oldest sister Arpie died in 1943 at age 31, from bacterial endocarditis, an infection in the heart resulting from complications of the flu. At the time, she was an instructor at UC Berkeley. I was just 17 when she first became ill, and 18 when she died.

Arpie was a special person—someone for whom I had great admiration and love. Arpie was special to everyone who knew her, and I still have notes and poems written to her by some of her Cal friends. She took special interest in my progress in school and pride in what I did. When home for Christmas vacations, she would go with me to pick out token gifts for any girl I happened to have a crush on at the time—these shopping excursions were mostly to Grants 5 and 10 cent stores, Woolworth or Roy's Drug store in Fowler. She was interested in my thoughts about a career, and when I expressed interest in becoming a lawyer, she bought me a copy of the book *Country Lawyer*, which I read repeatedly. I still have the book.

Her death was extremely difficult for me to understand, and impossible to rationalize. It took at least 15 years for me to believe that I would not die at age 31 just as Arpie had. I can't explain why I felt that way. Our church was more traditional and rather than emphasizing the celebration of Jesus' life, there was less interpretation of modern life problems and how to cope with them. By then, I was married with a family, and so to protect them, I carried a lot of life insurance, just in case tragedy struck. During high school, I was diagnosed with an enlarged heart because of my high school athletic activities. The doctor referred me to Dr. Evelyn Anderson, a UC San Francisco cardiologist at the time of Arpie's illness.

Our family was good friends with another family near Fowler, the father was of Greek ancestry, and the mother was Armenian and had grown up in the same village as Dad. Their son Leo, too had suffered great emotional distress when his mother died. He gave me some record albums and suggested I spend an hour each evening listening to them. They were classical pieces by Beethoven and Mozart and he told me that listening to music would help me cope with the loss of Arpie. In time I believed this helped me to adjust to the realities of losing my sister and to learn to live in the present moment. Gradually, I got over the feeling that Arpie's untimely death was a harbinger of a similar fate for me.

Other Family and Friend's Deaths

I faced Dad's death in 1953, when I was 28 years old and I took solace in the fact that he had lived 65 years, as a good and caring person. Dad's death was the result of poor medical practice rather than genetic failure. He died of blood loss during routine surgery to fix a duodenal ulcer. Had there been an intensive care room in the small hospital in Fowler, he would likely have survived. Mom died just 10 days before her 75th birthday. Sister Marian died at age 50 of pancreatic cancer, and brother Chuck died at age 67, also of pancreatic cancer. Perhaps the early period deaths within my family may be why I had fears of premature dying?

I understood the cause of Mom's death, from what now would be considered arterial disease, but she also suffered from thoracic cancer for over 9 years that went untreated. My brother-in-law George discovered that Mom had lived in an older apartment that had a non-vented natural gas heater. Though he replaced that heater, the cancer had apparently spread. Marian's death from cancer (liver and pancreas) and her husband Karl's subsequent death from the same cause about 12-13 years later are still a mystery as to the source. Chuck's pancreatic cancer appears to be from insecticide contamination of the ground water. Two neighbors, LeRoy Kevorkian and Carl Allberg had applied soil fumigants on their farms that were known to cause cancer, but the chemical had never been applied by us to our farm. Chuck had three dogs that had died prematurely over a 10-year period, and they also had liver/pancreatic cancer. So, I believe Chuck's cancer was not genetic, nor do I believe cancers of either Mom's or Marian's were genetic.

MY THOUGHTS ABOUT DEATH

Sometime later, after I was really committed to my successful professional work, I thought in terms of "if I die", and that attitude persisted for many years. More recently, reality set in after cancer was discovered in one of my kidneys; now it's a matter of "when I die". Apparently I now have no new health threats, but at my age, l am trying to live life to the fullest.

Do I still fear the possibility of death? Now that I am 91 years old, it cannot be that I fear a premature death, can it? I don't want to cease being alive, nor do I want to hasten death while I am in relatively good health. I've come to think that death is toughest on the survivors, those who have to cope with legal matters and the reality of the absence of someone who's been with them for many years and is no longer mortal.

Once death occurs I expect no cognitive relation with survivors, and will have no knowledge of what happens to them, or how well or poorly their lives continue. I believe all I will be able to do will have been done while I am alive, but I don't have any feeling about what my thoughts will be while in the process of dying. I presume any fears I have while alive will remain until the end of consciousness. But, will I care? Or, when will caring terminate?

In this framework those affected by death are the survivors, whose lives are changed and whose memories remain, good or bad. For the dead, I see death as a state of extinction.

Following surgery that resulted in the removal of a cancerous kidney in 2004, I had difficulty in breathing due to damage from intubation. While in the recovery room following this surgery I was extremely tired, and I consciously told myself to "let it go" (whatever that meant), but I also heard a voice tell me to "hang on and fight the problem". I still remember this mental conversation, and I am reminded that Mom was at Dad's bedside when he was possibly also struggling. He told her he wanted relief from being tired; he died following surgery.

Near Fatal Experiences of My Life

It has dawned on me that the Garoian family tree has persisted for thousands of years. I don't know how long, but it bothered me tonight that the line would end with son Lee. Then, I realized there is my grandson Ben Garoian, to carry on the line. I am not sure Ben understands that he may become "the end of the line" since he is an adopted son who has problems dealing with his adoption. I look forward to explaining to him why this is important to me.

Today I came across a note written on April 11, 2013 titled "Scares in my Life". I don't know why I wrote this reminder note to refresh my memory. During my lifetime, I faced several situations that could have resulted in my death, but for the miracles I attribute to a higher entity. Today may be as good a time as ever to record these stories during my lifetime.

The American Airlines Crash at Chicago

First on my list is a reminder of an American Airlines flight that crashed on departure from Chicago, destined for Sacramento. It was on a Friday in October, 1972. Fritz Mueller, a very good friend and my major professor for the Ph.D. from the University of Wisconsin, had asked me to present a research paper in Madison at a conference on "Measuring Economic Performance in the U.S. Food Industry". I hesitated, but Fritz persisted and I agreed because many of my friends who I would like to see, would be participating. As customary for me, I prepared my paper several weeks in advance. I had made flight reservations and purchased my ticket. On the Monday before the conference, I called Fritz and told him I was just swamped with work here in Davis, and asked him to present my paper. He expressed disappointment, but he agreed.

On Friday night after the conference, I was awakened by a nightmare and a message from my brain. The message said, "There was an airplane in the sky and it was in trouble". I went back to sleep after that "message", but on Saturday, I heard a news alert that all passengers and crew of an American Airlines flight had crashed on takeoff from Chicago O'Hare. I thought nothing of it until Lisa called and told me that I had been scheduled on that flight. The irony was that Lisa was working for Davisville Travel Agency and had written my ticket. The crash was a terrible event, and its effect would have been devastating on Lisa if I had been on that plane.

My Mercedes 230 SL Purchased in Paris

In 1975 I had qualified for a 12-months sabbatical from UC Berkeley to study how prices for farm products were determined in the communist countries. I had not made plans for transportation, thinking that I would take trains and airplanes for my travels. Discussions with Roland Wentzel made me realize public transportation would be very limiting for traveling to observe the farm areas of each country. As it turned out, I did this consulting for 13 years, making observations at the same farms and food processing plants from year to year, observing current indications of changes in each country. Changes in the availability of food supplies and prices are a vital indicator of future public discontent in such centralized countries.

As the result of our planning with the Wentzel's we decided I needed a car so I could travel in rural areas. We looked in the Paris newspapers and decided a small Mercedes 230 SL, with a cute pagoda-shaped removable hardtop would be a nice car to own and drive in Europe. I had never driven one, but it met my sports car desires. Barbara drove me to see the car—an orange car that reminded me of the OSU school colors. After I purchased it, Barbara took me to the government department to register and license the car. The next day I took off for Germany, to visit Elmar and Marleise Stuhler in Freising, a small town near Munich. I had made plans to stay with the Stuhler's. In a few days I intended to drive on to Belgrade, Yugoslavia, where I had a room set aside inside the U.S. Embassy compound.

Leaving the Wentzels and their roomy Paris apartment was tough. Packing the small Mercedes revealed I had not planned very well. I had several boxes of reference publications and books with me that were jam-packed in the car's small trunk, leaving the small space behind the front seat for my suitcases. I was to be on this trip for a year, so I should have packed more carefully. Well, I thought, I can leave excess materials with my friends scattered in Europe. Happy with this solution, I took off and headed east from Paris, my first destination being Stuttgart, where there was a factory-warehouse with parts available for older classic Mercedes cars that I owned. I wanted to go through that diminishing availability of parts for two 300 S roadsters that I had purchased in about 1963 with the guidance of Burt Wood in Oregon.

I hadn't driven a 230 SL Mercedes before, and I was fairly pleased with its performance. But as I approached the mountains between France and Germany I thought it was lacking power going up the hills. Still, I thought overall the car was okay and powerful enough. When I reached the higher mountains and curvy 2-lane road west of Karlsruhe, traffic was a bit heavier. I had been following a long lorie pulling a heavy load, and when I saw a stretch of two-lane road going up the hill and no traffic in the passing lane, I pulled out to pass. As I got to about midway between the driver wheels of the truck and the first axle of the trailer, I saw a car approaching in my lane, but illegally passing the cars traveling down the steep hill. I could not move further to the right, as the truck was adjacent to me, so I tried to speed up to get past the truck but my car was too underpowered to pass. I thought it better to be in a head-on collision than to be crushed by the weight of the truck. The only other last minute thought I had was, "God, why did I come to Europe to die?"

And then the answer came. Somehow, the two cars did not collide but passed with no space to spare and without a scratch on either. I thought then that my Lord had watched for my safety again. I kept on driving, albeit, I was very shaky. I continued driving nearly an hour until I reached the outskirts of Karlsruhe, where I saw a sign that said "Motel". I turned in, now about 4 p.m., secured a room and laid down on the bed but I was still too upset to sleep. I got up, looked around and found a liquor store where I bought a pint of gin, which I took to my motel room. Drinking that pint helped put me to sleep. The next morning I continued on to Oberturkhiem, just west of Stuttgart, my destination for the Mercedes old car parts warehouse. I bought a lot of rare parts not available elsewhere, so the stop was worth it, though I kept thinking I would like to find the bastard in the car that almost killed me. I was ready to have a word with him.

Fortunately the rest of the year's driving was without incidents. When I reached the Stuhler's house, I realized I needed a bigger and more powerful car. Elmar suggested we try a small farming town about 20 miles away and that is where we found a car that I bought. It was a 1967 Mercedes 4-door sedan, 2.5 liter engine with manual transmission. It was a lovely car, in immaculate condition, owned by a couple in their 50s. I liked this car so much that I brought it back to California, where it became my every-day car.

Cancer Surgery

In 2002, the third difficult episode of my life resulted when I went in for a routine matter and Dr. John Hoefer casually informed me I had not had a urine analysis for many years. Having no visible symptoms, I suggested that we check on it the next time blood work was due, but he was insistent. He gave me a small jar and told me to fill it with urine and he would have the results within 5 minutes. I complied, and he came back and said there is blood in the sample. I suggested the sample must have been contaminated. I tried to dismiss the possibility, since there had never been evidence of discoloration. He said it was microscopic, but I should have x-rays and a follow up with a kidney cancer specialist. The initial diagnosis was confirmed, so I asked for a second opinion. We agreed to have another x-ray in six months to monitor any change in the nodule's growth on the left kidney. There was a ½ inch growth visible on x-rays taken then. Still, I was reluctant, so I prevailed on Dr. Tom Brumley, my ophthalmologist, fellow wine maker, good friend, and Pierce-Arrow collector to arrange for me to have a third opinion, from a friend of his at the Napa Medical Clinic. Following that consultation, Nina and I agreed to the removal of the left kidney at Sutter West Hospital in Davis on February 8, 2004.

There was unexpected damage from this surgery, when removing the breathing tube used for intubation, my vocal cord muscles were damaged. The immediate result was sensitivity to smoke and dust that caused breathing problems. Over time worse symptoms developed that required equipment available at the UC Davis Hospital and more expert medically trained doctors neither of which were available at Sutter West Hospital. In time there were instances of immediate inability for me to breathe, and Nina would apply the Heimlich maneuver to vent air past the vocal cords—the problem was diagnosed by a young, brilliant otolaryngologist, Dr. Peter Belafsky of the UC Davis Medical College as a form of "spontaneous dysphasia that could be "controlled" by Botox injected into the vocal cord muscles. Since that first injection in 2005, I am given Botox injections about every 5 to 6 months as breathing problems return. The predictability of the next breathing problem is difficult, so we are more apt to remain within proximity of the UC Davis hospital and do less traveling. We fear that we shall be outside the confines of a medical facility with the ability to inject Botox, which would pose serious problems for me.

Did I Escape the Ravages of Chernobyl?

May is a pleasant month to be in Greece. I had visited Greece several times previously; once to visit the family of Stavros Kouroukalis, a graduate student at

Oregon State University, whose family came from the big island of Keffalonia. I took a ferry from Athens to Sami, a port city located on the eastern side of the big island; next I rode a bus across to Lexouri, on the western side. Traversing the island, I thought there was a village ahead where the residents were roasting a lamb over coals, but when the aroma continued and there was no city, I realized the fragrance was from native oregano plants.

I enjoyed that trip so much that years later I went back for several weeks. Stavros' relatives operated the hotel where I stayed, and the restaurant where I ate my meals. There are wide beaches from which the locals would take me fishing and in the evenings the fish and octopus we caught were served to us.

In Athens I visited the famous (and inexpensive) Agora antique market, the historic Acropolis, and then on to the southern parts of Greece, including Olympus, the home of the Olympics. I stood on the winners' mound and felt like a champion.

It was several years later, in 1986 that my associate Kirby Moulton and I were on a research project investigating the economics of producing and processing tomatoes in Greece, Turkey, and Israel. This included several days in Athens interviewing academic and government officials before we went north into the Peloponnese Peninsula to observe the processing facilities and to go into the country to see tomato fields beginning to be harvested.

It was here that we received news that the Chernobyl nuclear power generating facility in the Ukraine had suffered destruction. The first report stated that the cloud debris was moving north, and we felt safe from radioactive fallout because we were miles south of the area. Then, the winds shifted and we were now in the direct path of where the nuclear fallout would envelope us.

Television reports advised people to leave the outdoors, and to avoid eating strawberries, green vegetables (including salads), fresh meats, and to avoid drinking milk. What to do? We were here because we needed to be in the fields that were now in the path of the nuclear fallout. We decided we could hasten our field work and be gone in several days, so we continued our outside work, not knowing just when the nuclear fallout would reach us.

We felt we would be more secure in Istanbul in a few days and then depart to the south near Adana, where we would be very safe from fallout. The fact that we did not suffer burns, breathing problems and other symptoms during the rest of the trip was reassuring.

Is it possible that both Kirby and I suffered from the nuclear fallout while we were in Greece? I have been told it may take many years for atmospheric nuclear fallout to cause cancer to those exposed. In 2002, 16 years after the exposure in Greece, routine urine tests showing microscopic evidence of blood was found in my urine. We chose to monitor any further developments each six months for one year to see if the cancer had increased in size. When doctors observed a modest growth, the entire kidney was removed in 2004.

Kirby died of cancer in May, 2011, about 25 years following our exposure. I believe he showed cancer symptoms about eight years later than I did. Our both developing cancer following the exposure in Greece is likely to be mere happenstance. On the other hand, who knows?

Gallbladder Attack

On October 8, 2012, I awoke with severe chest pains that we feared was a heart attack. By 2 a.m. I was in the emergency room and by 4 a.m. the doctor wanted to surgically remove my gallbladder. Nina and I resisted the temptation, and I was kept in the hospital for observation to see if the infection would subside. With both Marian and Chuck having died of pancreatic cancer, I wanted assurance the pancreas was okay. The surgeon still wanted to operate, but we held out until we had an opportunity to confer with Dr. Peter Belafsky; meanwhile we cleared the pre-op tests, had a conference with the surgeon selected for the procedure, and told this surgeon our concerns with intubation. He told us that Dr. Peter Belafsky had been the best man at his wedding, and that he would talk with Peter. Several days later, and one day before the scheduled surgery, both doctors recommended we consider a change in diets to see if we could forestall surgery. The concern was that the damaged vocal cord muscles could close completely as a result of the surgery and I would not be able to breathe. That would require a tracheotomy with a permanent tube inserted to bypass the damaged muscles. I went on a fat-free diet, very little red meat, no dairy fats, and more vegetables. It is now 30 months since changing the diet, and thankfully I have not had a recurrence.

WHAT'S IT ALL MEAN?

If you have read this far, you likely have wondered "What was the purpose of these various ramblings"? or, "Surely there was *something* I must have missed, since we all survive health problems." Your questions are warranted, I suppose.

First, I was profoundly affected by the death of my lovely sister Arpie, one of the nicest persons I have known. At her age of 31, after working so hard and under such financial struggles, only to have the benefits to be withheld by death was a bitter pill. I am not the only one to wonder if the God we both worshiped existed. And, if He did exist, why was He such a punitive God to have taken away such a lovely person? I have never really overcome these feelings. Today, as I write these words, my eyes tear up, as I miss Arpie so very much.

I learned that "fairness" is not an answer, either. Was it a random action, and God made a mistake in selection that took Arpie by mistake? I'm still angry, and confused. For many years, I thought that God would come back and take me too; I expected to die at age 31 as Arpie had.

I've been kept alive by my God with assistance from doctors and medicines. At age 17 I learned that I had an enlarged heart, but I wasn't aware of any problem. It was diagnosed by Dr. Neilson, during a pre-athletic exam required by the high school. He arranged for me to be an out-patient of a cardiologist, Dr. Evelyn Anderson at U. C. San Francisco hospital. That kept me out of the military draft. In subsequent years, tests have shown the heart has returned to a normal size, with no apparent indications of and lingering damage from the prior diagnosis.

When I was about 35, I returned to Corvallis from a week's conferencing in New Orleans, with my good friend Paul Mohn. The first day back at work, I gasped for breath, and my colleague Ray Teal called our mutual family doctor, Dr. Clyde Kerneck, who immediately came from the hospital a couple of blocks away from our office building, and he hustled me off to the hospital. They found nothing wrong except a very high cholesterol reading above 450. I was immediately put on a no-fat diet, and monitored thereafter. When medicines became available to lower cholesterol, I was put on them as well as keeping on the low fat diet. Without this warning, I likely would have remained on my normal diets, and died by age 50.

I suffered a hemorrhagic stroke in 2008 so Nina immediately called 911 and had me delivered to the Emergency Room. After a series of tests, the diagnosis was "that the leakage in a capillary has stopped, and no further bleeding had occurred. I was diagnosed with high blood pressure, so I have been on medication to lower readings since. In March of 2013 I began to use about ½ teaspoon of powdered cinnamon with my cereal, with the result I was experiencing lower readings. Gradually, the amount of medication was reduced by the doctor, and I have not been on medication since about July, 2013, only the cinnamon with my cereal. At their suggestion, I monitor readings twice daily, and if the readings turn high, I have instructions on what medication to take.

As of now, I am on cholesterol reduction medication three times weekly, and back on the lowest dose of blood pressure medication available to maintain the low readings of the past several years when taken with cinnamon.

CAUTIONS

While I expect to find cures from doctors and hospitals, I have found that relying on them is not without problems. Like many people who lack a background in medical education I rely on doctors to properly diagnose ailments and prescribe treatments. Unfortunately, that is not an assurance that treatments or medicines prescribed will not create additional problems that would likely not occur.

Finding medicines that worked well in lowering blood pressure readings is an example. Unfortunately, medicine manufacturers cannot make medicines exactly like those made by the original company because of patent laws. They often make generic substitutes based on the original active medication, but they use "inert" additives that are different. Presumably, these carriers are inert, but with experience, I find they are not. I have been shunted from one brand to another for controlling blood pressure, with about 20 that have caused damning side effects. In the most damaging result, one medication caused a side effect of gout and joint pain that was not present before taking that medicine. My doctor's response was "don't worry about that, I have medicines that will solve that pain problem". Shifting to that additional medicine, I found that I developed pain in my left shoulder, and x-rays "showed" I had a rotator cuff problem, that was treated with cortisone injections. The problem continued, and the joint problem spread to the right shoulder. Briefly, what was happening was apparently the gout medicine was dissolving the cartilage between the shoulder joints, which left me with a diagnosis of "arthritis", when I had not previously suffered from this disease. While gout, with its occasional pain, is seldom a problem, the "arthritis" remains constantly. I was offered Tylenol to relieve the pain.

I preferred to relieve the pain with more natural methods, so I investigated the literature. For several years I have used a brand of "joint fluid" (Wellesse) sold by Costco that has worked well. I also consume cinnamon to relieve inflammation. I have also started eating about 2 ounces of hummus, which is made from chick peas. Then I have reduced red meat and animal fat consumption as well as eating more seafood and greens as salads.

The results? I no longer regularly take pain medication for arthritis, and my ability to reach forward, up and backwards has increased substantially. There is an occasional spasm of pain during cool, moist climate, but for most times, I am not having the excruciating pains I had before going to natural herbs and diets.

The point I am making is that I do believe in preventive maintenance for my body as well as for my cars. I believe my life has been prolonged, and the quality of life has been very good. I like to be pre-warned; my diet has changed without much help from medical doctors, whose training in nutrition is almost nil. For me, taking care of health issues before they become serious has been a healthy strategy, but I have not relied on the traditional medical industry for all of my health problems.

I have experienced a number of life saving events in my near 92 years, and I cannot explain why the events that saved my life came to happen. True, in some instances, such as the air flight, I made the choice not to proceed on the trip. But, some guidance compelled me to reverse a decision. Because I cannot explain the reasons for the actions that have saved my life, I have accepted the following verse:

> **"I believe in the sun even if it isn't shining,**
>
> **I believe in love even when I am alone,**
>
> **I believe in God even when he is silent."**

{Author is unknown to me}

In March and September 2016 I experienced gall bladder attacks that resulted in acute pancreatitis. In conversations with my primary care physician, a surgeon and Dr. Peter Belafsky, an otolaryngologist (and also dear friend) we agreed on surgery to remove the gall bladder in December.

I'm told this may be a life-threatening event which I must endure. Despite this, I believe in the concept of the three tenets written above: the sun, love and God will prevail.

CHAPTER SEVENTEEN

The Family's Lost Art of Humor and Philosophy

I am unsure if the Garoian's of my family were ever a humorous lot, but my Dad had talent for being a great story teller and a practical joker. There may be reasons for the family's failure to generate a comedian. But surely, a philosophy should linger and not be lost.

What's funny about being a survivor from a family that once occupied 14 houses in one village and were wiped out? Even I, the youngest and last survivor of the nuclear family feels he never had a youth, but was an adult from the beginning. We all climbed the social and economic wall we faced, clawing our way from the bottom to a higher level of stature.

Dad seems to be the exception; he liked playing practical jokes on people, including on Mom. Despite being financially in straights, he'd drag Mom from one second hand store to another, always finding fault with appliances that Mom needed, never buying one in these stores. He had already bought a new top-of-the-line washing machine and needed to have Mom out of the house so it could be installed and be a surprise for Mom when they returned home, empty handed. I know she would have been satisfied with any of the items they had looked at because they were better than not having any at all.

As a youngster I would laugh at the stories Dad would tell to visiting friends. Perhaps he worked hard to lighten the burden of a tough life. I think that inspired Chuck, who in his later life became a good story teller too. This was in a period of his life when he had moved his family to Brazil and Uruguay to become a fruit farmer. His wife was stressed because she did not speak Spanish or Portuguese. She proceeded to purchase airline tickets for herself and their two children, withdrew all of their money from the local bank, and left him destitute. It was after that experience that I recognized Chuck's story telling capabilities, and his authoring a book of imaginative stories.

Certainly I am not a story teller. When repeating a joke, I forget the punch line. Likewise, Marian was a serious person, but Isabel was less serious than either Marian and me.

So, what's left for a humorless person like me? Over time, I have relied on philosophy mainly from others that impress me. I offer some of these below, with the hope a reader will find them interesting, too.

"If you go on biting and tearing one another, take care. You will end up in mutual destruction". —Letter of Paul to the Galatians: Gal. 5:1, 13-18

"He who separates is lost." —Unknown

"The true character of a person is revealed by how he treats others when he is not asking for favors". —Unknown

Life isn't about waiting for the storm to pass—It's about learning to dance in the rain. —Unknown

12th Century Armenian Belief:

"What is left to me of life? That which I gave to others. Strangely only that. All that went to others, came back, sweetened". —V. Tekeyan

The clock of life is wound but once, and no man has the power to tell just when the hands will stop, at late or early hour. Now is the only time you own. Live, love, toil with a will. Place no faith in time. For the clock may soon be still". —Unknown

THE PRINCIPLES OF ATTITUDINAL HEALING

1. The essence of our being is love.
2. Health is inner peace. Healing is letting go of fear.
3. Giving and receiving are the same.
4. We can let go of the past and of the future.
5. Now is the only time there is and each instance is for giving.
6. We can learn to love ourselves and others by forgiving rather than judging.
7. We can become love finders rather than fault finders.
8. We can choose and direct ourselves to be peaceful inside regardless of what is happening outside.

9. We are students and teachers to each other.

10. We can focus on the whole of life rather than the fragments.

11. Since love is eternal, death need not be viewed as fearful.

12. We can always perceive others as either extending love or giving a call
for help.   —Author unknown

Less profound, these are some great ways to deal with the common burdens
of everyday life:

- Accept some days you're the pigeon and some days you're the statue.

- Always keep your words soft and sweet, just in case you have to eat them.

- Drive carefully. It's not only cars that can be "recalled" by their maker.

- If you can't be kind, at least have the decency to be vague.

- If you lend someone $20 and never see that person again, it was probably
worth it.

- Never put both feet in your mouth at the same time, because you won't
have a leg to stand on.

- When everything is coming your way, you're in the wrong lane.

- Birthdays are good for you. The more you have, the longer you have lived.

- You may be one person in the world; but you may be the world to one person.

- Some mistakes are too much fun to make only once.

—Author unknown

Regarding Confidence

Living is like pouring water out of a tumbler into a Coca Cola bottle—If"n
you're scared, you cain't do it. If'n you say to yourself, "By Dang, I Can do it."
By Dang, you won't Slosh a drop.   —Author unknown

"I feel sorry for people who don't drink. When they wake up in the morning,
that's as good as they're going to feel all day".   —Frank Sinatra

Cliff Calvin, at the bar Cheers was explaining the Buffalo Theory to his
buddy Norm. Here's how it went:

> "Well ya see, Norm, its like this. A herd of buffalo can only move
> as fast as the slowest buffalo. And when the herd is hunted, it is the
> slowest and weakest ones at the back that are killed first. This natural
> selection is good for the herd as a whole, because the general speed and
> health of the whole group keeps improving by the regular killing of the
> weakest members. In much the same way, the human brain can only

operate as fast as the slowest brain cells. Excessive intake of alcohol, as we all know, kills brain cells. But naturally, it attacks the slowest and weakest brain cell first. In this way, regular consumption of wine eliminates the weaker brain cells, making the brain a faster and more efficient machine. That's why you always feel smarter after several glasses of wine." Makes sense due to its logic.

An Irish Ballad

After I retired from the University of California, I moved to Cork, Ireland to accept a position in teaching and research funded as a "chair" by the Bank of Ireland. I ended up staying on the faculty of University College, Cork for slightly over seven years. It was a wonderful experience, and one I will not forget. The country was lovely, the university was famous, the students were extremely bright, and the people generally were the nicest I have every lived with. It was here at Queen's College, in Cork that a young, self educated boy in 1849 was named the first mathematics professor who introduced a new system of algebra, named for him as Boolean algebra. Nearly 100 years later, Boolean Algebra provided the mathematical procedure that enabled the development of the computers that we now use.

Every several months, Professor Denis Lucy, department head of Food and Dairy Economics, and the representative (director) of the Irish Division of Education, and I would meet somewhere in the Republic for meetings, and during the evenings we would relax in a pub with a bottle of Paddy's Irish Whiskey, made in Cork. After enough drinks, our guest from Dublin could be coaxed to sing and act an Irish Ballad titled *"Danny Boy"*. I greatly loved those performances, and the Ballad, and do even now; I have asked Nina to have it sung at a service or memorial after my death.

As I understand the background, an "ancient" Irish Chieftain is bidding farewell to his son. The lyrics make my mind and emotions flow, I am touched so much by this ballad.

> **Oh Danny boy, the pipes, the pipes are calling**
> **From glen to glen, and down the mountain side**
> **The summer's gone, and all the roses falling**
> **'Tis you, 'tis you must go and I must bide.**
> **But come ye back, when summer's in the meadow**
> **Or when the valley's hushed and white with snow**
> **'Tis I'll be here in sunshine or in shadow**
> **Oh Danny boy, oh Danny boy, I love you so.**

And if you come, when all the flowers are dying
And I am dead, as dead as well I may be
You'll come and find the place where I am lying
And kneel and say an "Ave" there for me.
And I shall hear, tho' soft you tread above me
And all my grave will warmer, sweeter be
For you will bend and tell me that you love me
And I shall sleep in peace until you come to me.
I'll simply sleep in peace until you come to me.
And I shall rest in peace until you come to me.
Oh Danny Boy, Oh, Danny Boy, I love you so.

White Ashes, a Buddhist memorial

Another thoughtful piece, this from Buddhist roots is titled *"White Ashes"* from Rennyo's Letters commonly read at a funeral service:

"When I deeply contemplate the transient nature of human life, I realize that, from beginning to end, life is impermanent like an illusion. We have not yet heard of anyone who lived ten thousand years. How fleeting is a lifetime!

"Who in the world today can maintain a human form for even a hundred years? There is no knowing whether I will I die first or others, whether death will occur today or tomorrow. We depart one after another more quickly than the dewdrops on the roots or the tips of the blades of grasses.

So it is said. Hence, we may have radiant faces in the morning, but by evening we may turn into white ashes. Once the winds of impermanence have blown, our eyes are instantly closed and our breath stops forever.

Then our radiant face changes its color, and the attractive countenance like peach and plum blossoms is lost. Family and relatives will gather and grieve, but all to no avail?

"Since there is nothing else that can be done, they carry the deceased out to the fields, and then what is left after the body has been cremated and has turned into the midnight smoke is just white ashes. Words fail to describe the sadness of it all.

"Thus the ephemeral nature of human existence is such that death comes to young and old alike without discrimination. So we should all quickly take to heart the matter of the greatest importance of the afterlife, entrust ourselves deeply to Amida Buddha, and recite the nembutsu. Humbly and respectfully."

AMEN

CHAPTER EIGHTEEN

…AND THEN I MET NINA

I've reached a stage when its time to say finis to this history and to either stop, or to talk about modern times. Perhaps this chapter should have come earlier in my memoir. I've done things during my life of which I am proud, and some I regret. There comes a time when the memoir ceases because one's life ends. My option is to stop it while I can by less terminal methods.

Professional travel has been an important part of my career. For two years, United Airlines presented certificates to me indicating that I traveled a million miles on their airplanes. I developed close ties with a few travel agencies, one of which was Patterson Travel in Davis, where Carroll Terra made most of my schedule arrangements. One year a red-haired lady went to work at Patterson's, but mainly doing production work behind the counter.

A few years later, Carroll and this red-haired lady decided to leave Patterson and opened a travel agency of their own, which they named Terra and Hendrickx. I shifted my business along with this fledging company's move to independence.

For about 10 years Terra and Hendrickx sent me around the globe many times, and I learned that the red-haired lady's name was Nina. She began to make my reservations, too. In 1983, I took an early retirement from UC Davis and traveled to Cork, Ireland, where I remained until 1988. I was home for about 6 months, when I took a one-year appointment at a graduate engineering and agricultural economics university in France as a visiting professor. In 1990,

Nina.

I returned to Davis, and began international economic consulting on a full-time basis.

Meanwhile, T&H remained my travel agents. Each January the company invited its customers to a winter party, which I had never attended. In 1995 I was again invited, but I was in Modesto for a consulting session with my partner, Al Spina. Returning home, I decided to stop by the T&H office while their party was underway, and I was greeted by a holiday peck on the cheek, first from Carroll, and a bit later, the first ever, by Nina. She gave me a glass of nice wine from the back of their office, and when that needed refilling, an attractive younger blonde lady came along and offered me a refill, but from a carafe, which I declined and told her I was enjoying a different wine from the back room. After a frustrating moment, she brought Nina to me and I was introduced to Tami, Nina's second daughter. I'm sure I made a negative impression with her on that night.

About a week later, I called Nina to make reservations for another trip with difficult overseas connections. When we got that schedule worked out, I asked Nina if she had a significant "other" in her life, but she hesitated several moments, and then asked me why I was asking, saying "Lee, aren't you married?" I told her I had been divorced for 5 years, and she mellowed a bit to allow me to ask her to go to a wine tasting the following Sunday afternoon.

I was late picking her up because though she lived only 2 blocks from me, I had been knocking on the wrong door, where I could hear music and voices, but no one answered. I went back home and called Nina and we soon realized that I had gone to the wrong house—she thought I had stood her up. This was not a good start.

Our trip took us to Napa, and I introduced her to Roland and Barbara Wentzel, he being a former student of mine, and both my good friends for over 30 years. They were invited to a multi-family dinner, so they asked us to join them; they called the host, and we were welcomed. At about 9:30 we made moves to leave to drive back to Davis, but my friends, not knowing the nature of the friendship between Nina and me urged us to stay over in the small, detached apartment I used while I was visiting them. Nina was quite embarrassed, we declined, and I dropped her off at her house.

Several weeks later I invited her to join me on a Classic Car Club weekend tour to Lake County, and she accepted with the understanding that we would have separate rooms. That worked out well, too, but my German Shepherd, Auggie, who traveled with us would have preferred joining Nina, but I didn't allow that.

Later, in talking with Al Spina, he said, "you are lucky you have met a good Catholic lady with conservative upbringing". I soon realized he was right, and I have been very happy about that choice.

We dated for nearly 2 years and in 1997, we were married by Fr. Richard Blinn with Nina's four daughters, son, and their families present. It has been a lovely marriage that I wish had happened years earlier. Getting acquainted with four married daughters and a son has not been the easiest experience. They had enjoyed frequent drop-in visits with their mother whenever and as often as they pleased. Now, there was an intermediary to compete with for her time. Over the years, it has gotten easier.

In February 1996, we used air miles to pay for a trip to Ireland. We flew into Cork from London, and were met by Con and Colette O'Sullivan, who loaned us a car for our use while we were in the country. Our first few nights were spent with Denis and Sheila Lucy, who had moved to an ocean front house at Crosshaven, County Cork on the Irish Sea near the port of Cork. I had convinced Nina that southern Ireland in winter was mild, since there were a variety of palm trees that thrived in the warmth of the warm water from the Caribbean Gulf Stream. Actually I had never been so cold in all my years in Ireland, and we had a tough time keeping warm. The worst time was in the morning as we showered and dressed, using a bathroom lacking heat. After leaving the Lucy's house we warmed up in the car as we drove into Kinsale, a lovely resort town just south of Cork. Our plan was to drive west from Kinsale to spend the next night at Blair Cove Inn, with the expectation of higher temperatures as we headed closer to the Gulf Stream. It never happened.

We spent the next night at Blair Cove Inn, also on the water, in a stable that had been converted into several picturesque apartments, each with cozy fireplaces in a comfortable living room, a kitchen, dining room, and 2 baths and bedrooms. We drove south to Land's End to a small fishing and farming village on a spit that led into the ocean. We stopped at a store where we purchased half a smoked salmon, a loaf of rustic bread, local farmhouse cheeses, and several bottles of French wines. And, we found some paperback books. There wasn't much else needed, and we enjoyed the warmth of the fireplace as we ate, frolicked in the living room, and then went off to bed.

The next morning we traveled north to the Berra Peninsula. Temperatures were cold enough that we believed the remaining salmon would be properly stored in the car's trunk; actually that was true for several days, and we picnicked with the remaining salmon, after buying new loaves of Irish bread as we continued our travels northward. We even drove through slushy snow as we crossed into the Dingle Peninsula and headed to Galway.

Nina was looking forward to searching for the Horsley family tree and her father's history, but she was near certain that it would be very difficult because records were incomplete. Nina's daughter Peggy had found that to be the case in her attempts. However, Nina had family correspondence that identified a small village in the region where we were traveling called Lizzycasey. This was the phonetic spelling of the village from her father's family memories. Either Colette or Sheila thought she knew the correct name, and we were able to locate it. All that remained of the village was a small country store, a pub and a small gasoline station. We took a picture of the village sign, talked with the owner of the pub about the village history, and continued on our trip.

We drove south to Mallow where we met up with Denis and Kay Murphy, good friends from my years of work in Ireland. Con and Colette joined us for dinner, and then we went on to O'Sullivan's house where we spent the night, before our flight from Cork the next day.

Our agenda was from Cork to Heathrow Airport in London, which went very well, and we had several hours layover at Heathrow. We wandered around for a while, and then decided to check our bags and to claim our assigned seats. Standing in line, bags on the floor besides us, two nicely dressed gentlemen approached from behind, and introduced themselves as making a survey, and would we be willing to be included? We agreed, and indicated for them to start. Very diplomatically they asked if would we mind, for privacy reasons that included opening luggage, stepping into a nearby room? After some small talk about our travels, and a look at our ticket itinerary, they started to remove, unfold, and set aside every bit of clothing within our possession. Finding nothing of interest, they repacked our luggage, thanked us for participating, and took us back to the head of the line, and walked away.

It was only later after we picked up a London newspaper, that we realized we had been targeted by Scotland Yard in their search for two suspects responsible for dynamiting Brighten Castle the previous day. Their suspects were described as an Irish lady with red hair, accompanied by a man who appeared to be a Middle Easterner. Nina and I met the descriptions. But aside from the description, I knew we were not the individuals they wanted. Nina is too gentle, and so honest, that one look at her would have made them aware of her gentle persona. I guess I looked the part, something that has happened to me all over Europe. I easily pass for Spanish, French, and Italian. When visiting a large department store, in Alexandria, Egypt, a well-dressed Egyptian lady came up to me jabbering about something in her Arabic language. My Egyptian host laughed and told her *he* was the Egyptian, not me.

Nina is a lovely person. Seldom judgmental about any person, she manages to see the better side of any issue or person, including me. She has a melodic greeting that is contagious when receiving a telephone call from a friend.

Nina has the best time-management practice of anyone I know, and I will never learn how she manages time so efficiently. There is no waste of this precious resource. If she has 5 minutes, she will go back to an earlier task, even for those few minutes. It isn't that she is a nervous person, it's that she seems to break every task into small bits, and takes on a job with the intention of accomplishing something constructive.

And she is generous in dealing with others. She serves as a volunteer with the local hospital auxiliary, earning the respect of her peers who have elected her to one or another office. She is extremely talented in the arts—especially in painting, sewing, and designing quilts that are attractive. I've lost count of the groups she quilts with, nearly all of them being donated to homeless people, or those from low-income families. She's also made quilts for her family members for many years, including grandchildren as they graduate from high school.

Have I mentioned patience? That trait seldom goes with anyone talented in the arts, but Nina is "patience" personified. I've learned patience from her, and from our lovely German Shepherd Foxy—a double effect from two of my best friends. There must be something that connects patience and caution, but I am not sure. Nina has both wrapped up together.

For a while after our marriage, I suspected Nina still adhered to the menu of boiled potatoes and meat, some dietary habit typically existing in the midwest. Then it dawned on me. She raised her five children for many years into adulthood as a single parent. Then, to keep her finances on a modest level, she worked part-time in the Davis library. As I write this I realize how she became such an efficient manager of her time—with growing children, maintaining a house, and earning income by working outside her family house, she had to learn to be a multi-tasker. Hmph, it is not an inherent skill after all, but then, I didn't know her mother, did I? Maybe she had a role model when she was growing up.

I got diverted from the meat and boiled potatoes topic didn't I? It took Nina only a small time to realize that good food, well prepared, is a nice way to spend time with ones you love and to be rewarded for the effort. In the beginning of our marriage, Nina was still working full-time at the travel agency she co-owned with Carroll. But soon, weekends took on a different time and tempo and she began to participate more in meal preparation, often showing me better preparation techniques I did not know. Then, as we began to work together in meal preparation, cooking took on another dimension for us both—she taught me cooking techniques and skills, and I added the diversity of menus from my living in many parts of this green earth. Even now, after about 18 years of marriage, we work together planning, prepping, and cooking our meals. We eat very well, thank you!

Nina already enjoyed wines when we started dating. She was the master of buying boxed white wines, while I drank mostly red wines, especially the wines I had made with Roland Wentzel and Tom Brumley (my ophthalmologist). She is the "point man" for quality of white wines when I need an honest taster.

From these comments, have I made Nina sound like the perfect woman? Not intentionally but I hope I have given her an opportunity to let all of these good characteristics and virtues emerge. I may have contributed to her increased consumption of fresh fruit that we enjoy for breakfast each morning, and to new recipe adventures.

But then, she grew up in North Dakota, where wheat, corn, and sugar beets are plentiful, but fresh vegetables and fruits that I was accustomed to picking from the trees each morning did not grow.

She hails from Neche, a small town in North Dakota, just a few miles from the Canadian border. The area is made up of northern European immigrants that had come to Canada then trickled south. Her parents farmed typical crops of the region, mainly wheat. She has one sister, Shirley, who with her husband farmed in the southeast of the state, near Wahpeton. We enjoy visiting Shirley and her two sons and their families; her two surviving daughters reside in Seattle.

A HAPPY MARRIAGE STORY ABOUT OUR WINE

During a 10-day period in September 2014 we followed my whimsical wish, "I'd like for us to make some wine". A group of our friends helped contribute to make it become reality. The next problem was "What kind of wine should we make?" Not a red wine, because Nina doesn't drink red wines. What choice is left? A white wine, because that's the wine of Nina's choice, and on occasions I like it too. So, we agreed on a choice.

We decided to model our wine after a friend, Richard Dousdt's winemaking style because we enjoyed the wine and it reminded us of him. His wine was crafted from grapes grown in his New Zealand vineyards and we were fortunate to be the recipients of many cases; it quickly became our house wine of preference.

But, where could we get grapes of the quality of New Zealand? I called the Wentzel's (whose names appear many times in this memoir) who I knew would be able to help us find a source. We found ourselves in a new grape growing region and were fairly well prepared to harvest grapes. Barbara Wentzel joined us in the vineyard and served as liaison with the farmer whose grapes we harvested.

Laden with several hundred pounds of grapes, ambition, but ill prepared to move forward, we worked the night until bedtime and stripped the berries from the stems. We placed the berries in a container that another friend had supplied for us, along with fermentation chemicals.

For several days we struggled, until the chemicals did their job, to turn grape juice into wine. Then, our friend showed up again, laden with more materials and equipment to handle the wines from the fermentation containers into curing containers, and left us with his admonition that, he will "continue to oversee the wines." We never saw him again. We were now left to our own errors and omissions.

Nina and Lee enjoying a relaxed evening in Yerevan, Armenia, 2002.

The juice turned into wine, ready to be transferred to carboys for further finishing and "fining". We used a food grade plastic hose to transfer the wine into another 5-gallon glass carboy. As I lifted the 75 pounds of wonderful wine to another rack, it slipped from my hands, and we lost the jar and the wine— beautiful wine. We struggled more carefully with the remaining 10 gallons (to fill 50 wine bottles in the future).

This is the experience of our life and marriage: an idea, a hope, with friends who spontaneously join us, who contribute to the mellowing of a concept into something that wasn't the original purpose. It then became the part of a new wholeness that we couldn't have anticipated, and which remains what has become the charm of our friends who moved into our lives, who saw us through a process, and then left to contribute to others. I suspect that is life as the fortunate are able to live it. Regardless of how our wine turns out, though we expect it will be the "best we have enjoyed", it is the result of our friends' efforts that melded into one life of ours.

It remains a good life, and I'm grateful to Nina for asking me to put much of it into writing.It was Nina who suggested I write my memoir about five years ago. Her patience in allowing me to do so, at my pace, reflects her tolerances that attract me.

In January 2016, we celebrated Nina's 80th birthday. After 20 years of marriage, what could I present to her as a gift? I opted for a history of her life titled "Nina Horsley, Her First 80 Years," a book contributed to by her family and friends, edited by Nancy Ottum, and compiled without her knowledge. She loved it as much as I love her.

Chuck, likely at Arpie's apartment in Berkeley. Arpie was proud of Chuck, who she liked to have dressed in a suit that was appropriate attire for the Bay Area. He spent a summer with her, while employed as a dishwasher.

Chuck in his high school senior yearbook photo, likely 1941. He was a member of the 143rd Infantry of the California National Guard that was called into active duty around 1941, just after this picture was taken. At the time, he was enrolled in Reedley Junior College as a forestry major. He transferred from the infantry to the Air Force and was trained as a machine gunner in the North Africa Campaign. Later he was sent to the India-Burma Theater where he served for 5 years as the base interpreter.

Above: Marian and Lee, circa 1962-68. Lee's work took him to Los Angeles where he would stop to visit Marian and her family several times a year.

Right: Lee's photo that was in the Cal Poly yearbook. In 1945-46, he served as editor of *El Mustang*, the student newspaper and as the student body president in 1946-47.

Marian was a nifty dresser. After graduating from the UC Berkeley School of Nursing, she married Dr. Karl Schmidt, a pediatrician who was also a regionally renowned oils artist. When we visited them, Karl would always gift a painting to us. Karl opened his office in Burbank, CA and Marian worked as his nurse. He was also on the UCLA medical school faculty, part-time.

Marian, posing at the rear entrance of their first house. Upon visiting them, I was surprised at her culinary abilities when I was served a lobster thermador that was truly a work of art. Isabel and Marian both prepared enjoyable meals, which should not have been a surprise because they had Mom as the Inspiration.

George Kaloostian in his usual pleasant mood, here likely shown in China following WWII. Isabel and George were among the earliest groups who toured China; Isabel would tell how she enjoyed Chinese cooking and when she would remark about the pleasant flavors, the Chinese would respond, "Enjoy the food, but don't ask about the ingredients."

Adrienne, Chuck's daughter, pictured in her southern California backyard. Adrienne acquired my financial interest in the Garoyan home ranch after Chuck's death and later leased the farm to another farmer. She graduated with a degree in accounting and worked as a CPA until recently when she changed careers to become a real estate agent.

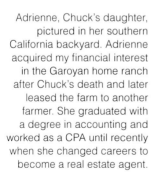

Above: Isabel, Elaine and me in Riverside, CA while celebrating Isabel's birthday. Elaine lived near her parents and frequently would look in on them.

Below: Isabel and Lee, photo taken in Riverside about a year before Isabel's death. As always, Isabel looked lovely, had a clear mind and was a social, friendly person like her father.

Isabel was the tomboy of our family. She was the first daughter to drive a car and the first to milk the family cow. Of my sisters, she was the one who I recall picked grapes on the farm, even after her marriage to George. She was the one who took me to the outdoor privy before bedtime because I was afraid of goblins.

In this photo, she is a 4th-grade teacher who so inspired her students that many kept in contact with her even into her retirement. I can imagine she would have been one of my favorite teachers had she taught when I was in school.

In many ways, Isabel was her "Father's daughter." She was a joiner and an organizer as was evident in her support of George's presidency of the American Entomological Society.

In many ways she and I shared some characteristics: Mom had blue eyes and so do we and we have lived the longest in the family—Isabel at 95 and me 90 years. She was a special soul, like Mom and Arpie.

Lisa and me. Lisa has a natural talent for composition like her grandfather and was recognized by her high school and OSU teachers for her abilities to craft interesting compositions. She gave it up to raise purebred Arabian horses and to become a CPA.

As a youngster, Lisa and her brother Lee would work in the Oregon fields harvesting strawberries, raspberries and green beans. Being a very frugal individual, she saved money for her favorite cause, raising Arabian horses.

We are pictured after interviewing the dog, Auggie, who became our pet.

Above: Daughter Lisa, Isabel, Elaine and me. Lisa and Isabel had a special connection, they shared the same birthday, June 23, only 37 years apart. This was a memorable visit to Isabel on perhaps her last birthday at the retirement home where she had lived for a year. Prior to living here, she lived alone after George's death. She always enjoyed helping others less fortunate.

Below, left to right: My niece Paula Lunbury (youngest of Marian and Karl's 3 daughters), her daughter Anna, me, Grace Lunbury, Nina, and Paige Lunbury. They were visiting us in Davis from Ft. Collins, CO. Grace is now married and lives in New Zealand.

Top Left: Karen is the first daughter of Marian and Karl Schmidt. She is standing with her daughter Felicia Connors. They both reside in North Carolina.

Top Right: David Harrington and Karen on their wedding day. We welcome David into the Garoyan family, and hope this memoir will provide him with a solid background of the family.

Left: Leon III family. Pia, Lee, and Ben, residents of Scottsdale, Arizona. Lee retired from a career with American Express and Pia is a renowned interior decorator. Ben (now 17), is the heir apparent to carry on the Garoyan family traditions and name, a task we believe he will do graciously.